Trials of the self

MANCHESTER
1824

Manchester University Press

STUDIES IN EARLY MODERN EUROPEAN HISTORY

This series aims to promote challenging and innovative research in all areas of early modern European history. For over twenty years it has published monographs and edited volumes that make an original contribution to our understanding of the period and is particularly interested in works that engage with current historiographical debates and methodologies, including race, emotions, materiality, gender, communication, medicine and disability, as well as interdisciplinary studies. Europe is taken in a broad sense and the series welcomes projects on continental (Western, Central and Eastern Europe), Anglo-European and trans-cultural, global histories that explore the world's relationship with Europe during the sixteenth to eighteenth centuries.

SERIES EDITORS

Sara Barker, Joseph Bergin, Laura Kounine and William G. Naphy

Also available in the series

Full details of the series are available at www.manchesteruniversitypress.co.uk

Trials of the self

Murder, mayhem and the remaking of the mind, 1750–1830

Elwin Hofman

MANCHESTER UNIVERSITY PRESS

The right of Elwin Hofman to be identified as the author of this work has been asserted by them in accordance with the Copyright, Designs and Patents Act 1988.

Published by Manchester University Press
Altrincham Street, Manchester M1 7JA

www.manchesteruniversitypress.co.uk

British Library Cataloguing-in-Publication Data
A catalogue record for this book is available from the British Library

ISBN 978 1 5261 5314 2 hardback

First published 2021

The publisher has no responsibility for the persistence or accuracy of URLs for any external or third-party internet websites referred to in this book, and does not guarantee that any content on such websites is, or will remain, accurate or appropriate.

Typeset
by Deanta Global Publishing Services, Chennai, India

'I've really been trying to self-improve lately. [...] I'm focusing on trying to get back to the truest version of myself.'
'How do you know that getting back to your truest version of yourself is gonna be an improvement?'

– Dialogue between Geoffrey and Josh in *Please Like Me* (2016)

Contents

Abbreviations

AC-ANT	*Assize Court of Antwerp*
AC-BRA	*Assize Court of Brabant*
AC-WEST	*Assize Court of West Flanders*
ADM-POL	*Administrative Archives: Police*
CAB	City Archives, Brussels
FA	Felix Archives, Antwerp
FIK	*Court of the First Instance of Kortrijk*
HA	*Historical Archives*
MA	*Modern City Archives*
NA	National Archives, Brussels
NA2	National Archives 2 – Joseph Cuvelier Repository, Brussels
OCAK	*Old City Archives, Kortrijk*
PCAP-C	*Privy Council Austrian Period – Cartons*
SABE	State Archives, Beveren
SABR	State Archives, Bruges
SAK	State Archives, Kortrijk
V	*Vierschaer (High Tribunal)*

Acknowledgements

It is only appropriate for a book in which confessions figure so prominently to begin with a confession of my own. So I confess: acknowledgements are my favourite part of many books. They are at once their most intimate and their most formalistic part. People speak personal words and thank their closest friends; pretending to be naively sincere and unaware of the fact that everyone writes almost the exact same things. Acknowledgements, it has been observed, are displays of the author's scholarly networks, competences and identities. They are, in effect, cleverly disguised CVs, covering everything from mentors to marital status.

As is common in acknowledgements, I have to start with the work of others. This book would not have existed were it not for many generous scholars who read portions (or all) of it and were willing to discuss my research. Tom Verschaffel has always been my first resort for all my questions. His insights are always fundamental, his demeanour calm and convivial, his comments inspiring and encouraging. Dana Rabin, Geertje Mak, Henk de Smaele, Johan Verberckmoes and Kaat Wils have been exceptionally helpful by thoroughly reading an earlier version of this text and providing essential comments. I have further benefited from feedback and encouragement from the other scholars at the Cultural History research group in Leuven, particularly Jo Tollebeek, Pieter Huistra, Nelleke Teughels, Andreas Stynen, Liesbet Nys, Timo Van Havere, Raf De Bont, Joris Vandendriessche, Jolien Gijbels, Veronique Deblon, Tinne Claes, Kate Kangaslahti, Marjoleine Delva and Matthias Mcirlaen. Their intellectual and moral support has been invaluable. Elsewhere, Sara Cosemans, Brecht Deseure, Josephine Hoegaerts, Theo van der Meer, Magaly Rodriguez Garcia, Xavier Rousseaux, Pieter Spierenburg, Dorothée Sturkenboom and Tine Van Osselaer all commented on parts of my research, from early proposals to chapter drafts. I am immensely grateful for their time and their insights. The editors and reviewers for Manchester University Press made valuable suggestions when this book was reaching its final stages.

The research for this book would not have been possible without two fellowships of the Research Foundation – Flanders and a travel grant to Chicago from the same foundation. I further benefitted from fellowships of the KU Leuven internal funds and of the Belgian American Educational Foundation. I am also grateful to Jan Goldstein and Nicole Eustace, who welcomed me at the University of Chicago and at New York University and gave me opportunities for exciting exchanges of thoughts.

While giving all these thanks, I have shown some of the networks in which I have participated and the grants and research stays I have received. I have displayed an awareness of the debts I have incurred and, at the same time, I have claimed authorship over this book. I have repeated a few clichés, but stayed clear of others ('writing is a solitary activity', 'any remaining errors are my own'). At the end of their acknowledgements, however, scholars need to display personality, authenticity and sociability; perhaps they should even exhibit a sense of humour. As such, people from partners and parents to pets and long-dead singer-songwriters often make appearances. Family names can generally be omitted from this part, casting a sense of mystery over the identity of these individuals. As such, I thank Liesbet, Sam, Tine and Pieter, Andreas, Ann-Sofie and Heleen, Josh, JL and the other Tom. I thank Ender and my parents, for their unwavering support and their interest in my research. Entirely in accordance with recent tradition, my final words of gratitude are for Ben. I thank him, for his support, his down-to-earthness, his humour and his tenderness.

Like the self, gratitude is entangled with interiority, with emotions, with responsibility, with individuality and with personality. Like the self, gratitude is elusive and difficult to approach. As one critic has argued, it is a meagre reward to be included 'on a list that looks like the bcc line of a mass e-mail'. But there is a solution: rather than approaching gratitude as an abstract concept, I hope to put it into practice.

How to do the history of the self: an introduction

Jacob Mol was to answer to charges of the attempted murder of his wife before the Antwerp criminal court. Mol, 36, a fruiterer, had always had a difficult relationship with his spouse. They married in 1741, but after eight weeks, Mol left her, 'because she came home every day with three or four women'. He re-joined her a few weeks later, but they fought all the time, verbally and physically. They separated, got back together, separated again, got back together, had a row 'over the maid and because his wife was keeping up with other women' and separated again. They were even officially separated by the church court and Mol started living with another woman. But, Mol claimed, his wife kept harassing him. Eventually, she 'lured' him to come and live with her again. When he got home in the evenings, he would often find her in bed with another woman. On two occasions, he joined them for intercourse. On 20 February 1750, however, things went wrong and Mol stabbed his wife after a row. He left her for dead.[1]

Six days later, the Antwerp magistrates interrogated Mol. After establishing his name, age, place of birth, trade and marital status, judges asked for his motivations, questioning 'how he had lived with his wife'. Mol started telling a long story, explaining their whole married life, up to the moment that he stabbed her. He described some of the fights they had had, and, eventually, how his wife had angered him by continually insulting him the evening of the incident. 'Mort Dieu', he had said, 'I won't bear this any longer'. His wife had then blown out the lights and he had grabbed a knife and stabbed her. When the judges asked him why, he said he had done it 'because he was in fury and huge anger'.

The case of Jacob Mol marks the beginning of a tendency, in the criminal justice system and beyond, towards a greater interest in the 'inner' side of men and women in the late eighteenth and early nineteenth centuries. Not that people's inner sides were wholly neglected before 1750; but deep, individual and inner motivations, feelings and passions became increasingly central concerns. Through this increasing attention for the inner, people's 'self' was formed and transformed in different ways. This remaking of the

mind is the subject of this study. Using trial records and other sources from
Belgium and elsewhere in North-Western Europe, I show that criminal justice stimulated people from a wide variety of backgrounds to practise a
deeper and more inner self after around 1800. But this history is neither
self-evident nor straightforward. Jacob Mol, the people around him and his
judges practised the self in several interacting and conflicting ways. These
practices show the complexity of the self, the power mechanisms involved
and the hazards of the archives.

Histories of the self

The self is notoriously hard to define. Most people have a sense of what the
self is, but find it hard to describe it precisely. Attempts at studying the self
in history and across cultures further complicate the concept, and so does the
plethora of terms scholars have used to address related notions: the individual, the subject, identity, the soul, the person, personality, the I, the ego. I will
not hazard a strict definition. I follow Jan Goldstein in loosely circumscribing
the self – in a European context – as 'individuated mental stuff'.[2] The history
of the self as I will study it in this book is the history of thoughts and feelings
about who we are, to some extent apart from collectives and to some extent
apart from the body. It relates to broader concepts, such as 'psyche' and
'mind', which I will again use in a loose way: these terms refer to thoughts
and feelings, rather than to bodies and actions, but can never be seen as
entirely apart from people's bodies and actions. Different degrees of individuality and embodiment, and, as we will see, constellations with several other
characteristics, can be encompassed within these loose circumscriptions.

The interest in the history of the self dates back at least to the Swiss cultural historian Jacob Burckhardt.[3] In *Die Kultur der Renaissance in Italien*
(1860), he proposed that the autonomous, secular and rational individual,
so characteristic of the ideology of the Western elite of his own time, had its
origins in renaissance society.[4] In his wake, 'the rise of the individual' has
become a master narrative for the history of the West. Unlike Burckhardt,
however, many scholars have situated its breakthrough in the eighteenth
century rather than the sixteenth.[5] Also unlike Burckhardt, some have contended that the history of the self is more than the history of individual
autonomy. As Charles Taylor has argued in his magisterial *Sources of the
Self* (1989), the late eighteenth century was also crucial for creating a new
sense of inwardness, a sense of inner depths. The self became a 'true nature',
an inner moral source people had to discover.[6]

The analyses of Taylor and his predecessors mainly relied on the works
of philosophers who explicitly articulated ideas about the individual and

the self. In reaction to this elite perspective, more recent historians have often taken a broader perspective. In *The Post-Revolutionary Self* (2005), Jan Goldstein has traced the advent of a holistic self in post-revolutionary France. Around 1800, the idea that the individual psyche was unitary and indivisible, as put forward by Victor Cousin, replaced the sensationalist idea that the mind was fragmented; an idea that many people started to see as morally and politically undesirable. Goldstein's work had strong ties with intellectual history, as she discussed the competing psychological theories of sensationalism, Cousinianism and phrenology. However, her scope was also much broader, as she argued that education and cultural life propagated Cousin's idea of an *a priori*, unified self throughout France.[7]

Even broader in its use of cultural sources, and perhaps more hostile to intellectual history, was Dror Wahrman's *The Making of the Modern Self* (2004), a study of the 'unstructured intuitions' that underlay people's fundamental assumptions about 'who they were and who they could be'.[8] To discover these fundamental assumptions, he has studied a wide variety of cultural sites: scientific treatises, plays, novels, sermons, memoirs, magazines, pamphlets, ballads and more. Wahrman has argued that the modern self was a particular conception of identity, one that presupposes an 'essential core of selfhood characterised by psychological depth, or interiority, which is the bedrock of unique, expressive individual identity'.[9] This conception of self had its origin, in England, around 1780. Before, people considered their identity to be more malleable and more turned towards others.

Along with Jerrold Seigel's intellectual history of the self since the seventeenth century, Wahrman's and Goldstein's studies have become standard references for the history of the self in the eighteenth and early nineteenth centuries.[10] They argue that in this period, a modern or post-revolutionary self was made. Goldstein suggests that this self was class-specific and explicitly speaks of a 'bourgeois self'. Wahrman seeks to include a whole cross-section of society in his analysis, but his reliance on printed sources obscures the experiences of illiterate and semi-literate people. Yet social historians have stressed that we may not simply assume that common people did not participate in or influence cultural practices of the better sorts.[11] As Anna Clark has recently argued, people could adapt and exploit elite writings about the self for their own purposes.[12] Little research has been conducted into the changing self-conceptions of common men and women in the eighteenth and early nineteenth centuries. As a result, the history of the self remains incomplete and we cannot adequately assess the impact of the 'modern self'.

Even apart from this class specificity, recent historians have criticised the very concept of the 'modern self' (or 'post-revolutionary self', for that matter), as it obscures the complex constellations of ideas and practices of the self. Intellectual historians have found that in the late eighteenth century, when this modern self supposedly emerged, competing ideas about the values of social determination, anti-individualism and self-abandonment remained prevalent.[13] Some autobiographical writings, moreover, remained remarkably devoid of introspection or inner sentiment.[14]

As a result, some historians have begun to stress the diversity of ideas and practices of the self rather than major shifts in its history.[15] Laura Kounine, for instance, has recently challenged 'the idea that we can – or indeed should even attempt to – identify and map distinct and changing understandings of the "self" over time'.[16] In her study of self and emotions in sixteenth- and seventeenth-century German witchcraft trials, Kounine suggests that the search for the 'modern self' should give way to analyses of 'multifaceted, variegated, and at times conflicting notions of personhood' according to specific situations within a time period.[17]

I suggest in this book that we can – and indeed should – trace changing conceptions of the self over time, but in a way that departs from the often too all-encompassing way the concept of the 'modern self' has been used before, and with more attention for common and illiterate people. To do so, I propose three methodological innovations for the study of the history of the self: first, to study how 'institutions', in this case institutions of criminal justice, have formed and transformed the self. Second, to approach conceptions of the self as a set of several discourses that can coexist in several constellations. And third, to study practices, rather than 'ideas' or 'experiences' of the self.

Institutions of the self

In the second essay of his *Genealogy of Morality* (1887), Friedrich Nietzsche went in search of the origins of the self. He found them in the coming of 'society' and the 'state'. The state and its powerful leaders created institutions of justice and punishment to protect themselves against people's 'instincts of freedom', such as animosity, cruelty and the pleasure of raiding and destroying. Not being able to 'discharge' these instincts outwardly, people pitted their instincts against themselves. Their instincts 'turn inwards' and become their 'soul', their 'bad conscience': 'The whole inner world, originally stretched thinly as though between two layers of skin, was expanded and extended itself and gained depth, breadth and height in proportion to the degree that the external discharge of man's instincts was *obstructed*'.[18] For Nietzsche, the state and its institutions of punishment founded a conception of the self as reflective, interior and autonomous.[19]

Almost a century later, French philosopher Michel Foucault was inspired by Nietzsche and historicised his ideas, most famously in *Discipline and*

Punish (1975). Foucault agreed with Nietzsche that the individualised and autonomous self was a product of coercion and power mechanisms of discipline and surveillance, many of which he argued developed in the eighteenth and nineteenth centuries.[20] In the first volume of *The History of Sexuality* (1976), Foucault added that the prime method for people in Western, Christian society to establish a truth about themselves was through confession. People were to examine and form an interior self, which received the status of a true nature simply because of the form of confession.[21]

Before Foucault, and to some extent still since, many historians of the self did not heed much attention to the role of power or institutions of the self. They studied ideas and experiences of the self in treatises and novels, plays and letters, autobiographies and diaries. On the basis of such sources, they have described the increasing autonomy of the individual, the discovery of inner depths, and the growing stability of the self. Such accounts often fail to acknowledge why and how the self changed. In Foucault's wake, some sociologists and historians, including Nikolas Rose and David Sabean, have called to attention how powerful institutions, such as churches and governments, mandated the formation of particular selves, in more historically specific ways.[22] They have shown that we must take the institutions that have suggested, promoted and mandated certain conceptions of self seriously. This approach is not without risks, however. It is tempting to assign too much power to institutions to autonomously determine and dictate particular conceptions of self. Foucault, Sabean and Rose have all been criticised for not giving enough attention to the failures of institutions to impose their conceptions of self, to ordinary people's ways of dealing with these institutions and to the ways they could influence them from the bottom up.[23]

I propose to study what I will call 'institutions of the self' in a different way. The power differences between representatives of certain institutions and ordinary people dealing with them should not obscure the importance of everyday interactions to enact these power differences and to negotiate different models of the self. Institutions of the self, such as criminal courts, churches, schools and medical facilities, are important not because they singlehandedly dictated people's conceptions of self, but because they solicited, arbitrated, recorded and communicated these conceptions and gave them an official status.

This approach to 'institutions of the self' borrows from Ute Frevert's research on the importance of institutions such as law, family and religion in the history of emotions. Frevert has argued that the emotional codes institutions set up have important repercussions for how members of these institutions – citizens, family members, believers – feel and express emotions.[24] Institutions such as criminal justice had a wide reach and thus far-reaching implications. Even if not everyone came directly in touch with the law or the Church, and even though these institutions were not unified and proposed several, often conflicting messages, their discourses and practices were forces to be reckoned with by almost all.

In spite of Nietzsche's and Foucault's attention for the role of penal institutions in the history of the self – or perhaps because of it – historians have not extensively explored the self in criminal justice. Yet it was a powerful institution of the self. In eighteenth- and nineteenth-century Europe, all inhabitants of a country were subject to its laws and could in principle be tried if they were suspected of violating them. Most people recognised the power of the criminal justice system and many even used it for their own purposes, filing complaints and testifying as needed. By doing so, as Julie Hardwick has suggested, people 'borrowed the authority of the state through its courts to endorse particular solutions', and in turn, 'judges whose verdicts endorsed the prevailing opinions in the local community encouraged an increasing resort to the courts which expanded the role of the state'.[25] The criminal courts, then, made people from all layers of society give an account of themselves and they steered this account in a particular direction. Magistrates proposed, promoted and regulated certain discourses of self in dialogue with a large number of people, including many people from lower social groups, who received only a limited education and did not take part in philosophical or literary communities. Criminal courts offer a privileged opportunity to study the self among less privileged people.

The case of Jacob Mol illustrates the power of criminal justice as an institution of the self. After he had stabbed his wife, thinking she was dead, he put on his best clothes, went to a friendly officer of justice and asked to be taken to prison. The officer, however, first took Mol home again, to check whether his wife was really dead. This happened not to be the case; in fact, she had only suffered minor injuries. Mol was surprised, but still insisted that he be taken to prison for interrogation, validating the authority of the criminal justice system. Once in court, Mol's self became a topic of discussion: his judges asked him to reflect on his responsibility, feelings and motivations. But Mol did not simply accept the suppositions of his judges. Rather than agree that he had wilfully attempted to kill his wife, he denied his responsibility, arguing that he had only acted in a fit of anger after her continuing defiance. The criminal court did not simply dictate a model of the self, but provided an occasion to discuss and arbitrate Mol's self.

The influence of criminal justice reached further than to the people directly involved. Criminal justice was at least in part a public performance. Arrests caused a stir in local communities, leading to gossip and discussion; criminal trials were sometimes witnessed, reported and publicly debated (even if parts of the trial often took place in private); executions attracted huge crowds – I will discuss the historical specificities of these events later on. Through these public rituals, the criminal justice system communicated which discourses of the self were acceptable. Thus, criminal courts tried to influence how their audience should deal with certain behaviour and how they should think about, for instance, responsibility or interiority.

Through everyday interactions and discussions, the conceptions of self debated by criminal courts could spread. Many people knew (or thought they knew) how the courts worked and tried to turn this to their advantage.[26] As Carolyn Steedman has observed, 'law mattered to eighteenth-century people out of necessity, because it was there – in their face – shaping and dictating the lives they led, the love they felt, the labour they exchanged for livelihood'.[27] Even if they did not wish to deal with the law, people *needed* legal knowledge when they were called in as witnesses, arrested as suspects, or convicted and wanted to obtain a pardon. They had to learn how legal institutions worked and what these institutions' preferences and procedures were. They did so by seeing, hearing and discussing proper ways of dealing with justice – and therefore also acceptable discourses and practices of the self. Because criminal justice stood firmly in people's lives, its influence extended beyond suspects and witnesses and onto their families, friends and communities.

For this reason, studying the criminal court as an institution of the self also reveals the impact of other institutions, discourses and practices, including medical advice, occupational regulations and local and family customs. The Church is probably one of the most influential among these. Although it had a crucial role to play in eighteenth- and nineteenth-century people's conceptions of self, I will only attend to this institution in a limited way in this book. Elsewhere, I have discussed Catholicism, penance and selfhood more extensively, and others have attended to Catholic and Protestant projects of self-formation in various European regions.[28] Conceptions of the self inspired by religion – or medicine, philosophy, occupation or family customs – find their way to this book in as far as they affected people's discourses and practices in criminal courts.

My approach to the history of the self through institutions of criminal justice connects to recent trends in the history of crime and criminal justice. Many older histories in this field have tended to focus on legal norms and texts. When they did attend to the self, as Michel Foucault did in *Discipline and Punish*, they have often focused on grand trials and punishments rather than on the extensive procedures and negotiations that preceded them. Recent historians, such as Rebekka Habermas, Katie Barclay and Laura Kounine, have adopted the perspective of 'doing justice', giving more attention to the role of the actors of criminal justice, their different degrees of power and their negotiations, spaces, bodies and emotions.[29] This approach allows us to sketch a history of the self that takes into account the diversity and complexity of the practices of criminal justice and the contingency of its history. Criminal justice did not simply regulate the self from above, but was above all a place where the self became a topic of discussion.

Discourses of the self

Before we give closer attention to the institutions of the self, I must return to a more fundamental question: in what way can the self be said to have a history? What form should such a history take? In the 1990s, a fierce debate raged among anthropologists. Is the self is a 'peculiar idea within the context of the world's cultures', or rather 'a universal, like culture'?[30] Following Marcel Mauss' earlier work, Clifford Geertz had claimed that the person, which he equated with the self, is conceived in the Western world as 'a bounded, unique, more or less integrated motivational and cognitive universe, a dynamic center of awareness, emotion, judgement and action organised into a distinctive whole and set contrastively against other such wholes and against its social and natural background'. This was, he argued, different in most other cultures.[31]

Several anthropologists took issue with this view. Two critiques are interesting for my purposes here: Melford Spiro has argued that all cultures make some distinction between 'self' and 'other', as is demonstrated by the presence of a pronoun signifying 'I' in every known language. Even in cultures where the existence of an inner self was explicitly denied, in practice, he argued, people did use such a self-concept: the autonomous, egocentric and independent self was quite common outside the West.[32] Another strand of critique focused on the unitary view on the Western self: several anthropologists argued that there are many different conceptions of self in the West as well, and that Geertz's view on the Western self was mostly derived from written philosophical traditions, not from analyses of experiences.[33]

These arguments are reminiscent of a debate that has preoccupied historians of homosexuality for a long time. Inspired by Mary McIntosh's 1968 article on 'the homosexual role', many historians and sociologists started to argue that the Western conception of homosexuality was not universal, but historically constructed.[34] They have been labelled 'constructionists' and opposed to 'essentialists', who argued that a 'homosexual essence' of some kind has always existed.[35] 'Essentialists' heaped up anecdotal 'evidence' of homosexuality in past times, while 'constructionists' argued that it was only in the late nineteenth century (or, for some, the eighteenth century, or earlier, or later) that the homosexual, as a distinct being desiring sex and love with people of his or her own sex, came into existence.[36]

The debates soon became tiresome and new scholars sought a way out of them. With her *Epistemology of the Closet*, Eve Kosofsky Sedgwick laid the foundation of what became known as 'queer theory'. She argued against a 'Great Paradigm Shift' with the 'birth of the homosexual', for it obscured the incoherence and instability of 'homosexuality as we conceive of it today'. The concept of 'homosexuality', she wrote, is defined and used in overlapping, contradictory and conflicting ways. Older ways of conceiving sexualities continue to interfere with new ideas.[37]

Queer theory's criticisms have inspired historians of sexuality to reflect on matters of continuity and change, coherence and incoherence and stability and instability. David Halperin has most fruitfully adapted his earlier ideas on the construction of homosexuality to accommodate Sedgwick's criticisms. In *How to Do the History of Homosexuality*, he claimed that every history of homosexuality should start from modern notions of homosexuality, in all their incoherence. Historians should then disintegrate this concept, trace the genetic origins of its different aspects and locate their convergences. They should distinguish modern homosexuality from these earlier discourses, but also acknowledge continuities. Such a project, he claimed 'would be able to capture the play of identities and differences within the synchronic multiplicity of different but simultaneous traditions of discourse that have existed through the ages as well as the play of identities and differences across the various diachronic transitions within each of them over the course of time'. Halperin then distinguished four categories of understandings of male sex and gender deviance, and sketched their histories and their relations to the modern category of homosexuality.[38]

In light of these debates, it seems useful to adopt a similar approach to the history of the self. By adapting the history of the self to some of queer theory's insights, by starting from modern notions of self, destabilising them and tracing the histories of their different and contradicting aspects, we can move beyond the impasse between universalists and peculiarists. Some aspects of the ideal-typical 'modern self' recur across different cultures and periods, while others are rather less common. They can appear in various constellations. The history of the self, then, is not the history of a natural object, but a history of the constellations of discourses that make up the self.[39]

For the remainder of this section, I distinguish four axes along which the self is and has been conceived. They are linked and overlap in important ways, but all have their own specificities. The 'modern self', interior, stable, whole and in control of itself, is one specific constellation of these axes. Although the discourses on the axes I discern seem mutually exclusive, this is not necessarily the case, as the self and its conceptions are always unstable and full of paradoxes. The four axes are (1) interiority and outer orientation, (2) stability and malleability, (3) holism and fragmentation and (4) self-control and dispossession. While the first of each of these variables has traditionally been considered to be constituent of the 'modern' conception of self, the others continue to disturb this self.

(1) Interiority, a sense of inner depths in varying degrees, is perhaps one of the most crucial elements in the historiography of the modern self, playing a pivotal role in the works of, among others, Charles Taylor and Dror Wahrman. Yet discourses of the outward-oriented self are equally interesting, and continue to disrupt discourses of interiority: there are those discourses that imply that the self is mainly socially orientated, for instance through shame or embarrassment, and there are those discourses that consider the body to be the most important element of the self, for instance in neuroscience, phrenology and criminal anthropology. Narratives of interiority and bodily or social orientation both appear throughout history.

The sense of an inner self may be combined with a sense that this inner self is a 'true self' and that one needs to live accordingly. Jean-Jacques Rousseau has often been identified as one of the great proponents of this 'authenticity'.[40] But interiority does not always suppose authenticity. It seems that, before the late eighteenth century, and in many social circles also afterwards, there was a social obligation to conceal aspects of the inner self.[41] Awareness of a 'true self' did therefore not necessitate attaching great significance to it.

(2) The second axis that I would like to discuss concerns stability and malleability. Dror Wahrman has most lucidly argued that the modern self is a stable self. He has observed that in the eighteenth century up to around 1780, 'identity play' – crossing borders of gender, race and class – was possible and to a certain extent acceptable, for instance at masquerades. This changed with the advent of a stable self at the end of the eighteenth century. The borders of identity categories, or at least some of them, were no longer to be crossed: the popularity of masquerades diminished; people no longer saw children as *tabulae rasae*, but as born with particular characteristics which they could not overcome. They had a stable self.[42]

However, the nineteenth century of course also had its share of crooks, con-artists and transvestites, crossing boundaries and playing with different identities. Moreover, as Wahrman himself has noted, some identity categories, such as nation and religion, became looser and more changeable from the late eighteenth century on.[43] Again, there were conflicting discourses. A sense of a stable self has always been disrupted by discourses of fluidity and malleability.

(3) Connected to the question of the stability and malleability of the self, are discourses of autonomous self-control (being in control of yourself, self-possession) and losing this control, 'dispossession'. The autonomous individual has had many historiographical births – in antiquity, in early Christianity, in the twelfth century, in the renaissance and in the seventeenth, eighteenth, nineteenth and twentieth centuries. Unlike people from a usually only loosely defined 'earlier era', the 'modern individual' was able to make his (or her, but more often his) own decisions, independent of a larger collective.[44] It seems, however, that some degree of autonomy, some degree of agency and an ability to make self-conscious decisions, was present in every time. The degree to which people acknowledged this 'reflexive basis of selfhood' has however strongly varied, as Jerrold Seigel and other intellectual historians have shown.[45]

More tangible, perhaps, than discourses of self-control are discourses of dispossession, discourses of not being in control. Again, intellectual historians have made essential analyses of discourses of social and biological determination, or, as Charly Coleman has done, of the ways in which people surrendered themselves to God.[46] Far less research has been devoted to the use of discourses surrounding lack of self-control in practice. Particularly interesting are discourses of what Dana Rabin has called 'displacement of self': individuals who are normally in control of themselves use these discourses to evade responsibility for their actions at certain times. By referring to drunkenness, possession or insanity, individuals could claim 'not to be themselves' while they did something, effectively denying control over themselves at these times.[47]

(4) Finally, we can distinguish discourses of holism and fragmentation. The importance of these discourses has been shown by Jan Goldstein, who has argued that the dominant 'sensationalist' psychology of eighteenth-century France portrayed the mind as fragmented, consisting of different mental faculties, operating somewhat independently, but nevertheless all knowable. In the nineteenth century, Victor Cousin and his followers put much more stress on a holist and *a priori* self. However, alternative discourses, such as phrenology, which offered a fragmented conception of the self in the nineteenth century, were always available. A sense of fragmentation became again more dominant after Freud's theory of the 'unconscious', which proposed that not all parts of the mind were known to itself.[48]

These four variables overlap, intersect and interact on many important points. It is therefore crucial to note that these are not separate histories. Distinguishing them has methodological advantages and allows us to be better aware of what, exactly, we are talking about when we are talking about the history of the self. It makes it possible, furthermore, to break up the idea of a single, unitary history of the self, and to consider convergences and divergences of different aspects of the self, through time and among different social groups.

It is most important to recognise, in these histories, differences along lines of gender, class and race, while at the same time questioning the viability of these very categories, destabilising and deconstructing them by analysing inherent mechanisms of power distribution. In this book, I will particularly attend to the role of gender and social status. I approach these terms not as stable categories, but use them as analytic concepts that were themselves much in motion in the eighteenth and nineteenth centuries. 'Social class' was not yet a common term nor a stable category in the period under discussion. In practice, however, people were well aware of the different opportunities that differences in wealth, education, profession and social networks brought along. The distinctions cannot always be sharply made, since the different aspects of social status did not always neatly align and are not always visible in the archival records. I will use the most commonly available variables, literacy and profession, as well as circumstantial indications, to assess how different discourses of the self related to different social backgrounds. I will show that, as far as discourses of the self in criminal court were concerned, social status played a limited, but distinct role. Indeed, some of the typical discourses of the modern self that has been ascribed to 'middle-class' or 'bourgeois' people were also employed by and applied to common and poor people – and in some cases, precisely those bourgeois people escaped them.

Gender is often clearer in the archival records, as it was in society, but its meanings are not self-evident either. Discourses of stability and malleability affected how important and rigid gender was as a category, just as it did for social status. But gender differences could also affect what sort of discourses of the self people related to. Expectations and norms of 'masculinity' and 'femininity' – I will use these concepts to refer to the often-overlapping expectations of men's and women's behaviour – brought along discourses that related to the self. As we will see in chapters 3 and 4, people sometimes expected women to give more importance to their inner sides (but sometimes, they saw a profound inner life as an important masculine trait); and they often thought that men were more in control of themselves (but they offered women fewer options for losing such control). Similar practices could be seen as both distinctly masculine *and* feminine.[49] Social status and gender thus related to the self in reciprocal and ambiguous ways that are nevertheless essential for our understanding of the history of the self.

Jacob Mol's 1750 trial illustrates the uses of the methodology I propose. At first, the case does not seem to reveal much about conceptions of self. But if we look for the discourses outlined above, they are clearly present. Most obvious are the discourses of autonomy and dispossession. By referring to his 'fury', Mol, who could sign his own name but was of little means, claimed that he was not in control of himself at the time of his crime. His words suggest that he was generally in control of his actions, but that this self-control was vulnerable to 'displacement' by the masculine incidences of strong passions and drunkenness. His judges, on the other hand, suggested a more stable self: by asking how he had lived with his wife, they expected continuity between their previous rows and his current actions. While Mol blamed his actions partly on his wife's misbehaviour, thus implying an outer orientation, both Mol and his judges also stressed interior processes: his own emotions and his own decisions. The records of Mol's interrogation therefore reveal a common man's conflicting conceptions of self.

Practices of self

'Scholars have written at great length about the emergence of individualism and autonomy as doctrines', wrote Lynn Hunt in *Inventing Human Rights*, 'but much less about how the self itself might change over time'.[50] She raises an important point: to what extent does thought about the self relate to the self, as it is experienced and practised? Can we know the self apart from its representations? Does the self even have a history if it is not a history of its representations? Some scholars arguing for the universality of the self have posited that it is indeed only the representation of the self that changes.[51] Many others seem to assume implicitly that only ideas about and representations of the self are, in fact, knowable, and that history as a consequence should only study these.

Historians working in other domains have, of course, encountered similar problems. Nowhere have they been addressed more explicitly – at least in recent times – than in the historiography of emotions. The history of emotions intersects at crucial points with the history of the self: emotions have, for instance, been considered to 'well up' inside a person (interiority), or to make a person do things 'in rage' that he or she would otherwise not do (displacement).[52] It is a domain that has known major developments over the last forty years. While emotions had already been discussed by early pioneers as Johan Huizinga and Lucien Febvre, emotions history primarily gained a firm theoretical grounding from the 1980s onwards.[53]

In 1985, Peter and Carol Stearns wrote a programmatic article for the history of emotions, in which they launched the term 'emotionology'. With this neologism, they referred to 'the collective emotional standards of a society', which they tried to recover primarily from advice literature.[54] In this way, they distinguished emotionology, emotional standards and expressions, from emotions themselves, which were far more difficult to study.

Studying emotionology had, however, as the Stearns's readily admitted, a distinct disadvantage: they did not capture actual experiences. What they did not recognise, but what critics did, was that by coining the term 'emotionology', they widened the gap between experience and expression, as if these two were unrelated.[55]

In 1997, William Reddy therefore proposed a different approach, with a different neologism: 'emotives'. With his theory of emotives, Reddy tried to find a balance between social constructionist and biological determinist approaches to emotions. Borrowing from speech act theory, he argued that emotives – verbal emotional expressions – were essential in shaping and managing emotions. Saying 'I am sad' is not just a statement of fact, but has self-altering effects and changes the feeling itself. Reddy therefore emphasised the vocabulary of emotion to study the history of emotions.[56]

Yet in a 2012 article, Monique Scheer found that the debate on whether historians had access to real experiences of emotions had not yet been adequately resolved. She has proposed an approach grounded in Bourdieu's practice theory. Emotions are not something people *have*, she maintained, but something people *do*. By claiming that a person does not feel prior to the 'doing' of an emotion, the gap between experience and expression of emotions disappears. Scheer consequently discussed four categories of emotional practices: mobilising (practices inducing an emotional state, e.g. penance), naming (like Reddy's emotives), communicating (emotional expressions, like crying) and regulating practices (emotional norms).[57]

At several points, Scheer's argument touched on the history of the self. Subjects, she posited, are nothing but the sequence of acts in which they participate. These acts encompass giving attention to 'inner' processes. People have to learn to cultivate an 'inner self', to be 'true to themselves'.[58] The self is not given and not only learned through theoretical instruction: interiority, autonomy, stability, wholeness and their counterparts are things that need to be done. Scheer's theory is therefore a fruitful starting point to develop a theory of self that can encompass, or go beyond, experience and expression. Looking for the practices that formed the self may help us to take the history of the self to a new level.

Let me first try to define, or delimit, what practices of self are. Practices of self are the things people do to shape, form and transform the self – the mental side of the individual. The self and a particular sense of self do not exist prior to these practices, but are created in them. People have to practise, have to *do* interiority or outer orientation, stability or malleability, autonomy or dispossession, wholeness or fragmentation. We can find these practices of self in historical sources through other 'doings and sayings' on which these practices are dependent and with which they intersect.

Adapting from Scheer's categories of emotional practices, I distinguish four overlapping categories of practices of self.

(1) A first category concerns what Michel Foucault has called 'techniques' or 'technologies' of the self, a concept he heavily relied on in his works and lectures of the 1980s.[59] Technologies of the self allow people intentionally to form and transform their self. They are the things people do to change or stay the same, to gain control or to lose it, to discover their 'true self', to please others, to live more authentically or to renounce themselves. They may produce the desired effect, or they may not. Well-studied examples include meditating, confessing, penance, examining your conscience, autobiographical writing, psychoanalysis or taking psychological advice. But there are less obvious examples: drinking alcohol to lose self-control, for instance, or reading philosophical treatises to learn more about how the self works. People can practise techniques of the self voluntarily, though this is not necessary. Someone else may stimulate or even force them to do something to alter their self. Mandatory psychological therapy, for instance, may be part of a conviction. The concept of 'techniques of the self' makes possible the analysis of both disciplining and liberating techniques of forming and transforming the self.[60]

(2) A second category of practices of self is made up of what Jan Goldstein has called 'self-talk', or what Monique Scheer has termed 'naming practices'. These are the practices by which people explicitly talk or write about their self, their inner or outer orientation, their wholeness or fragmentation, their autonomy or lack thereof. By saying that something was 'inner', people formed their sense of interiority, by claiming behaviour as a consequence of their true self or personality, they created this true self and personality. Self-talk can have the same self-altering effects that William Reddy claimed for his 'emotives'. The availability of a language to talk about the self therefore has a distinct influence on the way people practise their self.

(3) Interpretations are a third category of practices to consider. People may be seen as intentionally and unintentionally conveying aspects of their self through all sorts of actions. They and others can interpret these actions in varying ways and these interpretations in turn influence the self. When people explain behaviour, they often link this to the self: they can refer to internal or external circumstances, to true selves or to temporary displacements. In doing so, they again form and transform the self.

(4) Regulating practices are Scheer's final category and I use it here as well. This term refers to social norms concerning the self, often connected

to institutions of the self and conveyed in self-help manuals, philosophical and moralising literature and by people like judges, teachers, preachers and psychologists. These norms are written or promoted with the goal of changing and regulating other people's selves. People are sometimes explicitly instructed to live authentically, to explore their self or to renounce their self-interest; at other times, they are implicitly told that they will be held accountable for their behaviour, that their self is whole or that they cannot change. They may also be taught that the unified self is a fiction, a bundle of perceptions, or, on the contrary, that it founds all human knowledge.

Looking for these four categories of practices of self in the available historical sources makes it possible to go beyond debates about experience versus expression, beyond debates about self-conscious expressions versus 'unstructured intuitions'. It is vital to recognise whether people themselves considered these as differences, but equally vital to recognise that expressions of self are never just expressions, but in fact make up the self itself.

From this perspective, the relevance of the case of Jacob Mol starts to become clear. Regulating practices were visibly at play in his trial: by asking Mol 'how he had lived with his wife', judges tried to impose a model of a stable self, by later asking him *why* he had stabbed his wife, they moreover tried to cast his actions as autonomous, wilful decisions. Mol, however, resisted these attempts to regulate his self, interpreting his actions and history in a different way, as we have seen, by stressing his temporary displacement. Through his anger, Mol practised dispossession. When Mol confessed his crime, this was, in the first place something his judges demanded. But in this particular case, it was not only a regulating practice, as Mol himself had actively sought to confess his crime. Mol turned himself in to justice, he insisted that he be taken to prison for interrogation. While his motivations are not made clear, this could be interpreted as a technology of the self, actively seeking to come clean and practising honesty and authenticity.

The chapters in this book are ordered in a way that reflects the different practices of the self: chapter 1 deals with regulating practices and technologies of the self, discussing the priorities of criminal justice and the ways people tried to use it for their own purposes. In chapters 2 and 3, I discuss interpretations of the self in criminal court as I analyse how people tried to portray their actions as universal and rational; or as the result of a 'displacement' of the self. Chapters 4 and 5 discuss the most explicit forms of self-talk, dealing with feelings and the concept of an inner nature. Although the differences between these practices are not clear-cut, they point towards the different means by which the self was established.

Once and future Belgium

Through these three innovations – studying the self through institutions of criminal justice, attending to different and conflicting constellations of discourses of the self and approaching the self as a practice – this study is a plea for, and an example of, a new way to do the history of the self. It contrasts with the traditional historiography of the self by placing common people front and centre in the analysis and staying clear of all-too-encompassing narratives of the coming of the 'modern self'. At the same time, this approach still allows me to track changes over time, as institutions and practices evolved and discourses converged in new ways.

Most of the institutions, discourses and practices of the self that I discuss in this book were situated in the region that is currently Belgium, between c. 1750 and c. 1830. This is the period when, according to many scholars, the 'modern self' was made. It is therefore an excellent period to interrogate whether we can trace changing conceptions of the self over time, as well as to questions the social differentiation of these conceptions.

I have chosen to focus on Belgian archives for two reasons. First, its legal records are exceptionally rich. Thousands of interrogation transcripts and witness statements from all over the period have survived. Criminal trial records have been much better preserved than in many French or German regions, where often either the eighteenth-century or the nineteenth-century records are incomplete. Second, the country is interesting because of its close affinities with the rest of Europe. 'Belgian' history in this period is not the history of a national state. A Belgian history between 1750 and 1830 is also an Austrian, French and Dutch history.

Belgium only became an independent country in 1830. In 1750, although people had already started to use the term Belgium, historians generally refer to the region as the Southern Netherlands. In the South-East of what would later become Belgium, the Prince-Bishopric of Liège was an autonomous part of the Holy Roman Empire. The larger part, also called the Austrian Netherlands, was part of the Austrian Monarchy, a conglomerate which also included the Austrian mainland, the Bohemian Crown and Hungary. It was ruled by the Austrian Emperor but retained some autonomy; a local governor represented the emperor in most matters. In 1789, after longstanding dissatisfaction with the policies of Emperor Joseph II, the Belgians revolted to form the independent United States of Belgium in 1790. The independence was short-lived, as the region was brought back under Austrian rule the same year. The new emperor – Joseph II had passed away – could not enjoy his returned territories for long either, as the revolutionary French Republic conquered the region first temporarily in 1792 and then definitively in 1794. In 1795, what was by then called 'the former Belgium' became a part of the French Republic and later of the Napoleonic Empire. After Napoleon's defeat, the region merged with Liège and the Northern Netherlands (the former Dutch Republic) in 1814 and became a part of the Kingdom of the Netherlands. In 1830, Belgians felt insufficiently represented in this new country and declared independence. The resulting country had more or less the same borders it still has today.[61]

Not only politically, but also culturally, Belgium was entangled with its neighbouring countries. Dutch and French were the main languages used in the Southern Netherlands. Most people in the region that is now Flanders spoke a Dutch dialect, yet educated people most commonly read and wrote in French. French was the main language of high culture and of the central government, but local administrations and criminal courts in predominantly Dutch-speaking regions used Dutch.[62] The cultural influence of France was enormous and much greater than the cultural influence of the Dutch Republic. French novels, journals and treatises circulated widely and were read in coffee houses and learned societies and French plays were regularly performed. Original cultural productions show the influence of the latest cultural tendencies in neighbouring countries.[63] Culturally, the region was in many respects similar to a French province, even before it was politically integrated in the French Republic.

The cultural frames of reference for Belgium's inhabitants also extended beyond their own local communities through their religious affiliations. The vast majority of Belgians were Catholic; the share of Protestants, Jews and atheists was negligible. Since the seventeenth century, the Southern Netherlands had become a model of the success of the Counter Reformation. Except during the revolutionary decade, church attendance was high and people generally observed their Easter duties, more so than in France.[64] This was perhaps the country's most distinguishing feature.

Institutionally, the Southern Netherlands were diverse, at least up to 1795. Counties and duchies, such as Flanders and Brabant, and larger cities, such as Brussels, Ghent and Antwerp, had a strong autonomy in the eighteenth century. In contrast with France, criminal justice was firmly controlled by the urban courts. These courts all had their own legal traditions. Nevertheless, most criminal courts roughly operated in a similar way. Although the Austrian criminal codes were never formally adopted, criminal courts followed procedures that were more or less inspired by the criminal code decreed by Charles V in the sixteenth century. Moreover, judges used similar legal manuals, often also Dutch and French legal manuals, to guide their decisions.[65] After the French annexation of the Belgian territories in 1795, the French revolutionary legal system was installed. Henceforth, criminal justice operated in the same way as in other French regions. In 1810, it was replaced with the Napoleonic criminal justice system, which would remain in place with minor modifications even after the French were defeated, up to 1867. Even afterwards, the Belgian legal system continued to operate in quite a similar way to the French.[66]

Due to all its intertwinement with other European countries, historians have often claimed that Belgium was at the 'crossroads' of European history. In 1900, Belgium's most famous historian Henri Pirenne wrote that the country was 'a microcosm of western Europe'.[67] Some scholars continue to make such arguments up to this day, even if the precise constellation of laws, institutions, languages, religion, economy and culture led to some very specific situations. In any case, it does make Belgium an interesting case study of European history. While I will give some attention to the legal, social and cultural specificities of the different cities and regions I study, and of the Southern Netherlands as a whole, I especially seek to address how the specificities of each case can illuminate the broader European history of the self. The manifold political, legal and cultural changes that occurred in Belgium between 1750 and 1830 provide an opportunity to interrogate similar changes that occurred on a European scale. Throughout this book, I will therefore firmly place the Belgian developments within their European context, especially comparing, as far as the existing historiography allows, with the most closely related major powers in continental Europe – France and the German territories. The transformations of the self in Belgium were, I will show, part of a much wider shift in many European regions.

The smell of the archives

Records of the institutions of justice and policing are my main sources in this study. I will therefore often discuss crimes and criminal justice. This is, however, not a systematic legal or crime history. I have mined legal records for insights in the thoughts and feelings of eighteenth- and nineteenth-century people. As such, I discuss various cases and various crimes throughout the different chapters for what they can tell us about the history of the self. I have not always been methodical in my source selection and followed trails that simply seemed interesting. Criminal trial records form my main corpus, but I occasionally refer to police reports that did not lead to trials, to pardon letters and to criminal case discussions in the Privy Council. This has resulted in a broad perspective on eighteenth-and nineteenth-century life and culture, rather than a systematic history of crime and criminal justice.

Nevertheless, I have followed a few principles when selecting sources. I focus on four types of crime: homicide, suicide, sodomy and prostitution. I selected these four crimes for diverse reasons. Homicide was severely punishable, generally by death. The diverse homicide cases – murder, manslaughter, infanticide, parricide, duelling, poisoning – therefore generally contain the most thorough investigations, are plenty in number and have generally been well-preserved. Suicide and sodomy are both interesting because they were serious crimes at the beginning of this period. Sodomy was not only an unspeakable sin, but also punishable by death. The possessions of someone who committed suicide could be confiscated, so his or her family would inherit nothing; and the deceased's body could be dragged through the streets and hanged upside down. After 1795, however, both acts were (at least officially) decriminalised. This makes for interesting comparisons through time. Moreover, both crimes directly relate to questions of the self: in the case of suicide because the self decided to end its own life, in the case of sodomy because the question of motive could focus on (or deny) inner nature. Even though the number of both suicide and sodomy cases was limited, sodomy cases especially were sometimes very thorough. Finally, cases of prostitution are relevant because, like some of the homicide cases, prostitution could be interpreted as a more money-motivated offence. In comparison with the other crimes, prostitution was by far the lesser offence. There were no country-wide laws concerning prostitution, but some cities had municipal ordinances forbidding commercial sex. It was, however, at particular moments, one of the most frequently prosecuted minor infractions in larger cities. Punishments varied from expulsion and short-term confinement to public whippings. Combined with the other cases, prostitution cases give us access to the diverse spectrum of criminal investigation tools and procedures.

The necessity of selecting also means that I have not been able to study in detail the many trials records for other crimes. These choices have their consequences for the stories I am able to tell, and perhaps for the interpretations that result from them. Throughout this book, we encounter the histories of pain and remorse, poverty, honour and duelling, drunkenness and witchcraft, sentimentalism and nature. However, the histories of high politics and international relations, the public sphere, capitalism, industrialisation and emerging consumerism are less visible in this study (though not entirely absent), in part because of the types of crimes and sources I have focused on. So, although I have good reasons to focus on the crimes I have, it may well be possible to write a history of the self through the criminal records with a very different focus.

For the old regime period, I have studied the records of urban courts in three cities: Brussels, the capital, Antwerp, the country's third-largest city and main port (and hometown to Jacob Mol), and Kortrijk, a smaller town near the French border. For major cases, these courts also had jurisdiction over their surrounding countryside and smaller villages. Hence, their records provide a diverse sample of both people from the cities and from the countryside and of both French-speaking and Dutch-speaking citizens (though the latter were more numerous). After the annexation of Belgium in the French Republic in 1795 and the installation of a new criminal justice system, I have studied the criminal or assize courts with seats in Antwerp, Brussels and Bruges, responsible for the most serious crimes in the provinces in Antwerp, Brabant and West-Flanders, and the correctional courts in Antwerp, Brussels and Kortrijk that dealt with less serious crimes.

As a rule, I have only studied those cases for which witness statements or suspect interrogations have been preserved. As my research progressed, I have sometimes expanded my boundaries: because of the low number of sodomy cases, I have been more exhaustive in trying to collect 'all' sodomy cases in the Southern Netherlands. I have also added some cases that I encountered in the archives of the Privy Council and in the archives of the Council of Flanders, particularly on prostitution, sodomy and suicide. At other times, I have set additional limits: due to their bad condition, some of the homicide cases in the Assize Court of West-Flanders could not be studied, and as the number of cases was too high in the Assize Court of Brabant, I selected cases opting for as much diversity and breadth as possible. In sum, I have studied approximately four hundred court cases. In addition, I have also studied some eighty requests for grace between 1750 and 1795. For this sample, I selected all homicide cases from the first two boxes of each decade among the grace requests preserved in the archives of the Privy Council.[68]

The selection of these cases is not, and cannot, be neutral. As scholars of postcolonial and queer studies have shown, the histories that archives and records allow us to write are shaped by power. Police officers, judges, clerks and archivists determine in part which discourses are recorded, preserved and made accessible. They make possible certain histories, but not others.[69] Indeed, the preservation of criminal records has not always been self-evident. This study took me to trial records in various conditions: some archives were well inventoried, some only minimally, some not at all. Some documents were in peak condition, others were mainly dust.

The old regime archives of criminal justice were preserved with practical intent: when a convict applied for grace, which could happen many years after the trial, the court was to give its advice, preferably by referring to the witness statements and interrogations of the initial trial. Sometimes the Privy Council even asked them to copy the entire investigation for review. Upon reaching a verdict, the court clerk bagged the files relating to a case and the clerk or an officer of justice generally preserved them. But archival practices were not always smooth: in 1769, for instance, Rombout De Smet requested grace for the homicide his brother had committed eleven years earlier. The governor forwarded his request to the Brussels magistrates for their advice. They were unable to locate the records of their earlier investigations, as the prosecutor had recently deceased: 'We have searched the chambers of his office and his home, but all in vain'. They even wrote to the Paris police, where De Smet had fled after his crime, to enquire whether the files had been sent there. No, the lieutenant of the Paris police replied, adding that 'if, as you suppose, the files had been sent to me, they would certainly have been found, as the files in our depots are in meticulous order'.[70]

The documents that were deemed valuable for preservation were therefore those that established the evidence and circumstances of the crime. A typical trial record before 1795 – such as the file of Jacob Mol's trial – would contain records of preliminary witness hearings by a delegation of judges or the prosecutor. It would likely also contain a medical report certifying death and its cause in murder cases, an arrest warrant if the suspect was not immediately caught, the interrogation of the suspect, interlocutory judgments, the charges of the prosecutor and the retort of the defendant. If applicable it would also include attestations in favour of the defendant, witness hearings on the request of the defendant, a rejoinder by the prosecutor, sometimes the verdict and a report of its execution and sometimes a copy of a pardon letter and the advice of the magistrates. Most cases do not contain all of these documents. Records of prostitution trials, for instance, are generally very summary in nature; it is not difficult to relate this to their weak position and frequent arrests. Pleas by lawyers are usually not kept in trial files (though most defendants were not allowed a lawyer anyway), nor are detailed reports of the actual court sessions or justifications of the verdicts. In a few cases, legal advice sought by the judges has been preserved.

After the French annexation, the records of the abolished urban courts were to be transferred to the registries of the newly established courts of the first instance, although in many cases, they continued to be preserved locally, often in attics or town hall basements. Eventually, many of the trial records ended up in city archives. The archives of the newly established courts were dealt with in a different way: initially, the courts themselves kept them and only in the second half of the twentieth century they transferred them to the state archives. As archivists deemed the number of cases too high to preserve all of them, they have often destroyed trial records of the police and correctional courts when they were transferred to the state archives.[71]

The content of the new regime trial records was, to some extent, similar to before. More than before though, court files also served to document that the proper procedure had been followed, in case a defendant would appeal to the court of cassation, which would annul any trial that had not followed proper procedure. Clerks generally recorded every stage of the trial, even if only by a single sentence, and many administrative documents were preserved – orders for imprisonment, reports of the jury drawings, summons of witnesses and the like. The establishment of a professional police force in major cities resulted in the inclusion of police reports in many case files. Detailed reports of court sessions, witnesses' statements at the actual trials, pleas and reports of the deliberations of juries or judges were absent. These belonged to the oral part of the trial and were not written down.

The availability of particular criminal court documents thus relates to the power of the courts and of the archives: the documents were preserved to legitimise their actions. Both before and after 1795, witness statements and suspect interrogations are the most interesting documents for my purposes. The existence of such documents is not self-evident. For most British courts, for instance, they are non-existent, as trials were mainly oral affairs. In the Southern Netherlands, however, as in France, Germany and the Northern Netherlands, a criminal trial was wholly or partially a written affair. Witness and suspect statements were therefore crucial evidence of the correct workings of justice and necessary for handling pardons and appeals. In contrast, up to the 1830s, unlike in Britain, there were few published criminal trial reports, even after trials became public in 1795. The practices of recording and preserving in order to authorise power have therefore shaped the analyses in this book.

Making the records

If the recording and preservation of documents were up to clerks and archivists, the production of these documents was a process of negotiation. They neither show only the perspective of the judiciary, nor provide access to the pure voices of the common people. I will closely attend to the circumstances of the suspect interrogation and its influence on the resulting records in chapter 1. For now, let us consider witness statements: to what extent can they inform a history of the self that seeks to include common people?

Witnesses provided crucial evidence in eighteenth- and nineteenth-century criminal cases. A police officer, a prosecutor or a magistrate heard them, locally or in the courthouse. In any case, the interrogator heard them separately, behind closed doors and without the presence of the suspect. A clerk was present to record the interrogation. In principle, the interrogator should not ask specific questions during this hearing (except for the witness' name and quality): legal commentators all over continental Europe stressed that witness depositions were not interrogations.[72] While it is obvious that on many occasions they did ask specific questions, the clerks sometimes (but not always) edited these out. After they had completed their statements, the clerk should read out the recorded statement to the witnesses, who had to confirm and sign it, or if they were unable to write, draw a mark. Neighbouring countries observed a similar procedure.

Magistrates and police officers certainly had much power in shaping the records of witness statements. They made clear that they had specific goals: they wanted reliable testimony that they could use to secure a conviction and they often pushed their investigation in a certain direction. Magistrates sought a story they could understand in terms of the law. Moreover, as witnesses made their statements, they had to swear an oath that they would speak the truth, which made them liable to prosecution for perjury.[73] In the trial against Laurent Spinoy in 1824, a local court secretary reported that after witness hearings, he spread the rumour that some witnesses would be arrested for perjury, with the (successful) intent of getting them to reveal more information.[74] Although few trials for perjury were held, some magistrates reminded witnesses of this possibility to get them to be more cooperative.

Magistrates further influenced how witnesses' statements would be recorded when they dictated a witness' declaration to their clerk. They often omitted questions and sometimes summarised witnesses' answers. While French and Belgian legal manuals remained vague about this, some German legal scholars explicitly recommended magistrates to summarise and thus only have legally relevant information written down.[75] In the ancien régime, clerks consistently wrote witness statements down in the third person. In the new justice system, practices varied: some clerks and officers continued to write them in the third person, while others started to use the first person (and some switched back and forth within one statement). They probably altered expressions they deemed vulgar, vernacular or colloquial. During the French period, trials were conducted in French and statements by Dutch-speaking witnesses were written down in translation.

Although we should not underestimate the power of magistrates and clerks, they could not make the witness statements all by themselves. Many witnesses liberally testified about things that were not relevant to the case at hand. From the resulting records, we know that at least in some cases clerks wrote down legally irrelevant statements, even if it is unclear to what extent they did so consistently. If magistrates and clerks altered the record of what people said, they had to make sure that they did not distort witnesses' words so much that they would not confirm them. Recorded statements perhaps did not reflect exactly what they had said, but they did reflect something they found 'sayable'. While people crafted a story, they also negotiated their truth.[76]

Witnesses could also advance their own agendas in their testimonies. Many were well aware of what would be counted as mitigating or aggravating circumstances and stressed or omitted certain facts in accordance with their relationship to the defendant.[77] At the same time, they created an image of themselves before justice and stressed their own moral superiority, knowledge or resourcefulness. For many witnesses, justice was something they could manipulate.[78]

How, then, must we read these strategic records? They do not provide access to the 'pure' voices or selves of the common people or even of the people who testified. This is not only the case because magistrates asked specific questions, intimidated them or distorted their words, but quite simply because there are no 'pure' voices.[79] What people said in court, they said in a particular legal context, with particular pressures and circumstances, with particular goals. Like every other historical source, legal records only provide 'situated testimony'.[80] That people found things worthy of saying and having recorded in a particular context makes them valuable. We should not worry too much about whether they were voicing their 'true beliefs' or their 'actual experiences': witnesses were crafting a story about a crime, a story based on imperfect memories, infused with elements of stories told and heard before, in reference to a situation of power difference.[81]

Unless the parties involved explicitly questioned particular elements, whether a story was true or whether people were 'authentic' does not matter as much as the fact that they said it and clerks recorded it. Witnesses and magistrates agreed that this was something that *could* have happened, something that was 'thinkable' and 'sayable'. Trial records are not interesting because they show a world beyond the judiciary, but because they show a dialogue between the judiciary and the world beyond. People tried certain strategies, learned which practices and discourses of the self were acceptable and which were not. If the discourses of self reported in court were not 'truthful', the fact that they were reported and recorded required people to relate to them. Legal records reveal practices by which the self was done, they reveal the presence of certain discourses of the self and they show how people negotiated the self in the institution of criminal justice.

Because they were a part of the institution of criminal justice, trial records do not just tell us something about the people involved in a trial. As I have argued above, through the power of the court, people's stories, discourses and practices had a wider impact. In the old regime, in the Austrian Netherlands as in France and most German territories, witness statements did not become public, but people could of course tell others about their experiences. The notable exception was the Antwerp court, where in some cases witnesses had to repeat the statements they had first given privately in the public court session.[82] In this way, they could reach a far greater audience. This practice became standard in all courts after 1795, with the adoption of the new French procedures. The press even started to report some of the public witness statements. These testimonies were often similar to previous private statements. If not, the judge could have their previous statement read aloud.[83] The negotiations of discourses and practices reported in the trial records could therefore inspire a wide audience, especially after 1795.

By their very nature, some aspects of self and society do not or only rarely show up in criminal courts. In this, however, trial records are not different from other sources to study the self: Rousseau or Hume, novels or diaries, educational plans or psychological manuals all provide a specific and contextual access to the self. Criminal court records have the distinct advantage of involving the lives of a broad cross-section of society, including many ordinary people, who do not often show up in other sources.

Reading the records

The density of criminal records precludes a straightforward approach to reading and interpreting the self in trial records. My approach to these documents has been to subject them to multiple, partially structured analyses. For each case, I first read through the entire case record, giving particular attention to accusations, witness statements, interrogations, conclusions and verdicts. I then made structured notes of the cases, summarising them and transcribing elements that seemed particularly relevant to my research: practices of the self, discourses of the self, discord between the parties involved, emotional practices and discourses, personal reflections, unusual proceedings and generally any detail that struck me as interesting – even if I did not yet know how to interpret it. In a second phase, I entered these notes in a qualitative analysis software programme, Dedoose. As I reread all my notes, I started to 'code' them with particular tags that I developed as I went along. Tags could indicate particular practices of self or emotions (e.g. self-talk, laughing, confession), particular strategies of defence (e.g. poverty, young age, insanity), particular interpretations of crimes, the use of objects or places or just generally that something was remarkable. In a third phase, I consolidated a more stable set of codes and went through all the records again, adding or changing codes as relevant. This process led me to become intimately familiar with the cases and their logics.

When conducting my analysis, I used these codes in two ways. First, they provided a structured overview of each case, showing the internal sequence of relevant discourses and practices. Second, I could easily search for similar aspects across different cases, allowing for instance an analysis of diachronic change in the use of certain discourses, which could then easily be viewed in the original context of their case. While the software also allows for quantitative analysis, I have only used this as a heuristic device. Given the difficulty of interpreting discourses and practices of the self and the relevance of their context, counting codes would give an illusionary and dangerous sense of certainty and stability. Only in a few rare instances will I discuss precise numbers. What matters most for my analysis is how people said things, in what circumstances and with what effects. While I will not be able to avoid characterising certain phenomena as 'frequent', 'often' or 'increasingly', I think that the vagueness of these terms better captures the instability of historical knowledge.

I will often contextualise quotations from the archives, but for the sake of readability and conciseness I will sometimes quote fragments from the archives without much context. I will sometimes construct narratives as if they directly reflect a situation, without noting that these narratives are the result of my prior deconstruction of judicially situated narratives of one or several witnesses. I hope to strike a fair balance between deconstructing my sources and reconstructing a fluent historical narrative. If witnesses and suspects were often clever narrators in eighteenth- and nineteenth-century trials, I believe it is the privilege and the duty of historians to be so as well.

The case of Jacob Mol, as I have related it throughout this introduction, shows the different ways in which I will approach my sources. I initially told the story as if my reconstruction, based mainly on Mol's interrogation and the judges' conclusions, reflects what had actually happened. I do not know that, of course, but this initial reconstruction serves as a background to understand the strategies Mol and the courts used and to uncover conflicting discourses and practices of the self. I will close this introduction, again, in a more narrative style. In March 1750, Mol's parents wrote to the governor to obtain grace for their son. The governor asked the Antwerp magistrates for their advice, and they were sympathetic, agreeing with Mol's exculpating narratives of self. The crime, they judged, was 'not premeditated, but a sudden rage, which the victim may have given occasion to with her insults and her reproaches'. The 'wickedness' of the wife, who was a 'veritable fury', had, moreover, been established and Mol had turned himself in voluntarily. They therefore recommended to grant him grace. Mol was pardoned on the occasion of Good Friday 1750, on the condition that he paid the legal costs.[84]

Notes

1 Felix Archives, Antwerp (FA), *Vierschaer (V)*, 103 (Jacob Mol 1750).

2 Jan Goldstein, *The Post-Revolutionary Self: Politics and Psyche in France, 1750–1850* (Cambridge, MA: Harvard University Press, 2005), pp. 1–2; Elwin Hofman, 'How to do the history of the self', *History of the Human Sciences*, 29:3 (2016), 9–10. This introduction contains material that was first published in a different form in the latter article.

3 For a more extensive historiographical overview, see Elwin Hofman, 'Sources of the self from the renaissance to the 20th century', in Wade E. Pickren (ed.), *The Oxford Encyclopedia of the History of Psychology* (Oxford: Oxford University Press, 2020), doi: 10.1093/acrefore/9780190236557.013.685.

4 Jacob Burckhardt, *Die Kultur der Renaissance in Italien* (Basel: Schwabe, 1978).

5 E.g. C. B. Macpherson, *The Political Theory of Possessive Individualism: Hobbes to Locke* (Oxford: Clarendon, 1962); Louis Dumont, *Essais sur l'individualisme: une perspective anthropologique sur l'idéologie moderne* (Paris: Seuil, 1983).

6 Charles Taylor, *Sources of the Self: The Making of the Modern Identity* (Cambridge, MA: Harvard University Press, 1989).

7 Goldstein, *The Post-Revolutionary Self*.

8 Dror Wahrman, *The Making of the Modern Self: Identity and Culture in Eighteenth-Century England* (New Haven: Yale University Press, 2004), p. xv.

9 Wahrman, *The Making of the Modern Self*, p. xi.

10 Jerrold Seigel, *The Idea of the Self: Thought and Experience in Western Europe since the Seventeenth Century* (Cambridge: Cambridge University Press, 2005).

11 E.g. Tim Hitchcock and Robert Shoemaker, *London Lives: Poverty, Crime and the Making of a Modern City, 1690–1800* (Cambridge: Cambridge University Press, 2015), p. 17.

12 Anna Clark, *Alternative Histories of the Self: A Cultural History of Sexuality and Secrets, 1762–1917* (London: Bloomsbury Academic, 2017).

13 Seigel, *The Idea of the Self*; Charly Coleman, *The Virtues of Abandon: An Anti-Individualist History of the French Enlightenment* (Stanford: Stanford University Press, 2014).

14 Rudolf Dekker, 'Introduction', in Rudolf Dekker (ed.), *Egodocuments and History: Autobiographical Writing in Its Social Context since the Middle Ages* (Hilversum: Verloren, 2002), pp. 7–20; Arianne Baggerman, 'Autobiography and family memory in the nineteenth century', in Rudolf Dekker (ed.), *Egodocuments and History: Autobiographical Writing in Its Social Context since the Middle Ages* (Hilversum: Verloren, 2002), pp. 161–73; Arianne Baggerman, Rudolf Dekker and Michael Mascuch, 'Introduction', in Arianne Baggerman, Rudolf Dekker and Michael Mascuch (eds), *Controlling Time and Shaping the Self: Developments in Autobiographical Writing since the Sixteenth Century* (Leiden: Brill, 2011), pp. 13–32.

15 E.g. John Jeffries Martin, *Myths of Renaissance Individualism* (Basingstoke: Palgrave Macmillan, 2004); Moshe Sluhovsky, *Becoming a New Self: Practices of Belief in Early Modern Catholicism* (Chicago: University of Chicago Press, 2017).

16 Laura Kounine, *Imagining the Witch: Emotions, Gender, and Selfhood in Early Modern Germany* (Oxford: Oxford University Press, 2018), p. 136.

17 Kounine, *Imagining the Witch*, pp. 18–20.

18 Friedrich Nietzsche, *On the Genealogy of Morals* (New York: Random House, 1967), pp. 84–5. Even earlier, John Locke already noted the affinities between

self and criminal justice, claiming that the self was a 'forensic' concept, crucial for the operation of justice: John Locke, *An Essay Concerning Human Understanding*, ed. Peter Harold Nidditch (Oxford: Clarendon, 1975), bk. II, chap. 27, paras 18, 20, 26.

19 Cf. Judith Butler, *Giving an Account of Oneself* (New York: Fordham University Press, 2005), pp. 10–15.

20 Michel Foucault, *Discipline and Punish: The Birth of the Prison* (New York: Vintage Books, 1995).

21 Michel Foucault, *The History of Sexuality. Volume I: An Introduction* (New York: Pantheon Books, 1978); Michel Foucault, *Mal faire, dire vrai: fonction de l'aveu en justice* (Louvain-la-Neuve: Presses Universitaires de Louvain, 2012).

22 David Warren Sabean, 'Production of the self during the age of confessionalism', *Central European History*, 29 (1996), 17–18; David Warren Sabean, *Power in the Blood: Popular Culture and Village Discourse in Early Modern Germany* (Cambridge: Cambridge University Press, 1984); Nikolas Rose, *Inventing Our Selves: Psychology, Power and Personhood* (Cambridge: Cambridge University Press, 1996); Nikolas Rose, *Governing the Soul: The Shaping of the Private Self*, 2nd ed. (London: Free Association Books, 1999).

23 Harry Oosterhuis, *Stepchildren of Nature: Krafft-Ebing, Psychiatry, and the Making of Sexual Identity* (London: University of Chicago Press, 2000), pp. 13–15; Kounine, *Imagining the Witch*, pp. 17–19; Mathew Thomson, *Psychological Subjects: Identity, Culture, and Health in Twentieth-Century Britain* (Oxford: Oxford University Press, 2006), pp. 6–7.

24 Frank Biess *et al.*, 'History of emotions', *German History*, 28:1 (2010), 75.

25 Julie Hardwick, *Family Business: Litigation and the Political Economies of Daily Life in Early Modern France* (Oxford: Oxford University Press, 2009), p. 123. See also Shannon McSheffrey, 'Detective fiction in the archives: court records and the uses of law in late Medieval England', *History Workshop Journal*, 65:1 (2008), 66.

26 Laura Gowing, *Common Bodies: Women, Touch and Power in Seventeenth-Century England* (New Haven: Yale University Press, 2003), p. 13.

27 Carolyn Steedman, *History and the Law: A Love Story* (Cambridge: Cambridge University Press, 2020), p. 223.

28 Elwin Hofman, 'A wholesome cure for the wounded soul: confession, emotions, and self in eighteenth- and nineteenth-century Catholicism', *Journal of Religious History*, 42 (2018), 222–41; John Bossy, 'The social history of confession in the age of the Reformation', *Transactions of the Royal Historical Society*, 25 (1975), 21–38; W. David Myers, *'Poor, Sinning Folk': Confession and Conscience in Counter-Reformation Germany* (Ithaca: Cornell University Press, 1996); Caroline Muller, 'Ce que confessent les journaux intimes: un nouveau regard sur la confession (France, XIXe siècle)', *Circé. Histoires, Cultures et Sociétés*, 4 (2014); Coleman, *The Virtues of Abandon*; Sluhovsky, *Becoming a New Self*; Sabean, *Power in the Blood*; Thomas Robisheaux, 'Penance, confession, and the self in early modern Lutheranism', in Marjorie Elizabeth Plummer and Robin Barnes (eds), *Ideas and Cultural Margins in*

Early Modern Germany: Essays in Honor of H.C. Erik Midelfort (Farnham: Ashgate, 2009), pp. 117–30; Kounine, *Imagining the Witch*.

29 Rebekka Habermas, *Thieves in Court: The Making of the German Legal System in the Nineteenth Century* (New York: Cambridge University Press, 2016); Kounine, *Imagining the Witch*; Katie Barclay, *Men on Trial: Performing Emotion, Embodiment and Identity in Ireland, 1800–45* (Manchester: Manchester University Press, 2019).

30 Clifford Geertz, '"From the native's point of view": on the nature of anthropological understanding', *Bulletin of the American Academy of Arts and Sciences*, 28 (1974), 31; Martin Sökefeld, 'Debating self, identity, and culture in anthropology', *Current Anthropology*, 40 (1999), 429.

31 Geertz, '"From the native's point of view"', 31.

32 Melford E. Spiro, 'Is the Western conception of the self "peculiar" within the context of the world cultures?', *Ethos*, 21 (1993), 107–153.

33 D. W. Murray, 'What is the western concept of the self? On forgetting David Hume', *Ethos*, 21 (1993), 3–23; Dorothy Holland and Andrew Kipnis, 'Metaphors for embarrassment and stories of exposure: the not-so-egocentric self in American culture', *Ethos*, 22 (1994), 316–42; Sökefeld, 'Debating self'.

34 Mary McIntosh, 'The homosexual role', *Social Problems*, 16 (1968), 182–92.

35 Edward Stein (ed.), *Forms of Desire: Sexual Orientation and the Social Constructionist Controversy* (New York: Routledge, 1992).

36 Among 'essentialists', John Boswell has been most prominent: John Boswell, *Christianity, Social Tolerance, and Homosexuality: Gay People in Western Europe from the Beginning of the Christian Era to the Fourteenth Century* (Chicago: University of Chicago Press, 1980). For many 'constructionists', the first volume of Foucault's *History of sexuality* has provided a theoretical point of departure: Foucault, *The History of Sexuality*. An authoritative account is David F. Greenberg, *The Construction of Homosexuality* (Chicago: University of Chicago Press, 1988).

37 Eve Kosofsky Sedgwick, *Epistemology of the Closet* (Berkeley: University of California Press, 1990).

38 David M. Halperin, *How to Do the History of Homosexuality* (Chicago: University of Chicago Press, 2002).

39 Cf. Nima Bassiri, 'What kind of history is the history of the self? New perspectives from the history of mind and brain medicine', *Modern Intellectual History*, 16:2 (2019), 665.

40 Barbara Carnevali, 'Rousseau et l'authenticité. Le concept d'authenticité chez Rousseau', in Yves Citton and Jean-François Perrin (eds), *Jean-Jacques Rousseau et l'exigence d'authenticité. Une question pour notre temps* (Paris: Classiques Garnier, 2014), pp. 23–34.

41 Eveline Koolhaas-Grosfeld, 'Behind the mask of civility: physiognomy and unmasking in the early eighteenth-century Dutch Republic', in Arianne Baggerman, Rudolf Dekker and Michael Mascuch (eds), *Controlling Time and Shaping the Self: Developments in Autobiographical Writing since the Sixteenth Century* (Leiden: Brill, 2011), pp. 247–66.

42 Wahrman, *The Making of the Modern Self*, chap. 7.

43 Wahrman, *The Making of the Modern Self*, pp. 278–81.

44 Cf. Roy Porter, 'Introduction', in Roy Porter (ed.), *Rewriting the Self: Histories from the Renaissance to the Present* (London: Routledge, 1997), pp. 1–14.

45 Seigel, *The Idea of the Self*.

46 Coleman, *The Virtues of Abandon*. I adapt the term 'dispossession' from Coleman, who uses it in a more limited way, to refer to positive aspirations, not to unintended losses of self-control.

47 Dana Rabin, *Identity, Crime, and Legal Responsibility in Eighteenth-Century England* (Basingstoke: Palgrave Macmillan, 2004).

48 Goldstein, *The Post-Revolutionary Self*, chap. 7.

49 Josephine Hoegaerts, *Masculinity and Nationhood, 1830–1910: Constructions of Identity and Citizenship in Belgium* (Basingstoke: Palgrave Macmillan, 2014), p. 6.

50 Lynn Hunt, *Inventing Human Rights: A History* (New York: W. W. Norton, 2007), p. 33.

51 Sökefeld, 'Debating self'.

52 Cf. William M. Reddy, 'Historical research on the self and emotions', *Emotion Review*, 1:4 (2009), 302–15.

53 For recent overviews of the field and its methods, see Rob Boddice, *The History of Emotions* (Manchester: Manchester University Press, 2018); Barbara H. Rosenwein and Riccardo Cristiani, *What Is the History of Emotions?* (Cambridge: Polity, 2018); Jan Plamper, *The History of Emotions: An Introduction* (Oxford: Oxford University Press, 2015); Susan J. Matt and Peter N. Stearns (eds), *Doing Emotions History* (Urbana: University of Illinois Press, 2014).

54 Peter N. Stearns and Carol Z. Stearns, 'Emotionology: Clarifying the history of emotions and emotional standards', *The American Historical Review*, 90 (1985), 813.

55 Josephine Hoegaerts and Tine Van Osselaer, 'De lichamelijkheid van emoties. Een introductie', *Tijdschrift voor geschiedenis*, 126:4 (2013), 454.

56 William M. Reddy, 'Against constructionism: the historical ethnography of emotions', *Current Anthropology*, 38:3 (1997), 327–51; William M. Reddy, *The Navigation of Feeling: A Framework for the History of Emotions* (Cambridge: Cambridge University Press, 2001).

57 Monique Scheer, 'Are emotions a kind of practice (and is that what makes them have a history)? A Bourdieuian approach to understanding emotion', *History and Theory*, 51:2 (2012), 193–220.

58 Scheer, 'Are emotions a kind of practice', 200.

59 Luther H. Martin, Huck Gutman and Patrick H. Hutton (eds), *Technologies of the Self: A Seminar with Michel Foucault* (Amherst: University of Massachusetts, 1988), p. 18.

60 Jan Goldstein, 'Foucault's technologies of the self and the cultural history of identity', in John Neubauer (ed.), *Cultural History after Foucault* (New York: de Gruyter, 1999), pp. 43–4.

61 On the territorial and political history of Belgium in this period, see Jane C. Judge, *United States of Belgium: The Story of the First Belgian Revolution*

(Leuven: Leuven University Press, 2018); Jan Roegiers and N. C. F. van Sas, 'Revolution in the North and South, 1780–1830', in J. C. H. Blom and Emiel Lamberts (eds), *History of the Low Countries* (New York: Berghahn, 2006), pp. 275–316.

62 Tom Verschaffel, *De weg naar het binnenland: geschiedenis van de Nederlandse literatuur 1700–1800, de Zuidelijke Nederlanden* (Amsterdam: Bert Bakker, 2017), pp. 27–32.

63 Michèle Mat, 'Boeken, ideeën, genootschappen in het Oostenrijkse "België"', in Hervé Hasquin (ed.), *Oostenrijks België, 1713–1794: de Zuidelijke Nederlanden onder de Oostenrijkse Habsburgers* (Brussels: Gemeentekrediet, 1987), pp. 239–62; Bram Van Oostveldt, *Tranen om het alledaagse: Diderot en het verlangen naar natuurlijkheid in het Brusselse theaterleven in de achttiende eeuw* (Hilversum: Verloren, 2013); Jeroom Vercruysse, 'Les pamphlets de la Révolution belge (1787–1791) et les Lumières philosophiques', *Revue belge de philologie et d'histoire*, 91:2 (2013), 317–26; Ilja Van Damme, 'Zotte verwaandheid. Over Franse verleiding en Zuid-Nederlands onbehagen, 1650–1750', in Raf De Bont and Tom Verschaffel (eds), *Het verderf van Parijs* (Leuven: Universitaire Pers Leuven, 2004), pp. 187–203.

64 W. Rombauts, *Het Paasverzuim in het bisdom Brugge (1840–1911)* (Leuven: Nauwelaerts, 1971); Liliane Voyé and Karel Dobbelaere, 'Portrait du catholicisme en Belgique', in Alfonso Pérez-Agote (ed.), *Portraits du catholicisme. Une comparaison européenne* (Rennes: Presses Universitaires de Rennes, 2012), pp. 11–61.

65 Jos Monballyu, *Six Centuries of Criminal Law: History of Criminal Law in the Southern Netherlands and Belgium (1400–2000)* (Leiden: Brill, 2014), pp. 15–18.

66 Monballyu, *Six Centuries*, pp. 27–33.

67 Henri Pirenne, *Histoire de Belgique: des origines au commencement du XIVe siècle* (Brussels: Henri Lamertin, 1900), p. viii. For antecedents, see Tom Verschaffel, *De hoed en de hond: geschiedschrijving in de Zuidelijke Nederlanden, 1715–1794* (Hilversum: Verloren, 1998), p. 301.

68 National Archives, Brussels (NA), *Privy Council Austrian Period – Cartons (PCAP-C)*, 587–647.

69 McSheffrey, 'Detective fiction in the archives', 65–6; Steven Maynard, 'Police/archives', *Archivaria*, 68 (2009), 159–82.

70 City Archives, Brussels (CAB), *Historical Archives (HA) Trials*, 10449. On the early modern legal archives, see also Harald Deceulaer, 'Introduction', in Harald Deceulaer, Sébastien Dubois and Laetizia Puccio (eds), *Het pleit is in den zak! Procesdossiers uit het ancien régime en hun perspectieven voor historisch onderzoek. Acta van de studiedag gehouden op het Algemeen Rijksarchief (11-03-2013)* (Brussels: State Archives, 2014), pp. 9–38.

71 Karel Velle, 'Gerechtelijke archieven en lokale geschiedenis (19de-20ste eeuw)', in Jan Art (ed.), *Hoe schrijf ik de geschiedenis van mijn gemeente?* (Ghent: Stichting Mens en Kultuur, 1996), pp. 232–9.

72 Benoît Garnot, 'La justice pénale et les témoins en France au 18e siècle: de la théorie à la pratique', *Dix-huitième siècle*, 39:1 (2007), 102.

73 Monballyu, *Six Centuries*, pp. 414–23.

74 State Archives, Beveren (SABE), *Assize Court of Antwerp (AC-ANT)*, 1378, Exhib. 63.

75 Peter Becker, '"Recht schreiben" – Disziplin, Sprachbeherrschung und Vernunft. Zur Kunst des Protokollierens im 18. und 19. Jahrhundert', in Michael Niehaus and Hans-Walter Schmidt-Hannisa (eds), *Das Protokoll: Kulturelle Funktionen einer Textsorte* (Frankfurt am Main: Peter Lang, 2005), pp. 52–5.

76 Cf. Elizabeth S. Cohen, 'She Said, He Said: Situated Oralities in Judicial Records from Early Modern Rome', *Journal of Early Modern History*, 16:4–5 (2012), 417–18.

77 Gowing, *Common Bodies*, p. 13. On the idea of 'law in society' for the history of sexuality, see Stephen Robertson, 'What's law got to do with it? Legal records and sexual histories', *Journal of the History of Sexuality*, 14:1/2 (2005), 161–85.

78 Cf. Garnot, 'La justice pénale et les témoins', 103–5.

79 Frances E. Dolan, *True Relations: Reading, Literature, and Evidence in Seventeenth-Century England* (Philadelphia: University of Pennsylvania Press, 2013), 112–53. See also John H. Arnold, 'The historian as inquisitor: the ethics of interrogating subaltern voices', *Rethinking History*, 2:3 (1998), 379–86.

80 Cf. Cohen, 'She Said, He Said'.

81 Gowing, *Common Bodies*, p. 14; Amy Gilman Srebnick, 'Does the representation fit the crime? Some thoughts on writing crime history as cultural text', in Amy Gilman Srebnick and René Levy (eds), *Crime and Culture: An Historical Perspective* (Aldershot: Ashgate, 2005), p. 19.

82 Edmond Poullet, *Histoire du droit pénal dans le duché de Brabant, depuis l'avénement de Charles-Quint jusqu'à la réunion de la Belgique à la France, à la fin du XVIIIe siècle* (Brussels: Hayez, 1870), p. 314; Wim Meewis, *De vierschaar: de criminele rechtspraak in het Oude Antwerpen van de veertiende tot het einde van de achttiende eeuw* (Kapellen: Pelckmans, 1992), pp. 72–101.

83 Monballyu, *Six Centuries*, pp. 428–33.

84 FA, V, 103 (Jacob Mol 1750).

1

The self in court: procedures of conscience and confession

In 1757, Joanne Catherine Janssens stood trial for breaking banishment and complicity to murder before the magistrates in Kortrijk. Janssens was involved with a band of vagrant 'Egyptians'. According to witness statements, they had broken into the house of Joannes van Gampelaere near Tielt on 15 September 1757. Janssens, who was acquainted with Gampelaere's wife, had talked her way in and then the rest of the band had burst in, robbed the house and stabbed the owners. The Kortrijk magistrates sent word to other cities to arrest all gypsies and two women were arrested in Ghent, one of whom was identified as Janssens. She was transferred to Kortrijk, where she denied that she had been involved in the robbery and murder.[1]

The local magistrates soon found out that judges in Liège had previously convicted Janssens for robberies and branded her. She had been exiled from the Southern Netherlands. The magistrates seemed to agree that this allowed them to take harsher measures than usual. On 10 November, the prosecutor went to visit Janssens in prison. Having been imprisoned for almost a month, she asked him whether her case would come up soon. He replied that she could be imprisoned for a long time, as she had denied her presence in the murder. Janssens asked 'if she had been present, and if she confessed this, would she need to die?' The prosecutor said that he did not think so. She then confessed that she had been present at the murder scene, but had not been involved and had not been aware of what the others were up to.

Two weeks later, however, Janssens retracted this confession. She claimed that she had only confessed because the prison guard had recommended this. Nevertheless, the magistrates wanted their confession and condemned Janssens to torture. When she was brought to the torture chamber, Janssens immediately confessed that she had been present in the murder, but said that she had been forced by her companions to go along. A month later, the court condemned her to death by hanging.

In the quest for the truth, the judiciary personnel had threatened Janssens, lied to her and condemned her to torture.

How can we understand this criminal procedure? And what does it tell us about the self as practised in criminal procedures? In this chapter, I discuss the changing procedures of criminal investigation and criminal justice in the Southern Netherlands between 1750 and 1830 within their wider European context. My aim is not, however, to write a history of legal doctrines and practices – although that is a necessary part of my analysis. My aim is rather to analyse the underlying suppositions of the criminal justice system, looking for the conceptions of self that were inherent in the workings of criminal courts. The criminal trial was a technology for transforming the self, a technology that both legal staff and defendants used in different ways and to different ends. This chapter will provide an analysis of criminal trials as I argue that they became increasingly focused on people's inner sides, thus deepening these inner sides and making them more important, especially for women and common people. To do this, I will subsequently discuss criminal procedures in general, the uses of torture, the reforms of criminal justice, confession and resistance to it and the effects of giving an account of oneself in criminal court.

Procedures of truth

The legal system of the eighteenth-century Southern Netherlands was, in many respects, similar to how it had been since the late Middle Ages. In contrast with France, where an ordinance from 1670 regulated criminal procedure, and many other Habsburg territories, where the *Constitutio Criminalis Carolina* (1532) did the same (though less strictly), there was no unified criminal code.[2] Different towns, cities and counties had different regulations and legal procedures. There were central government regulations, regional state regulations and city regulations, local traditions and recommendations by legal scholars. This 'legal pluralism' gave the people involved in criminal justice a limited flexibility.[3] Nevertheless, even though each court had its own procedural peculiarities, most continental European courts operated in a similar way, in part resulting from the fact that they all referred to similar legal scholars to guide them.[4]

With some exceptions, urban courts monopolised criminal justice in the Southern Netherlands. Citizens could turn to informal or local means to resolve minor disputes, but major crimes were almost always brought before the aldermen of the nearest town or city.[5] The 'officers of justice' (the *hoogbaljuw* in Kortrijk, the *schout* in Antwerp and the *amman* in Brussels) were generally responsible for the detection and prosecution of crimes. Because they had few staff, they most commonly only came into action upon a complaint, or when someone found a corpse (surveillance and occasional raids in larger cities notwithstanding).

Once an officer of justice had learned of a serious crime, caught someone in the act or received a complaint, he was to investigate and inform the magistrates of his findings. In some jurisdictions, the officer of justice conducted this preliminary investigation himself; in others a delegation of the magistrates did this. They inspected the scene of the crime, called for experts to conduct a post-mortem and heard witnesses. Clerks wrote everything down more or less diligently.[6] If the initial investigation of a crime had been up to the officer of justice, the magistrates were to play a decisive role in the rest of the trial.[7] The magistrates consisted of the mayor (in Kortrijk) or two mayors (in Brussels and Antwerp) and between seven and eighteen aldermen of a particular town or city, sometimes accompanied by additional councillors. The central government selected them from a shortlist of nominees submitted by the current bench of aldermen (or other city notables) and appointed them for a limited term. They were always men and always members of aristocratic families or wealthy merchants and had generally not received legal training.[8] The magistrates based their decisions mostly on the written court records and acted as a single body. In the trial proceedings, as in most other documents, there are never indications of internal dissent. While magistrates undoubtedly held different opinions, they are difficult to retrieve.[9]

To decide whether a suspect was guilty, judges were not simply to trust their own opinion. In the thirteenth century, after the abolition of the judicial ordeals, Roman-Canon legal scholars developed an intricate system of proofs to determine the degree of a suspect's guilt. Most continental European secular criminal courts adopted this system by the sixteenth century. As a rule, judges needed 'full proof' to convict anyone to death. Such 'full proof' could consist of testimony by two independent and reliable eyewitnesses or of a confession corroborated by a few other indicators. For convictions of lesser sentences, lower standards of proof were required. For corporal punishment short of death, 'semi proof' – for instance testimony of a single reliable eyewitness – sufficed. Prostitutes could be expulsed or temporarily confined on the flimsiest of evidence.[10] Although courts officially still used the system of proof in the eighteenth century, they almost never applied the complicated arithmetic some legal scholars had proposed in earlier centuries. Most magistrates settled for the vague requirement that proof of guilt had to be 'clearer than daylight'.[11] This left the judges some room for appreciation of the evidence.

Like many of their French and German colleagues, judges in the Southern Netherlands almost always wanted a full confession before convicting someone to death – even if there was sufficient testimonial proof for a conviction. A confession was the 'queen of proofs'. 'However certain testimonial proof may be [...]', wrote the local alderman J. G. Thielen in his commentary on criminal procedure in 1789 (plagiarising his French colleague Daniel

Jousse), 'we can nevertheless reasonably say that this proof may be in error [...]; while a confession, and the knowledge of the accused, is incontestable'.[12] The central government officially discouraged any reluctance to convict anyone who did not confess, but it continued up to the eighteenth century.[13] In 1766, the council of Brabant argued that even when there was enough proof to convict a criminal, torture was a 'humane' instrument, for 'it served admirably to tranquilise the conscience and the heart of the judge', who was now sure he was not convicting an innocent man or woman.[14]

To obtain a confession from recalcitrant suspects, torture could indeed be a solution. But everywhere in Europe, its use in a judicial context was strictly regulated. Before magistrates could apply torture, they had to convict the suspect by an interlocutory sentence. They could only issue this sentence if the material fact of the crime had been proven, if the crime was capitally punishable and if there were strong indications of the suspect's guilt.[15] According to most European jurists, the court needed a 'half proof' (e.g. one reliable eyewitness).[16] The most common means of torturing suspects were flogging, stretching on the rack or the gradual tightening of a collar with metal pins on the inside. As in eighteenth-century France and Germany, if suspects confessed under these torments, their confession was only legally valid if they confirmed it afterwards, when they were free from pain or restrictions. If they did not confess or retracted their confession, they could not be convicted to death, but they could be convicted to a lesser sentence – or, in some cases, to another torture session.[17]

When the court was of the opinion that there was sufficient evidence, they closed the case and pronounced a sentence. The judges could find the suspect innocent or guilty, or they could release the suspect under caution because they were undecided. In both cases, they could condemn the defendants to the payment of the legal costs anyway.[18] The legal reasoning behind this was that they were partially guilty by portraying suspicious behaviour.[19] If they found a defendant guilty, judges pronounced punishments ranging from fines and short-term confinements on water and bread, over declarations of infamy and public whippings, to banishment and death in many varieties. As in most German courts, but unlike in most French courts, defendants generally had no possibility to appeal.[20] Convicts could only apply for grace, which I will discuss in the next chapter. If they did not, or if the monarch rejected their application, the court executed sentences as soon as possible.

The eighteenth-century criminal procedure did not generate much discourse on matters of the self or interiority. The 'law of proof', which guided criminal courts, aimed to find the truth about criminal acts, not about the criminals themselves. Criminal courts required proof that an individual had committed a crime and did not, at least in theory, care much about motivations or explanations. The criminal justice procedures thus promoted an outward-oriented self, perhaps malleable but rarely explicitly so. Above all, however, the individual psyche was marginal to the criminal procedure.[21]

The temptations of torture

Although torture was relatively rare in the eighteenth century across most of Europe, the practice demonstrates the law's attitude towards the self quite clearly. The justification of regulated judicial torture related to the Christian idea that pain and suffering were meaningful and productive. The classic idea behind torture was that by inflicting pain on suspects, their inherently sinful will would be crushed. While in severe pain, people would not be able to concoct false arguments. Pain – and not threats or promises, which defenders of torture decried – would lead to truth. A narrative revealed under torture – a spontaneous truth of the body – was therefore seen as more reliable than any voluntarily disclosed answer.[22] This implied a specific view of the self: the mind was deceitful, but the body would reveal the truth when the self lost control. Magistrates should destroy the will – a form of the self – to access the truth of the body. They could access a true account through the body, not through reflection or persuasion, not through the mind.

Clerks often recorded interrogations under torture in great detail, showing the importance and care given to them and revealing much about the ambiguities of the system in practice. A well-documented case is that of Jan Bailliu in 1780.[23] Bailliu stood accused of killing his wife, but he denied the allegations and claimed that she had died from natural causes. After a thorough investigation, the Ghent magistrates concluded that his story contained 'lies, variances and manifest contradictions' and found the evidence against him sufficient to warrant an examination under torture. On 4 September 1780, Bailliu was taken to the torture chamber. The executioner showed him the rack and the magistrates admonished him to speak the truth, but he persisted in his denials. The executioner stripped him naked and tied him to a chair with spikes. He put a collar with metal pins on him, which was attached to the walls of the room with tight ropes. Finally, the executioner attached heavy weights to his fingers and toes – but Bailliu continued to deny. At 15h30, the torture session began.

At 16h03, Bailliu 'hailed the mercy of the Lord and the Holy Mother of God'. At 16h06, he said 'to have been created for suffering'. At 16h15, that 'justice has no place anymore'. At 16h24, 'patience, if truth is no longer believed'. At 16h35, he shouted that 'If I am guilty for the world, I am not guilty for God'. And so he continued. On the one hand, Bailliu sought solace in his faith: suffering was justified in the imitation of Christ and divine mercy awaited him upon death. On the other, he discredited the criminal justice system and more particularly the magistrates who were interrogating him.

After an hour and a half, Bailliu joined in with one of the main critiques espoused by opponents of torture: 'Dictate me how I should tell the truth, and I will tell it', he repeated several times. 'Dictate my death and I will sign'. Slightly later, he concluded that 'being judge and being barbarian, it's more or less the same thing'. But then he again turned to a martyr's narrative: 'O joy, that I have to suffer without guilt'.

As the night fell, Bailliu became more recalcitrant. 'The more pain, the merrier', he shouted at 21h20. 'There is no pain that can be too much', he said at 5h35. He mocked the magistrates and the executioner, complementing the latter on his bondage skills. At 7h30, he started playing with the weights attached to his fingers, knocking on the rack and exclaiming 'Glockenspiel!'.

In between his defiant exclamations, Bailliu begged for mercy and promised that he would confess when released. When magistrates told him that he had to confess before his release, he always fell silent. But then, again, when the 24 hours were nearly over, he ironically expressed his sympathy with the executioner, telling him not to despair for it was almost over. After 24 hours of torture Bailliu was released – without a confession. As the magistrates could not convict him to death but were sufficiently convinced of his guilt, they sentenced him to thirty years of imprisonment in a house of correction.

Judicial torture is often interpreted as the epitome of the unbridled inquisitorial powers of the justice system over suspects. But in the interrogation under torture itself, the balance of power was not so clear. Indeed, the endurance of physical pain gave suspects a specific form of authority. The body in pain was a means of defiance. Tortured suspects could present themselves as martyrs, suffering unjustly and challenging their tormenters for it. Bailliu used his body in pain to assert himself as innocent: he remained in control of his self-narrative.

The Bailliu case was not exceptional. It has been found that in several regions in seventeenth- and eighteenth-century France, only between 3 and 15 per cent of those condemned to torture eventually confessed.[24] We do not have similar statistics for the Southern Netherlands and my own sample of cases in which courts applied torture is too small to draw conclusions. It seems, however, that torture was not an effective means to obtain a confession. Even if suspects confessed under torture, they had to confirm this confession 24 hours after they had been released from the rack. While the threat of further torture may have stimulated them to do so, some suspects retracted their confessions nonetheless.

Let us take a look at another examination under torture, in the case against Jean-Louis Allard. Allard, a twenty-year-old man from Hainaut, had been exiled for thefts. He was again confined on suspicion of thefts in 1772, but escaped his holding cell (while leaving the officer of justice a letter with apologies for his escape). He was arrested again and brought before the magistrates in Brussels later the same year, on suspicion of having murdered an elderly couple. After five interrogations, Allard kept denying the murder. The court condemned him to torture.

On 10 May 1773 at 9h08, Allard was attached to the chair and collar. The magistrates admonished him to tell the truth, but he stuck with his story. Initially, he was silent, but at 10h10, he began sighing and at 10h18, his body started curling. At 10h31, he asked for a confessor, moaned and called upon God several times. When admonished to speak the truth, he persisted that he already had. At 10h44, he moaned that he wanted to die for his sins, persisting that he had spoken the truth. At 10h56 he broke and asked to be released from the rack, confessing that he had committed the murder.[25]

After he gave some details on the murder, however, the magistrates did not immediately release Allard. They asked him to name his accomplices. Allard persisted that he had committed the murder alone. The magistrates were not convinced and repeated the question several times. Allard said, 'that he had committed them alone, that he wanted God to throw him in Hell if he had an accomplice'. He noted that if he had had an accomplice, nothing would keep him from confessing, as he was to die anyway.

The torture continued. At 13h35, the prisoner begged to be released, insisting that he had spoken the truth. He again called upon God to have the torments stopped. 'Take my life', he shouted at 14h30, 'so I don't have to suffer any longer'. At 15h, he finally confessed that he had had two accomplices – two people who had also been apprehended. However, the magistrates still wanted to clarify some details. At 18h42, finally, he was released from the rack. The next day, Allard confirmed his confessions, but he excluded the declarations about his accomplices. Once again, he insisted that he had committed his crime alone.

The dynamics of the Allard case were wholly different to those of the Bailliu case. While Allard also took refuge in his faith, he was unable to use his pain to shift the balance of power and mock his interrogators. He could not assert himself in the way Bailliu did. The pain was so unbearable that he preferred dying – and he therefore confessed to the crime. Initially, however, he did not want to implicate anyone else. Only hours after he had confessed his own crime, he told the magistrates what they wanted to hear: the two other suspects, one of whom had already confessed, were his accomplices. When he had to confirm this afterwards, he retracted this part, even while signing his own death warrant and risking further torture. Perhaps this was a sign of his exceptional loyalty to his accomplices. The judges interpreted it, however, as a sign of his exceptional loyalty to the truth. Allard's reluctance to implicate his accomplices led magistrates to conduct an additional investigation. They concluded that the confession of one of the supposed accomplices had been false. Allard had acted alone. The value of torture as an instrument to produce truth was both confirmed and contradicted. It was confirmed, as Allard hesitated to implicate his accomplices and the magistrates interpreted this as an important clue. It was also contradicted, as Allard did actually implicate accomplices and told magistrates the story they wanted to hear, just to be released from torture. Torture led to the truth that was eventually accepted, but not because the body in pain necessarily spoke truth. The success of judicial torture hinged on its failure.

Both the Bailliu and Allard cases could be supplemented with other cases of judicial torture. In 1777, magistrates in Kortrijk interrogated Antoine Femmechon under torture. He persisted in claiming his innocence for eight hours.[26] In 1792, the Antwerp judges tortured Philip Mertens seven times: he confessed each time, but retracted his confession after he had been released from the rack. Only the last time he confirmed his confession and was condemned to death.[27] All of these cases testify to the ambiguous position of judicial torture. Magistrates still hoped that it would bring truth, but all too often it implied untruth. Torture was a means for magistrates to crush the self, but defendants could use it to assert the self.

Calls for reform

The criminal justice procedures as described above were – very broadly – how they were operating in the 1750s. Even then, already, legal practices all over Europe were changing under the influence of an Enlightenment climate of critique. To properly understand how the self was practised in criminal courts, I need to make a detour along the manifold reforms of criminal justice from the 1780s to the 1810s. Reformers sought to establish a criminal justice system that was fairer and more efficient, while magistrates softened the perceived harsh edges of the system in practice.[28] Many eighteenth-century reformers focused their attention on punishment. They would contribute to the rise of imprisonment and discipline as a means to 'correct' criminals, rather than punish crimes, a movement that was particularly strong in the Southern Netherlands.[29] This movement implied a stronger focus on the self on the part of criminal justice: they became more interested in the individuals before them, and not only in the specific crimes they had committed. Many reformers believed that criminals were not inherently evil, but badly educated. Through a better penal system and better education, society could be perfected.[30]

Besides cruel punishments, judicial torture was a thorn in the eye of the reformers. Their critiques of torture related to changing conceptions of pain, body and truth. They argued that pain did not lead defendants to speak the truth, but made them say whatever the interrogators wanted to hear, so that the pain would stop.[31] Around 1787, an anonymous former councillor in the Southern Netherlands railed against torture: it was a 'barbarous practice', which 'produces false confessions, for the desire to stop suffering leads to a deceitful declaration during torture, which is then confirmed afterwards out of fear of seeing the torture recommence'.[32] As we have seen, Jan Bailliu echoed these sentiments during his torture session. While religious appreciations of pain continued to occur, some came to see pain as only negative, something which to avoid at all times.[33] Even proponents of torture no longer made explicit its traditional supporting doctrine – that pain destroyed the obstreperous will. Almost no one seemed to still accept that pain had truth value. To speak truth, one was to have presence of mind and free will – the free will that pain destroyed. The abolition of torture related to a greater appreciation of the self as the origins of truth, rather than an obstacle to the truth.[34]

At the same time, the movement against torture was also linked to the culture of sensibility. Reformers framed their cries to abolish torture as a humanitarian movement, inspired by fellow feeling and sympathy. Many people came to accept that people 'felt with' the pain which they saw being administered to others. It is from this background that Goswin de Fierlant, the prime criminal justice reformer in the Austrian Netherlands, denounced torture as 'injustice' and 'barbarism'; it is from this background he denounced that (possibly innocent) people had to endure such torments. Fierlant and other abolitionists, all sensitive men, sympathised with those who had to endure pain. Some abolitionists criticised judges who used torture because it showed their lack of sympathetic feeling.[35] As a result, through sympathy and sensibility, an orientation towards the body was supplemented with an orientation towards the feeling and thinking self.

The implementation of the proposed reforms was no easy matter. The central government in the Austrian Netherlands was eager to reform criminal justice, expecting that they would be able to curtail the power of local elites that still held a quasi-monopoly on the administration of criminal justice. They put Goswin de Fierlant to work developing a new criminal code, but his proposals, formulated in his *Premières idées sur la réformation des loix criminelles*, were unsuccessful, especially due to the resistance of provincial and local courts. Only some smaller reforms were implemented: in 1782 the government decreed that suicide would no longer be punished.[36]

In 1784, it decreed that local courts could only apply torture after they had obtained permission from the Privy Council. The Council did not frequently deny this permission, however.[37] The resistance of the provincial and local courts seems to suggest that they disagreed with the 'modern' legal ideas the central government propagated. However, while the courts heavily defended their right to use torture and capital and corporal punishments, their use declined throughout the country. It seems, therefore, that the resistance to the reforms from above was at least in part politically motivated: the courts and councils did not want to lose their autonomy.[38]

Revolutionising criminal justice

Elsewhere in Europe, people proposed similar reforms. The debates were fierce in France, where many found a minor reform of criminal procedure in 1788 insufficient. Discontent about criminal justice contributed to the French Revolution.[39] The *Declaration of the Rights of Man and the Citizen* stipulated that all men were born free and equal in rights, that limits on their rights were to be established in laws and that the laws should be applied to everyone in the same way. The declaration formally rejected arbitrary orders, unnecessary punishments and presumptions of guilt. These declarations proposed individual autonomy and clear boundaries between selves. More than in the old regime, the law was specifically interested in individuals.[40]

The general principles were put into specific criminal laws between October 1789 and October 1791. Transparency, equality, legality and proportionality were the central aims of the criminal reforms.[41] The new criminal justice system was very concerned with the rights of the accused and took inspiration from the English criminal justice system. The new laws forbade torture in all its forms and all defendants had the right to a solicitor. Out of distrust of the power of judges, the legislators decided that the government would no longer appoint magistrates, but that the people (i.e. propertied men) would elect them from among themselves for a limited period of time. Only actions explicitly defined by the law could be criminal, and the codes also stipulated the punishment for any given crime. There was no room for arbitrariness on the part of the judge. Moreover, popular juries, drawn for each case from a list of eligible citizens, would determine guilt in serious criminal cases.[42]

Three degrees of courts were installed: police courts, which operated on the smallest jurisdiction and treated minor offences; correctional courts, with larger jurisdictions and more important cases, such as theft and public indecency; and criminal courts (later called assize courts), with the largest jurisdiction and the most serious crimes. In addition to these courts, there was a court of cassation in Paris, to which all convicts could appeal if they thought their sentence was contrary to law or to their fundamental rights.[43] In minor cases, judges only heard suspects and witnesses in court and then formulated a verdict.[44] In cases before the criminal courts, the justice of the peace conducted a more extensive preliminary investigation and then a judge appointed as 'director of the jury' followed up. He drafted an act of accusation. A jury of accusation then had to judge whether the evidence was sufficient to conduct a trial, and to this end they heard relevant witnesses and the accused orally in session. If so, the case was brought before a jury of judgment, who again heard both parties' witnesses. The public accuser and the defendant or his or her counsel then gave their pleas. The president of the court formulated a number of questions for the jury to answer. If found guilty, the judges then sentenced the accused to the punishment stipulated by the law.[45]

A crucial change in the procedures of criminal justice was that juries were not to determine guilt on the basis of a system of proofs as in the old regime, but to trust their 'inner conviction' (*conviction intime*). The value of confessions, witness statements and all sorts of proof was no longer predetermined: juries had to weigh the evidence for themselves. In this way, the truth of the law was to be the same truth as the truth in society.[46] This new evaluation of evidence again presupposed a changing conception of the self on the part of the legislators. Inspired by the ideas of sensibility, legislators based this system on a socially oriented self. By seeing and hearing witnesses and defendants during the trial, they argued, jurors would feel with them and be able to come to a just verdict.[47] The whole concept of 'inner conviction' and its association with feeling and fellow feeling announced the increased orientation of criminal justice towards the interior – of the magistrate, the juror and the defendant.

In the course of their wars with the other European powers, the French Revolutionaries came to occupy the Southern Netherlands, first for a few months from the end of 1792 to the beginning of 1793 and then definitively in 1794. For most of this period, the old legal order kept functioning. Not without opposition, the regular French legal organisation was first introduced in the Southern Netherlands at the end of 1795.[48] Despite its revolutionary aims and French origins, the new criminal justice system was not entirely alien to the Southern Netherlands. Even while the introduction of defence lawyers, a centralised (rather than urban) criminal justice system and a partially public procedure were indeed novel, some practical arrangements remained similar. Many of the people charged with keeping order and providing justice remained the same while their titles changed.[49] The course of preliminary investigations, conducted by police officers or justices of the peace, in practice differed little from the investigations formerly conducted by the officers of justice. In some cases, when the laws were unclear, judges could even resort to ancien régime laws.[50] The local embeddedness of criminal prosecution – most criminals were only prosecuted when their environment complained – also remained. And even while the 'law of proof' was abolished, juries and judges kept favouring confessions as evidence.[51]

While the French introduced their new institutions in the former territory of Belgium (and in many other newly conquered territories), they continued to reform them. As first consul Napoleon gradually expanded his power and became emperor in 1804, some of the most revolutionary aspects of the criminal justice system were undone. The Napoleonic reforms focused on guaranteeing security, rather than defendants' rights.[52] Thus, in reforms between 1795 and 1810, the criminal investigation again became secret, written and inquisitorial up to the court session, which remained public, oral and accusatory. New laws replaced the director of the jury with the examining judge (*juge d'instruction*), who carried out most of the investigations and interrogations. They stipulated that judges were once again appointed instead of elected, replaced the jury of accusation with an indictments chamber – consisting of magistrates attached to the court of appeals – and entrusted the power to prosecute to an official public prosecutor and his substitutes. For some crimes, the new laws stipulated minimal and maximal sentences. Choosing between them was left for the judge to decide.[53]

The reforms culminated with the *Code d'instruction criminelle* of 1808 and the *Code pénal* of 1810 – both came in vigour in 1811. These two codes would regulate criminal justice in the Belgian region for a long period, even after Napoleon's defeat. Despite frequent criticisms, the codes remained in use with only slight modifications when the Belgian and Dutch territories were integrated in the United Kingdom of the Netherlands in 1815, and even after the Belgian independence in 1830, up to the Belgian criminal code of 1867.[54]

Bad conscience

Let us now look in more detail at the impact of all these procedural reforms. The French Revolutionary legal system put an end to the reigning system of proofs. The value of a confession – or of any other type of evidence – was no longer made explicit. However, this did not mean that judges and juries put less value on confessions: on the contrary, as they deliberated on their 'inner conviction', a confession became one of the most sought-after pieces of evidence.

Although eighteenth-century legal scholars frequently heralded a confession as the 'queen of proofs', many magistrates were not all that industrious

in obtaining such proof. Apart from relatively rare torture sessions, the interrogation of the suspect was the main procedure for obtaining confessions.
The law required at least one interrogation. But in most cases, magistrates
simply allowed suspects to tell their side of the story, which often entailed
a denial of all allegations. In his legal manual, alderman J. G. Thielen provided some advice on how to conduct interrogations: he suggested that
interrogators try to confuse suspects about what they were accused of, so
that they could accidentally confess or contradict themselves. Moreover, he
advised that magistrates did not ask questions in a logical order, again, to
increase the chance that suspects would contradict themselves. Finally, he
proposed to hear suspects as soon as possible, so that they did not have the
time to concoct lies. Experience shows, he wrote, that the first interrogation was usually the most useful one, with the least prepared answers.[55]
Implicitly, Thielen made clear that allowing suspects to overthink their case
would not be beneficial to discovering the truth. From this view, it is unsurprising that Thielen also defended judicial torture, which started from the
same principle.

The records of interrogations may not reveal the exact nature of interrogations – not all questions were reported, questions were perhaps formulated differently, answers may have been summarised – but they do show
that there were rarely any attempts to pressure suspects into confessing,
even in serious cases. The magistrates puzzled together the story of events as
they had learned them from victims and witnesses and rephrased this story
as questions. Most commonly, these took the form of 'Asked if he did not...'
or 'Is it not true that...'. Regardless of the suspect's denials, they generally
continued their interrogations along the line of the events as they had supposedly unfolded. Magistrates rarely used the attempts at confusion Thielen
proposed. As in many other regions, the recorded questions early modern
interrogators asked often seem scripted and monological – clerks just had to
fill in the answers of the defendants.[56]

A typical example is the case of Antoine Deleporte in Kortrijk in 1762.
Deleporte was a sergeant in a minor village near Kortrijk and stood accused
of battery resulting in the death of a forty-year-old woman. The woman
had suffered from poor mental and physical health, but was from a relatively well-to-do family. The magistrates considered the case as serious;
they heard many witnesses. But Deleporte's interrogation was very straightforward: after verifying his identity, magistrates first established whether
he was near the woman at the time of the incident (he acknowledged this)
and then asked him in chronological order about the passing of events.
Deleporte confessed that he had hit the woman, but only very lightly and
only after she had gravely insulted him. When the judges continued with
more serious accusations – that he had hit her again afterwards, that it

had resulted in serious wounds, that she had died from these wounds – Deleporte simply claimed that these were false allegations. The only 'trick' question came at the end, when they asked him whether he had fled from his house after the woman had died. Deleporte acknowledged that he had done this on the advice of two notable inhabitants of his village. There was no other pressure to confess to the more serious allegations.[57]

This is not to say that magistrates were not interested in confessions, indeed, in some cases magistrates went to great lengths to elicit confessions – in cases with torture, for instance, or as in the case of Joanna Catherine Janssens, with threats and promises, as I discussed at the beginning of this chapter. However, in comparison with later interrogation strategies, magistrates' techniques were rarely sophisticated and rarely played to suspects' feelings. An exception was the case of Peter Stocker, suspected of sodomy in 1781. After a long and detailed interrogation, in which Stocker denied having ever even thought about sodomy, judges asked him 'whether he knows that he has a soul that he must try to save'. Stocker confirmed that he knew this. 'How does he dare, then', judges continued, 'to keep denying the truthful truth, does he not fear to be abandoned by God, and that his soul will be torn out of his disastrous body to be thrown into the abysses of hell?' Stocker did not break immediately, but eventually 'voluntarily' confessed a month later. Judges played to Stocker's religious fears in a more sophisticated way than in the case of Janssens to get him to tell the account that they wanted to hear. This approach was, however, rare.[58]

With the new criminal procedures of the French Revolutionary criminal justice system, the practices of interrogators necessarily changed. Torture was abolished and suspects gained better protection: magistrates had to inform them immediately of the charges against them, for instance, rendering some of Thielen's techniques obsolete. But criminal investigators still valued confessions, as they convinced juries and judges more than any other proof. As a result, magistrates started to seek out new techniques of interrogation, techniques that did not so much involve physical violence or direct confrontation, but that often played to people's feelings and sought to portray the interrogator as an ally of the suspect.

The change is most striking if we compare Thielen's treatise on criminal justice with an extensive commentary on criminal procedure published in France in 1845 by Faustin Hélie and edited for Belgian purposes between 1863 and 1869 by J. S. G. Nypels and Léopold Hanssens. In the more recent work, the authors argued that confession had been quintessential in the old regime, but was now just one piece of evidence among others, though still a very usable one. 'Our modern legislation attaches all the proper weight to confessions, but has left its moral appreciation to the judge'.[59] The prime means to obtain a confession was an interrogation. Focusing on the mind by asking questions was the preferred method to get suspects to give an account of themselves.

Faustin Hélie made explicit the psychology underlying the value of confession: 'When a man confesses to having committed an immoral action, this declaration carries the presumption of truth, for it is not in human nature to undergo voluntarily the imputation of a shameful fact, when this imputation is false'. To confess, trust between confessant and confessor was required. The confessant 'had to overcome an instinctive repugnance to talking'. He could find the power to do so in 'the secret inspiration of conscience and in the innate love of truth, that double ray which still resides in his mind, despite his attempts to obscure them'. Confessing allegedly also gave suspects their inner peace back: 'truth has such power to alleviate and relieve suffering'.[60]

Clearly, much had changed since the days of Thielen. For Thielen, judges were to confuse and delude suspects and, if this did not suffice, they were guaranteed to find the truth through regulated violence. The truth could be extracted by the interrogator from the body of the suspect. In the vision of Faustin Hélie and his contemporaries, suspects were still reluctant to confess to their horrible crimes. But the interrogator could extract the truth by gaining the trust of the defendants, by stimulating their conscience and allowing them to regain inner peace by confessing. In part, the truth moved from body to mind (though the body could still be important in accessing the mind), and from the result of an open opposition to a seeming collaboration (though open opposition was never far away).[61] In this process, the self, inner depth, feelings and conscience became central concerns of criminal justice.

This was not only a change in legal manuals. After the installation of the new legal system, the criminal interrogation techniques recorded in interrogation transcripts became more sophisticated. While many interrogations were still rather straightforward, it became increasingly common to try to *convince* suspects to confess. Moreover, interrogators not only played to suspects' fears, but also to their hopes: they promised that confessing would bring relief. They played to suspects' consciences and likened confession in criminal court with confession in penance. In 1810, after magistrates confronted him with the wealth of evidence against him, agricultural worker Jean Ronse said that he would confess in a next session. The interrogator pressed him to 'tell the confessions that weigh on his heart now', but he refused.[62] When farmer Laurent Spinoy professed his innocence of a murder in 1824, the judge told him that 'he will have to answer on several points, and one hopes that he will then speak more frankly, and will in the meantime search his conscience, and unburden his soul'. The magistrate did not tell Spinoy, like Stocker, to think about saving his soul for eternity, but to consider the advantages in this life of 'unburdening' his soul by confessing.[63] Judges increasingly presented confessions as something advantageous for the inner life of the defendant, thus confirming the importance of such an inner life. A guilty conscience could be alleviated through confessing.[64]

Interrogators went further: they not only promised relief of conscience, but they actively sought to provoke feelings of shock, shame, guilt and remorse – they sought to create or at least reveal guilty consciences. By provoking these feelings and analysing suspects' bodies, they sought new ways to the truth. To this end, interrogators sometimes confronted suspects with witnesses, victims or objects connected to the crime. In these instances, clerks almost always wrote down the reactions of the suspects, or the lack thereof. In 1816, for instance, a magistrate showed field servant Henriette Meurisse a series of objects: a child's cap, a small shirt and some linen and asked her 'to contemplate and handle these things'. He then asked whether 'when seeing them, she doesn't feel interior movements [*elle ne se sentait point emouvoir les entrailles*]?' For four minutes, Meurisse kept a 'profound silence' and then started 'sighing and bitterly weeping' for several more minutes. In tears, she confessed that the objects had belonged to her infant. She had been abandoned by everyone and had 'on no-one's advice except the demon's' thrown her baby in a river.[65] In a rather macabre performance, some interrogators even confronted suspects with the corpses of their supposed victims. They confronted several suspected infanticides with the corpse of their baby, who often immediately confessed that it was theirs, sometimes while 'crying and moaning'.[66] Domestic worker Pascal Bastiaens received the same treatment in 1821. Before the post-mortem was allowed to take place, the justice of the peace took him to look at the corpse of a murder victim, and asked him then and there to 'tell how this event has come to pass'.[67] The magistrates expected that seeing the victim would move him in such a way that he could no longer hide the truth.

This new focus on conscience and remorse was not only a clever means to extract confessions. The criminal justice system in the early nineteenth century was increasingly bent on reforming criminals, especially with the use of prison sentences. If a suspect showed remorse, this was a first step in their trajectory towards a better life. It showed that they accepted the moral values that they had broken and decreased the 'moral culpability' of the criminal. From this perspective, it made sense to reduce the sentence of those who repented.[68] Initially, however, sentences in the new regime were fixed and did not allow for much clemency. Juries found some defendants who confessed infanticide innocent. Although they did not motivate these verdicts, it seems that the jury found the possible punishments too harsh.[69] After the Napoleonic reforms, judges could arbitrate between minimum and maximum sentences to consider the remorse of the suspect. In some cases, they also recommended convicts for grace. In 1829, domestic servant Katharina Lignel had killed her infant but was struck by remorse. A neighbour saw her 'wholly dismayed and half insane, saying that she was damned and could not hope for salvation and knew that she would be arrested by the gendarmerie within few days'. And indeed, she was, and she immediately confessed to the local mayor that she had murdered her child. The court condemned her to death, but several magistrates felt compassion for Lignel and recommended her for grace. The trial contains two reports sent to the king, asking to pardon her crime. 'Notwithstanding the cruelty of the crime', they noted, Lignel has 'from the beginning confessed her crime with an open heart' and she has shown 'sincere remorse' to the court. They recommended her for His Majesty's compassion. Her sentence was commuted to ten years of imprisonment.[70]

In other cases, however, there was no hope for a diminished sentence. And yet some suspects responded to the incitements to confess. They felt guilt. They acknowledged that they had committed a particular action and that this action was morally wrong. As such, the feeling of guilt was the outcome of a long historical process of 'culpabilisation'. It can be seen as the result of an attempt of religious and legal institutions to not just have people obey the law, but to have norms inscribed onto the body and into the mind. The Catholic ritual of penance played a pivotal role in this process.[71] If people broke certain norms, they had a 'bad conscience' – they felt guilty and uneasy. Feeling remorse was a way of recovering from these feelings of unease: its effect was to disconnect the disapproved action from the *true* self. If you practised remorse, you showed that your actions were a deviation from values that you actually held deeply and dearly. This whole process worked to promote the feeling of inner depth.[72]

This background helps to explain why and how suspects confessed crimes: relief was the central theme, relief of conscience and relief of the actual sentence. As we have seen above, some interrogators made this explicit. Even without these specific admonitions, some suspects referred to these images when they made a confession. In 1816, an interrogator confronted maidservant Isabelle Desmet with contradictions in the story she had told. She broke and declared that 'her conscience told her to tell the truth', before making a confession.[73] In 1814, day labourer Pierre Calland said that he 'wanted to tell the truth to relieve his conscience for God and for Justice'.[74] In 1820, weaver Cecile Louise Broucke asked for a new interrogation after she had denied all allegations, claiming she had 'sincere repentance of her mistakes and that she felt pursued by remorse which torments her day and night [...], and therefore had resolved to confess and say everything'.[75] Interrogators not only promised the relief of confession, but suspects also longed for it.

Interrogators in the old regime often just asked suspects to tell their side of the events relating to a crime. If they did attempt to pressure a suspect into confessing, they were often blunt, simply confronting suspects with evidence against their claims, trying to trick them and using religious imagery to impress them. If that did not work, torture was a possibility. Lacking the latter solution, in the new regime, interrogators used more sophisticated techniques and paid more attention to feelings and to the relief of conscience that confessing could bring.

The interest in conscience was not entirely new in nineteenth-century trial records: Laura Kounine has found some references to conscience and interiority in sixteenth- and seventeenth-century German witchcraft trials.[76] Such discussions seem to have been much rarer in French witchcraft trials of the same period, where, as Virginia Krause has argued, individual subjectivity was mostly absent.[77] However, limited research on the period around 1800 shows that in Germany and France, too, psychological interrogation techniques and attention for the inner side of the suspect were on the rise in the early nineteenth century.[78]

The proliferation of 'psychological' interrogation techniques and the increasing references to conscience (and its relief) among both interrogators and defendants in the early nineteenth century can be seen as evidence of the continuing movement towards a 'culture of confession'.[79] Like the Catholic Church, institutions of criminal justice promoted self-verbalisation. They not only stimulated confession, but also promoted the idea that confession would not come spontaneously, that labour was necessary to overcome the suspect's reluctance to confess. Eventually, it would bring them relief. By demanding and writing down confessions, they made them more real. The techniques they used to obtain confessions in the early nineteenth century created a sense of depth and promoted the idea of an inner conscience and feelings of guilt as important aspects of the self.

The new discourses of guilt and interiority were visible across genders and classes. I have encountered them among impoverished aristocrats, merchants, artisans and farmers, as well as day labourers and male and female servants. But, as the examples discussed above illustrate, the changes were most outspoken in the case of more modest people – servants and day labourers – and especially in the case of women accused of infanticide. In these cases, interrogators asked their most interior-oriented questions: they frequently confronted women with clothes or even with the corpses of their infants and explicitly asked how they felt when seeing them. Men of the middling sorts were more often, but certainly not always, spared from these explicit techniques aimed at eliciting interiority. As I will discuss in more detail in the next chapter, they were more commonly treated as rational beings.

It could be objected that the evolutions I have sketched are merely the result of changing prescriptions and practices of transcription. Indeed, with the installation of the French Revolutionary criminal justice system, administration expanded and bureaucracy became more precise. Interrogation transcripts were, in some cases, more detailed than before. So perhaps magistrates were already using the same techniques in the old regime, but clerks simply did not write them down. This would seem to limit the significance of the evolutions that I have described, but it does not. It points to the increased attention for the relevance of conscience, guilt and relief. Because of the powerful place of the criminal justice system in society, writing down references to these aspects of the self was never *merely* writing them down, but acknowledging and reinforcing their privileged position.

Resisting confession

In the face of overwhelming evidence, warnings of eternal damnation, and threats and promises, some defendants continued to deny the allegations. Most were rather straightforward, simply denying the imputed crimes. But defendants too had particular techniques to make their case stronger. Much like Bailliu under torture, suspects, while clearly in a subordinate position, could appeal to God, assert their moral superiority or play to the interrogators' sense of justice to convince them of their innocence.

The case of Gerard Deboysere in 1802 is unique for the perseverance of both the interrogator and the suspect. I will relate this case in some detail, as it illustrates many of the interrogation techniques discussed in the previous section, as well as how suspects could resist them. Deboysere, a fifty-one-year-old former police sergeant from Bruges, was suspected of murder and theft. His first interrogation was rather straightforward: the director of the jury asked Deboysere about his whereabouts and actions on the day of the crime, Deboysere answered. During the second interrogation a month later, the director of the jury pointed out numerous contradictions in his story and made many 'observations' of a more likely course of events. He became none the wiser and the interview was suspended as the suspect seemed indisposed.[80]

For his third interrogation, again a month later, Deboysere was taken to the crime scene, to the house where the murder had taken place. His guilt was clear, the director of the jury said. 'We have only taken him here to ask for a pardon of God and Justice on the scene of the crime', he said. 'And in consequence, we ask him to tell us whether he has committed the crime singlehandedly, or whether he has had other accomplices'. The magistrate performed a whole range of interrogation techniques: confrontation with the crime scene to elicit a reaction; invoking the respect required to God and Justice; not asking whether he committed the crime but asking who helped him. Deboysere was not easily cornered, however. 'If he has committed a crime, he is punishable', he said, 'but he has not'. He resisted confession by expressing his agreement with justice and his innocence at the same time.

The director of the jury pointed out the blood on the wall. Deboysere asked him what he wanted to obtain by doing so. Again, many questions followed about Deboysere's 'when and where'. Finally, the director 'observed that he has not been called here to confess, for his culpability is proven, but to unburden his conscience by declaring his accomplices, if any'. Deboysere repeated that 'his conscience [was] not burdened'. Any witnesses against him were lying. Conscience was given an important role in the interrogation.

Two months later there was another interrogation, back in the court of justice. This time, the declarations of witnesses against him were read to Deboysere. After a few statements, he lost his patience and ceased to answer the questions, denying the legitimacy of his interrogators. Upon every question, for dozens of questions, he only said 'I don't say yes, I don't say no', 'I don't hear anything, I don't say anything, I'm mute', or 'I say nothing, nothing can be proven'. Neither the interrogators nor Deboysere seemed to want to bend. At one point, Deboysere accused the interrogators of 'impertinence', and asked what the allegations against him were. He said that all were 'telltales and shit'. And then he continued in his refusal to answer questions: 'Why do you continuously want to reason with me? I say that I hear nothing'.

After some two hundred questions, the interrogators once again tried a new technique. 'A truly innocent man', the interrogator said,

> has no better defence than the truth. [...] He who speaks truth, always says it in the same way, without variation, because the truth is one and invariable. The suspect, conversely, has changed his answers all the time [...] and often denies things that are irrevocably proven. It results that the suspect has not used the truth to defend himself, which evidently proves that he feels that the truth can only show that he is guilty.

After a moment of silence (the transcription noted) Deboysere said 'madmen are in the madhouse' – another defensive technique, claiming insanity. And then he started to assert his innocence again. 'All what they have said is lies', or 'gossip', and 'all what he has said himself is the truth'. But the interrogators again continued and observed that his behaviour showed his guilt: 'this is not the behaviour of an innocent, but the behaviour that we have seen among the truly guilty, when they do not want to confess their crimes'. And then, they summed up his most important techniques:

1. Denying things that have been proven beyond revocation or doubt
2. Never saying the same thing twice

3. Treating witnesses like drunkards, liars and forgers
4. Claiming that the accusers had instructed witnesses on how to answer questions
5. Repeating often that witnesses who are his old friends will eventually testify in his favour
6. Saying that witnesses would speak differently in his presence
7. Talking nonsense and being extravagant each time he feels so cornered that he has no good replies to make.

Deboysere did not reply to this exposition. The interrogators therefore continued to hold out the evidence against him; Deboysere persisted in his denials. Once again, the director of the jury then decided to resort to another technique and confront Deboysere with his unusual behaviour in prison. He interpreted his body to draw conclusions about the mind; again, conscience and feelings occupied a central role; he explicitly used metaphors of interiority. Deboysere had woken up in the middle of the night and shouted that soldiers were coming to take him to the guillotine. He had told others that he had seen the bailiff reading aloud his death sentence. Surely 'the idea of the crime tormented his conscience'. Practising his best rhetorical talents, the interrogator continued: 'Imagining hearing his death sentence, was that not the effect of an inner conviction of the crime? The tambour he was hearing, was that not remorse rising in his mind, which, reproaching his crime, didn't leave him quiet during day nor night?'

No, Deboysere replied, they were wrong to imprison him, for this only showed his insanity. Again, however, the interrogators refused to accept this. The extravagances he had committed were, according to experts who had examined him, the effect of anxiety and agitation since the crime: 'This agitation will continue as long as he doesn't make a complete confession of the crime with which he is soiled'. Only confession would bring relief. In response, Deboysere said that he doubted that the experts claimed this, and questioned their authority, saying that they were only 'pulse takers'.

The final stage of the interrogation, which must have taken many hours, was approaching. One last time, the interrogators pointed out that his behaviour clearly showed that he had plotted to deny everything and use all the worst means of defence, but that this was a proof against him. Deboysere once again claimed that these were only bagatelles, 'and that he would take care not to confess a crime he hasn't committed. And if he has committed it, he wants to be punished'. One final time, the interrogators repeated that his was not the behaviour of an innocent man, 'who would conduct himself with respect towards his judges and justify himself cold-bloodedly and peaceably'. Deboysere did not reply and the interrogation was closed.

The evidence against Deboysere was rather thin. It consisted of many small clues, especially that of Deboysere's own suspicious behaviour. As a result, the rest of the procedure also took more time than was usual. His interrogation before the president of the criminal tribunal, generally only a formality, was longer than usual and was conducted twice, although it was never as extensive as his earlier hearings. Almost a year after the murder, the jury came to a conclusion: Deboysere was guilty of murder and theft and was convicted to death. Almost all possible techniques of interrogation and of resistance had been used in the case. It serves as testimony of the increasing resort of interrogators to the mind of the suspect, to his feelings and his conscience; but also to the importance they attached to obtaining a confession. Conversely, the case also shows the range of techniques suspects possessed to oppose their interrogators: claiming innocence, false witnesses, insanity, refusing to answer questions, exposing plots against him and confusing the magistrates – even if Deboysere was, in the end, less than successful.

The exchange between suspects and interrogators had important repercussions for self and identity. Suspects who resisted their interrogators defied the identity of a criminal. They self-verbalised, but not in a way acceptable to the magistrates. The latter tried to destabilise their stories and to get them to confess. As in the Deboysere case, they played to suspects' inner side, their 'conscience' and their 'inner conviction' to get them to confess. Suspects had to relate to this sense of interiority and generally went along, practising an inner orientation but not accepting the interpretation of the magistrates. But the attempts of interrogators to destabilise suspects' stories of denial could backfire. Indeed, in his continuous denials, Deboysere practised a strong sense of identity. It led him to exclaim at one point: 'I am innocent and I know who I am'.

Giving an account of oneself

So far in this chapter, I have discussed the varieties in the demands of the court for people to give an account of oneself. These were generally specific demands: magistrates were aiming to obtain a confession of a particular crime. Magistrates stimulated people to confess, to a lesser extent in the eighteenth century, with the use of torture, and especially in the early nineteenth century, with psychological techniques, by promoting guilt and remorse, which could be relieved by self-verbalising.

We arrive at the next stage of the criminal trial: the confession itself and its effects. In the chapters that follow, I will discuss the excuses and interpretations people gave in their confessions. For now, I stick to the form of their confessions, and the effects of this form. The criminal court demanded an account of the self, but also dictated to a large extent what form this account should take. Between 1750 and 1830, the form of confession became more individual and more focused on the confessant's interior feelings and motivations; but an assumption of responsibility remained crucial throughout the period.

Eighteenth-century legal commentaries contained some formal guidelines on the confession: once suspects started to confess, Fierlant noted among others, they should not be interrupted. Only when they finished their story should the interrogator ask additional questions. It was particularly important, he noted, to ask for the circumstances of the crime: where it had taken place, which weapons had been used, whether there were any accomplices or witnesses. Moreover, interrogators should insist that suspects reveal their motivations for committing the crime. If these were unclear, they should ask whether anyone had incited them to the crime.[81] In practice, eighteenth-century interrogators were rarely as thorough as Fierlant recommended. They were usually quite content if a suspect confessed to the crime. Only in a minority of cases did they explicitly ask suspects about their motivations. In many trials, however, suspects volunteered an explanation for their behaviour, describing it as the consequence of particular circumstances or conditions.

The formal requirements of a confession changed little in the new regime. Like Fierlant, French criminalist François Duverger noted that the judge should not be content with vague and general confessions and that he should ask for the reasons for and circumstances of the crime.[82] As interrogations became more thorough, it became more common to ask for detailed circumstances. Especially when crimes were deemed atrocious – such as infanticide – it was more usual to explicitly ask for motivations. For instance, after Maximilienne De Cerf had confessed to infanticide in 1819 and described the circumstances of her crime, magistrates asked her 'what may have been the motive that has engaged her to commit this crime?'[83] The need for confessions not only became greater in the new regime, the confessions also required more details and explanations – I will expand on this point in chapter 5.

An important change in the form of confessions, at least in the way they were written down, was the gradual switch from the third person to the first person. In the old regime, clerks usually wrote down interrogations, like witness statements, in the third person, in the Southern Netherlands as in France and Germany.[84] In the case of Peter Stocker in 1781, interrogators asked – as was standard practice – 'what *his* name was' and some questions later 'with whom *he* associated'. Clerks wrote down that he answered that '*he* was called Petrus Gommarus Stockart' and that '*he* associated with no-one in particular'. When Stocker confessed, he said that '*he* was prepared to make a true confession'. He related his many acts of sodomy and said that '*he* had only done it out of urge'.[85] Clerks thus even wrote very personal confessions down in the third person. This was the habit in all courts, even though there do not seem to have been any regulations demanding this form of transcription.

The installation of the new legal system did not change these practices. Interrogation transcripts continued to transcribe questions and answers in the third person. After the turn of the century, however, some courts started to occasionally record answers in the first person. In the case of Gerard Deboysere, for instance, questions were reported in the third person and answers switched regularly between the first and the third ('he hears or sees nothing', followed a few questions later by 'I hear nor see anything').[86] A similar thing happened in 1809, when an officer of the judicial police in Kortrijk interrogated Barbe Vandenhende, suspected of infanticide. The clerk wrote most of the interrogation down in the third person, including Vandenhende's lamentation that 'she suffered much [during the crime], but that she wanted to suffer a thousand times more and leave this world'. The officer 'asked her the reason why she wanted to suffer and die', and Vandenhende replied 'for the crime that I have committed'. All further questions, and all further interrogations, were again written in the third person.[87]

Police officers indeed seem to have been among the first to have started writing interrogations in the second and first person. In Ghent in 1806, an entire interrogation by a judicial police officer was written down as such: 'Where were you [*vous*] on 16 September in the evening?' 'I was in the Grand Theatre'. When the suspect was then brought before the director of the jury, the interrogation was again written down in the third person.[88] Gradually, however, clerks also started to write down interrogations before magistrates in the first person. The Antwerp courts were earlier than those in Brabant and West-Flanders to commit to this practice. The first of these transcriptions can be found in 1813, and the practice was standard by around 1820. In Brabant, first-person interrogation transcripts became common around 1828. In West-Flanders, it remained common to write interrogations down in the third person at least up to 1830. Only occasionally, interrogations before the court were written down in the first person. In this period of transition, it was not uncommon for interrogations to switch between different pronouns. While the precise timing of these changes is still unclear, by the early-to-mid nineteenth century, most French and German courts also adopted the practice of recording interrogations in the first person.[89]

There does not appear to have been any directive to advise this shift.[90] None of the legal manuals note anything about the use of third or first/second person when writing down interrogations. They simply stipulated that the transcription should be 'clear, precise, legible and without corrections' and that 'answers should be written down literally', which was the same advice that had been given to ancien régime magistrates – 'literally' was not generally taken literally.[91] In a manual for justices of the peace from 1852, a model for recording interrogations still displayed questions in the third person.[92] The evolution therefore seems to have developed from below. Together with the increasing length of interrogations, this connected to an increased concern for representing suspects' words more precisely. As such, it was also a form of 'subjectivation': as suspects' answers were written down in the first person, they became more personal and more individual. It reinforced the individualising effects of confessing. Suspects not only confessed in the first person, but now they also had to confirm a direct, first-person transcription of this confession.

Within these constraints, confessants were relatively free to mould their stories in the form they wanted. *Relatively* free, of course: they had to confess to the crime at hand and in a way that made it understandable to the judges. As Virginia Krause has shown for witchcraft confessions in the sixteenth century, this often led to confessions that were rather uniform.[93] While there is greater diversity in the confessions of the murderers, sodomites and prostitutes I have studied than among Krause's witchcraft confessions, the central theme is also that people take on a particular identity. In interrogations, people were called to reflect on themselves: were they murderers, were they sodomites? Suspects were summoned to self-identify with the accusation, to express it in the first person. Through this act of confessing (or of denying), they became someone different; they assumed a transformed self.[94]

Judiciary institutions did not simply summon people to self-reflect and assume an identity, they also steered them towards particular sorts of selves – as we have seen, selves with depth (inner guilt and remorse) and, as we will see in the next chapters, stable selves in control of themselves. Most confessions were more or less extensive stories, detailing what suspects were doing before the crime and how circumstances brought them to the crime. They gave an account of themselves, taking on or rejecting particular identities; bringing along excuses and mitigations (or not); contrasting their crime with their previous behaviour or suggesting stabilities. Most suspects did not go much further than what magistrates wanted – they confessed to their crimes and made them understandable. Some went to great lengths to explain their crime much more extensively. Famously, for instance, in France in 1835 the young farmer Pierre Rivière wrote a fifty-page memoir detailing what brought him to murder his mother, his sister and his brother.[95] The only one to come close to this form of confession – but on a much smaller scale – among the suspects I studied was Pierre De Mahieu in 1803. The case illustrates how a criminal action led to a proliferation of practices of the self.

Unlike Rivière, the De Mahieu family was part of the country's (impoverished) elite. The family had been ennobled in 1715, but had fallen on hard times a while before the revolution. Pierre Antoine Joseph was born in 1764. He joined the army and while stationed in Antwerp in the 1780s, he met Josine Doloit. She knew French, which was refreshing for De Mahieu, who did not speak Dutch. They married and after Doloit's father died in 1801, they moved in with Doloit's mother and sister.

On 19 September 1803, an officer of the *gendarmerie* heard shouting while on patrol in Antwerp. People informed him that De Mahieu had slaughtered his mother- and sister-in-law. He went to their house and found De Mahieu hiding in the attic, his hands covered in blood. He was arrested and taken away. On their way to prison, De Mahieu and his guards encountered Doloit, who shouted at them: 'De Mahieu, De Mahieu, what have you done!' 'I come from killing your mother and your sister', De Mahieu allegedly replied, 'and if you had been home, I would have killed you too!' Doloit fainted.

The substitute government commissioner interrogated De Mahieu the same day. His answers were recorded in the third person. Asked why he was arrested, De Mahieu immediately confessed that it was 'for having punished his mother-in-law and sister-in-law'. The interrogator then asked 'if it was the effect of the vivacity of the moment, or whether he had premeditated punishing them like that'. De Mahieu said that 'it was because of a vivacity in that moment, but that he had nevertheless for some time thought about punishing them exemplarily for the irregular conduct of his wife that his mother-in-law provoked'. De Mahieu took responsibility for his crime. He went on explaining that he had tried to lead his in-laws to virtue, to have them abandon their scandalous life but without success. The day of the murder, he had asked his sister-in-law not to demand his wife to prostitute herself for the benefit of the family. His sister-in-law hit him and then he hit her with a hammer. His mother-in-law came to help her; he took his knife and stabbed her. De Mahieu claimed that he had not intended to kill, only to punish.

Witnesses were heard. They stressed the virtuous behaviour of the Doloit family and suggested that De Mahieu's jealousy came forth from his frequent drunkenness. Another witness had heard that De Mahieu was often restless at night, getting up to check the house for intruders. De Mahieu's brother-in-law (his sister's husband) testified that De Mahieu had visited him in Brussels about six weeks before. He looked sad and could hardly eat; he seemed 'occupied by sinister plans and dark projects'. The brother-in-law 'pushed him to open his heart and tell him the cause of his chagrin', but he would not say anything, except that 'he would be talked about'.

Two weeks after his arrest, De Mahieu was interrogated anew, now more extensively and by the director of the jury. He was asked about his entire life course: how he met his wife, how they lived, where he worked, etc. – I have relied on his answers to introduce De Mahieu earlier. He freely disclosed his many disputes with his wife and her family, which centred on their perceived lack of virtue. He said that before his violent act, someone in the street had shouted 'she has danced despite you', which he took to mean that his wife led an unruly life. As De Mahieu 'loved virtue and loved an irreproachable life', he felt that he had to act.

After the interrogation, De Mahieu was given insight into the declarations against him. While he did not dispute the general accusations, he found that the statements did not detail his actions precisely enough and started writing a 'Reply to several declarations against me', addressed to the director of the jury. This memoir is written in clear handwriting, but contains many spelling errors and is sometimes difficult to make sense of. De Mahieu related what happened after the crime, now in the first person. He described in dramatic detail how terrible he felt:

> The movement of my mind and my body, my pen cannot describe. One must be in such an unfortunate event to feel its effects, and he who is not accustomed to crime feels it still more intensely, for the suffering he feels for his crime and the desperation of having committed it, and the rage in his heart against those who he believes being its author, this together brings the strongest man to delirium in spirit and body, so that he does not know what he is doing or saying, and such a man is so attacked in all parts of his body that all these parts are in movement. I am sure that if I had been bled three days afterwards, there would not have been any blood, for all my blood was frozen from the horror of my crime and I have kept a tremble that will never disappear.

De Mahieu practised feelings of suffering, desperation, rage and horror, placing these feelings explicitly both in the mind and in the body. He continued his memoir with correcting some specific witness declarations and ended by stipulating that: 'It is not myself that I seek to defend, but the duties I have to my family, but it is my character to be without detours and to say things like they are'. Two months later, De Mahieu's case came before the jury. They unanimously convicted him for premeditated murder. He was guillotined on 18 January 1804, dressed in a red shirt, on the central square in Antwerp.[96]

Comparisons with the case of Pierre Rivière are interesting. Both killed close family members, both wrote a memoir on their murder, both readily confessed their crime and both shared a sense of righteousness, believing their victims had provoked their treatment, and importance – people would talk about them. Both vividly testified of the horror they felt when they realised what they had done, while both also lacked the submission associated with remorse. But there are of course notable differences as well. Rivière's text was much more extensive, spanning about fifty pages, compared to De

Mahieu's three pages. Rivière was truly writing a history and had always intended to do so – it was part of his criminal plan. For De Mahieu, writing came more as an afterthought, to set the record straight.

The most obvious difference is, of course, that while the Rivière case attracted national attention in France, and the most renowned doctors investigated Rivière's sanity, De Mahieu's case was mostly a local affair and his sanity was never in the picture. There were elements that could have served such a course of investigation: his 'paranoia' about virtue, about possible intruders at night and his restlessness. However, they only served as indications of his premeditation, not of his insanity. It is testimony to the increased status and elaboration of psychiatric thought that Rivière's mind in 1835 attracted so much more attention than De Mahieu's in 1803. Although the court eventually declared that Rivière was not insane, he received grace for the death sentence (but later committed suicide).[97] The Antwerp trial promoted a conception of De Mahieu's self that was more in control of itself and more socially oriented. While witnesses and De Mahieu himself addressed his states of mind at some length, his interiority was, in 1803, not yet as central as it would later become.

De Mahieu's confessions and his memoir show the successes and the failures of the norms and feelings institutions of religion and law tried to enforce. De Mahieu was obsessed with virtue, his own virtue and his family's virtue. After he killed his in-laws, he confessed his crime and confessed his horror of what he had done, but he did not display remorse. He felt that he had to tell the truth, but was adamant that his version of the truth was the only one. There was no submission to the law. As such, his confessions and his memoir were not just the result of regulating practices of the court, the law or religion. De Mahieu actively strove to have his own version of the story accepted. *He* wanted to determine the true story about himself and his actions. He wanted to confess, he wanted to be tried, for it was the right thing to do. He used the criminal trial as a technology of the self, to become a better person again. He assumed control and actively accepted the identity of a murderer. Because his sanity was not investigated, he was able to remain in control in a way that Pierre Rivière could not.

The turn inwards

The ideas about and practices of criminal justice went through great changes between the mid-eighteenth century and the 1830s. While this is well-known, historians of criminal justice have had little attention for how closely intertwined legal procedures were with evolving conceptions of self. Conversely, scholars of the self have rarely addressed how deeply conceptions of self were implicated in the political project of criminal justice. My goal in this chapter has been to both introduce the general principles of criminal procedure in late eighteenth-century and early nineteenth-century Belgium, and to show how these principles implicated discourses and practices of the self.

The eighteenth-century criminal justice system was, admittedly, not very concerned with the self. Except in the most serious cases, the criminal courts mainly judged crimes, not criminal selves. They had some interest in their circumstances and the social status of the suspect – vagrants did not receive the same treatment as noblemen – but had only a marginal interest in the more individual background of a criminal. While a confession was a highly valued piece of evidence in the system of proofs, most interrogations were rather straightforward and did not try to penetrate to the suspect's inner self. The most incisive but rarely used method to obtain confessions was judicial torture. The ideology of judicial torture was based on the idea that truth resided in the body. It was a truth that was accessible through the destruction of the will, through the destruction of the self by the application of pain. The self was, for eighteenth-century criminal justice, often more a hindrance than an asset. Certainly, there were exceptions, but compared with the early-nineteenth-century trial records, concerns about interiority, feelings and motivations were remarkably absent.

The reformers of criminal justice in the late eighteenth century put the self in a more positive light. They decried torture and inhumane punishments and stressed that criminal justice should seek to change people, to change selves, rather than destroy them. From the late eighteenth century, therefore, criminal justice more and more started to take not crime but the criminal self as its object. This view was exemplified by the rise of 'houses of correction', discipline and prison sentences. But it also impacted criminal procedures. Magistrates no longer sought truth by inflicting pain on the body of the suspect, but through the feeling and thinking (though still embodied) self. The practices of criminal trials started to stimulate a more inner-oriented self from the late eighteenth century and especially early nineteenth century on. Interrogators started playing on suspects' feelings and on their consciences; they appealed to remorse. They promised suspects that if they confessed, they would feel better. They used some of the most inner-oriented approaches for defendants of the lowest social status, such as illiterate servants. By focusing so much attention on individual, inner feeling and conscience, the criminal court stimulated interiority, stimulated people so reflect on their inner lives and expand them.

And many suspects went along with this. Indeed, the 'turn inwards' of the criminal trial was not only carried by magistrates practising more sophisticated techniques, but also by the suspects themselves. Men and women of all social statuses showed remorse and hoped to obtain relief. The accounts about themselves that they were required to give had always led to the assumption of an identity. Increasingly, the self they practised in these accounts was *individual*. It was not only spoken in the first person, but also written down and confirmed in the first person. Moreover, the accounts became more oriented towards *feelings* and *motivations*. Through these practices in the criminal trial, people's inner sides expanded. While the criminal trials only directly affected a small number of people, they institutionalised practices of interiority and individuality. By attending to these practices, courts confirmed their validity and reinforced them. Because of their status as official institutions, they could indirectly influence many more people than just the suspects before them. While discourses of the self remained unstable and, as I will discuss in the next chapters, conflicting discourses arose at the same time, for many people, an inner orientation became a more important discourse in the early nineteenth century.

Notes

1 State Archives, Kortrijk (SAK), *Old City Archives (OCAK)*, 6676. Also for the following paragraphs.

2 This diversity incited complaints: see Poullet, *Histoire du droit pénal*, pp. 312–13. While Philip II had issued an ordinance on criminal procedure in 1570, this ordinance was limited in scope and not recognised in all courts.

3 Cf. Susanne Pohl-Zucker, *Making Manslaughter: Process, Punishment and Restitution in Württemberg and Zurich, 1376–1700* (Leiden: Brill, 2017), p. 15.

4 Monballyu, *Six Centuries*, pp. 15–18.

5 Maarten F. Van Dijck, 'Towards an economic interpretation of justice? Conflict settlement, social control and civil society in urban Brabant and Mechelen during the late middle ages and the early modern period', in Manon van der Heijden *et al.* (eds), *Serving the Urban Community: The Rise of Public Facilities in the Low Countries* (Amsterdam: Aksant, 2009), pp. 62–88. In France, the regional parliaments had more influence. In Germany, practices varied strongly by state.

6 Monballyu, *Six Centuries*, pp. 414–17.

7 Monballyu, *Six Centuries*, pp. 417–27; Poullet, *Histoire du droit pénal*, pp. 316–73.

8 Catherine Denys, *La police de Bruxelles entre réformes et révolutions (1718–1814): police urbaine et modernité* (Turnhout: Brepols, 2013), p. 47; Luc Duerloo *et al.*, 'Bestuur en politiek op een Schoon Verdiep', in Marnix Beyen *et al.* (eds), *Het stadhuis van Antwerpen: 450 jaar geschiedenis* (Antwerp: Pandora, 2015), pp. 171–216, p. 185; Niklaas Maddens, 'De nieuwe tijd', in Niklaas Maddens (ed.), *De geschiedenis van Kortrijk* (Tielt: Lannoo, 1990), pp. 216–17.

9 Denys, *La police de Bruxelles*, p. 48.

10 On the system of proof, see John H. Langbein, *Torture and the Law of Proof: Europe and England in the Ancien Régime* (Chicago: University of Chicago Press, 1977), pp. 4–12; Foucault, *Discipline and Punish*, pp. 36–41.

11 Goswin de Fierlant, 'Premières idées sur la réformation des loix criminelles' (ca. 1773–1782), fo. 941r. (NA, *Diverse Manuscripts*, 2119).

12 J. G. Thielen, *Forme et manière de procéder en criminel, calquées sur les ordonnances & quantité d'arrêts, & jugemens notables* (Herve: Imprimerie du Journal général de l'Europe, 1789), pp. 83–4. Daniel Jousse, *Traité de la justice criminelle de France* (Paris: Debure, 1771), vol. 1, p. 672.

13 Eugène Hubert, *La torture aux Pays-Bas autrichiens pendant le XVIIIe siècle: son application, ses partisans et ses adversaires, son abolition* (Brussels: Hayez, 1896), pp. 27–33.

14 Hubert, *La torture*, pp. 95–101.

15 Monballyu, *Six Centuries*, p. 424; Hubert, *La torture*, pp. 36–40.

16 Langbein, *Torture and the Law of Proof*, p. 5.

17 Hubert, *La torture*, pp. 36–60; Monballyu, *Six Centuries*, p. 425.

18 E.g. in the case against Jacquemijns in Brussels, 1791: CAB, *HA Trials*, 8146.

19 Foucault, *Discipline and Punish*, p. 42.

20 Monballyu, *Six Centuries*, p. 54.

21 Cf. Foucault, *The History of Sexuality*, p. 43; Monballyu, *Six Centuries*, pp. 109–16; Paul Friedland, *Seeing Justice Done: The Age of Spectacular Capital Punishment in France* (Oxford: Oxford University Press, 2012), chap. 4.

22 Lisa Silverman, *Tortured Subjects: Pain, Truth and the Body in Early Modern France* (Chicago: University of Chicago Press, 2001), pp. 7–10; Sara Beam, 'Rites of torture in Reformation Geneva', *Past & Present*, 214: suppl 7 (2012), 209–10.

23 The interrogation is transcribed in Hubert, *La torture*, pp. 148–52.

24 Silverman, *Tortured Subjects*, pp. 89–90.

25 CAB, *HA Trials*, 1086. Also for the following paragraphs.

26 SAK, *Goethals-Vercruysse*, codex 202.

27 FA, V, 125. See also Hubert, *La torture*, pp. 125–31.

28 Michel Porret, *Beccaria: le droit de punir* (Paris: Michalon, 2003), pp. 19–33; Piers Beirne, *Inventing Criminology: Essays on the Rise of Homo Criminals* (New York: University of New York Press, 1993), pp. 13–14.

29 Piet Lenders, 'De eerste poging van J.J.P. Vilain XIIII tot het bouwen van een correctiehuis (1749–1751)', *Handelingen van de Zuid-Nederlandse Maatschappij voor Taal- en Letterkunde en Geschiedenis*, 12 (1958), 167–87; Catharina Lis and Hugo Soly, *Te gek om los te lopen? Collocatie in de 18de eeuw* (Turnhout: Brepols, 1990); Marie-Sylvie Dupont-Bouchat, 'La prison pénale. Modèles et pratiques: "Révolution" ou "évolution"? (1775–1815)', in *La Belgique criminelle. Droit, justice, société (XIVe–XXe siècles)* (Louvain-la-Neuve: Academia-Bruylant, 2006), pp. 357–84.

30 Thomas Nutz, *Strafanstalt als Besserungsmaschine: Reformdiskurs und Gefängniswissenschaft, 1775–1848* (München: Oldenbourg, 2001), pp. 69–71.

31 See the essays on several different regions in Norbert Campagna, Luigi Delia and Benoît Garnot (eds), *La torture, de quels droits? Une pratique de pouvoir, XVIe-XXIe siècle* (Paris: Imago, 2014).

32 *Terribles et désolantes reflexions d'un ex-conseiller en premiere instance dans le Brabant: sur quelques abus de justice* (Imprimerie Patriotique, 1787), p. 6.

33 Cf. Joanna Bourke, *The Story of Pain: From Prayer to Painkillers* (Oxford: Oxford University Press, 2014), p. 273.

34 Silverman, *Tortured Subjects*, pp. 164–72.

35 On Fierlant's arguments against torture, see Eugène Hubert, *Un chapitre de l'histoire du droit criminel dans les Pays-Bas autrichiens au XVIIIe siècle: les mémoires de Goswin de Fierlant* (Brussels: Hayez, 1895), pp. 73–4. For the wider movement, see Karen Halttunen, 'Humanitarianism and the pornography of pain in Anglo-American culture', *The American Historical Review*, 100 (1995), 303–34, 80–2; Silverman, *Tortured Subjects*, pp. 174–5; Javier Moscoso, *Pain: A Cultural History* (Basingstoke: Palgrave Macmillan, 2012), chap. 3. On the movement of sensibility, see chapter 4.

36 Jos Monballyu, 'De decriminalisering van de zelfdoding in de Oostenrijkse Nederlanden', *Revue belge de philologie et d'histoire*, 78:2 (2000), 453–7.

37 Hubert, *La torture*, p. 118; Marie-Sylvie Dupont-Bouchat, 'La reforme du droit penal dans les Pays-Bas autrichiens à la fin de l'Ancien Régime (1765–1787)', in Georges Macours (ed.), *Cornua legum: actes des journées internationales d'histoire du droit et des institutions* (Antwerp: Kluwer, 1987), pp. 80–1.

38 Jos Monballyu, 'De Raad van Vlaanderen en de hervorming van het strafrecht (1756–1787)', *Tijdschrift voor Rechtsgeschiedenis*, 64 (1996), 47, 72–5; Xavier Rousseaux, 'Doctrines criminelles, pratiques pénales, projets politiques: le cas des possessions Habsbourgeoises (1750–1790)', in Michel Porret (ed.), *Beccaria et la culture juridique des Lumières* (Genève: Droz, 1997), pp. 237–40.

39 On the debates in France, see François Tricaud, 'Le procès de la procédure criminelle à l'âge des Lumières', *Archives de Philosophie du Droit*, 39 (1994), 145–67.

40 Hunt, *Inventing Human Rights*, pp. 136–7; Emmanuel Berger, *La justice pénale sous la Révolution: les enjeux d'un modèle judiciaire libéral* (Rennes: Presses Universitaires de Rennes, 2008), p. 19.

41 André Laingui and Arlette Lebigre, *Histoire du droit pénal. T. 2: La procédure criminelle* (Paris: Cujas, 1979), pp. 133–41.

42 Emmanuel Berger *et al.*, 'La justice avant la Belgique: tentatives autrichiennes, influences françaises et expériences néerlandaises (1780–1830)', in Margo De Koster, Dirk Heirbaut and Xavier Rousseaux (eds), *Tweehonderd jaar justitie. Historische encyclopedie van de Belgische justitie / Deux siècles de justice. Encyclopédie historique de la justice belge* (Bruges: Die Keure, 2015), pp. 33–4.

43 Berger, *La justice pénale*, pp. 25–6; Monballyu, *Six Centuries*, pp. 60–3.

44 Berger, *La justice pénale*, p. 80; Monballyu, *Six Centuries*, p. 428.

45 Monballyu, *Six Centuries*, pp. 429–31; Robert Allen, *Les tribunaux criminels sous la Révolution et l'Empire 1792–1811* (Rennes: Presses Universitaires de Rennes, 2005), pp. 26–48.

46 Foucault, *Discipline and Punish*, pp. 96–8.

47 Yann Robert, *Dramatic Justice: Trial by Theater in the Age of the French Revolution* (Philadelphia, PA: University of Pennsylvania Press, 2019), pp. 204–13.

48 By then, further reforms had been introduced, but the central principles of revolutionary criminal justice remained: Berger, *La justice pénale*, pp. 37–48, 80–3; Allen, *Les tribunaux criminels*, p. 21.

49 Denys, *La police de Bruxelles*, p. 310; Xavier Rousseaux and Axel Tixhon, 'Du "sergent à verge" à la "profileuse": pistes pour l'histoire des polices dans l'espace belge, du Moyen Age au 21e siècle', in Jonas Campion (ed.), *Les archives des polices en Belgique: des méconnues de la recherche?* (Brussels: Algemeen Rijksarchief, 2009), pp. 19–22.

50 Berger *et al.*, 'La justice avant la Belgique', pp. 36–7.

51 Cf. Xavier Rousseaux, 'Les tribunaux criminels en Brabant sous le Directoire (1795–1800). Acculturation et résistance à la justice républicaine', in J. Craeybeckx and F. Scheelings (eds), *De Franse Revolutie en Vlaanderen: de Oostenrijkse Nederlanden tussen oud en nieuw regime* (Brussels: VUB, 1990), p. 279.

52 Emmanuel Berger, 'La poursuite pénale sous le Directoire (1795–1799) et l'Empire (1811–1814) dans les départements belges. Evolutions et ruptures des modèles judiciaires français', in Emmanuel Berger (ed.), *L'acculturation des modèles policiers et judiciaires français en Belgique et au Pays-Bas (1795–1815)* (Brussels: Archives générales du royaume, 2010), pp. 85–98.

53 Berger, *La justice pénale*, p. 13; Berger *et al.*, 'La justice avant la Belgique', pp. 37–8; Monballyu, *Six Centuries*, pp. 27–60, 432–4.

54 On these modifications, see Berger *et al.*, 'La justice avant la Belgique', pp. 43–5; Sjoerd Faber, 'De verzachting van de Code Pénal in Nederland (1813) en België (1814–1815)', *Pro Memorie*, 15 (2013), 243–60; Monballyu, *Six Centuries*, p. 28.

55 Thielen, *Forme et manière*, pp. 52–61.

56 On eighteenth-century France, Maryvonne Lorcy, 'Stratégie et tactique dans la procédure criminelle du XVIIIe siècle d'après les archives judiciaires bretonnes' (PhD dissertation, Lille 3, 1987), p. 203. On Germany, Kounine, *Imagining the Witch*, p. 163.

57 SAK, *OCAK*, 8293.

58 FA, *Modern City Archives (731)*, 1514/2.

59 Faustin Hélie, J. S. G. Nypels and Léopold Hanssens, *Traité de l'instruction criminelle: ou Théorie du Code d'instruction criminelle* (Brussels: Bruylant-Christophe et compagnie, 1865), vol. 2, pp. 410–11.

60 Hélie, Nypels and Hanssens, *Traité de l'instruction criminelle*, vol. 2, pp. 411–12.

61 The change from opposition to seeming collaboration was also visible in the spaces of interrogation: Elwin Hofman, 'Spatial interrogations: space and power in French criminal justice, 1750–1850', *law&history*, 7 (2020), in press.

62 State Archives, Bruges (SABR), *Assize Court of West-Flanders (AC-WEST)*, 228–1081.

63 SABE, *Assize Court of Antwerp (AC-ANT)*, 1378.

64 Cf. Hélie, Nypels and Hanssens, *Traité de l'instruction criminelle*, vol. 2, p. 412. A similar evolution occurred in penance: Hofman, 'A wholesome cure'.
65 SABR, *AC-WEST*, 286–409. The same technique was also used in SABR, *AC-WEST*, 320–723.
66 National Archives 2 – Joseph Cuvelier Repository, Brussels (NA2), *Assize Court of Brabant (AC-BRA)*, 1924 and 2231; SABR, *AC-WEST*, 395–1431.
67 NA2, *AC-BRA*, 481–1733.
68 Susan A. Bandes, 'Remorse and criminal justice', *Emotion Review*, 8:1 (2016), 17; Foucault, *Mal faire, dire vrai*, p. 208.
69 E.g. SABR, *AC-WEST*, 200–784, 230–1097 and 320–723; NA2, *AC-BRA*, 2231 and 2275. Cf. Karine Lambert, *Itinéraires féminins de la déviance: Provence 1750–1850* (Aix-en-Provence: Université de Provence, 2012), pp. 44–5.
70 SABR, *AC-WEST*, 398–1459. The commuted sentence is reported in Sibo van Ruller, *Genade voor recht: gratieverlening aan ter dood veroordeelden in Nederland 1806–1870* (Amsterdam: Bataafsche Leeuw, 1987).
71 Hofman, 'A wholesome cure', 225–8. On culpabilisation, see Jean Delumeau, *Le péché et la peur: la culpabilisation en Occident (XIIIe–XVIIIe siècles)* (Paris: Fayard, 1983); Marie-Sylvie Dupont-Bouchat, 'Culpabilisation et conscience individuelle. L'individu, l'Église et l'État à l'époque moderne (XVIe–XVIIIe s.)', in *La Belgique criminelle. Droit, justice, société (XIVe–XXe siècles)* (Louvain-la-Neuve: Academia-Bruylant, 2006), pp. 75–105.
72 Bandes, 'Remorse and criminal justice', 17.
73 SABR, *AC-WEST*, 277–336.
74 SABR, *AC-WEST*, 262–213.
75 SABR, *AC-WEST*, 320–723.
76 Kounine, *Imagining the Witch*, chap. 3.
77 Virginia Krause, *Witchcraft, Demonology, and Confession in Early Modern France* (Cambridge: Cambridge University Press, 2015), pp. 36–7.
78 Elwin Hofman, 'Corporeal truth: conscience, fear and the body in French criminal interrogations, 1750–1850', *Cultural and Social History*, advance access (2020); Michael Niehaus, '"Wirkung einer Naturkraft". Das Geständnis und sein Motiv in Diskursen um 1800', in Jo Reichertz and Manfred Schneider (eds), *Sozialgeschichte des Geständnisses: zum Wandel der Geständniskultur* (Wiesbaden: VS Verlag für Sozialwissenschaften, 2007), pp. 43–73.
79 Cf. Peter Brooks, *Troubling Confessions: Speaking Guilt in Law & Literature* (Chicago, IL: University of Chicago Press, 2000), chap. 5; Chloe Taylor, *The Culture of Confession from Augustine to Foucault: A Genealogy of the 'Confessing Animal'* (Abingdon: Routledge, 2009).
80 SABR, *AC-WEST*, 164–446. Also for the following paragraphs.
81 Fierlant, 'Premières idées', fo. 807r.
82 François Duverger, *Manuel des juges d'instruction 2* (Niort: Robin, 1844), vol. 2, p. 460.
83 NA2, *AC-BRA*, 2231. A similar situation is reported in 1802 in NA2, *AC-BRA*, 304–661.

84 There are some examples, however, of interrogations partially transcribed in the first person, especially when torture was applied, e.g. Krause, *Witchcraft, Demonology, and Confession*, pp. 118–20; Paul Cohen, 'Torture and translation in the multilingual courtrooms of early modern France', *Renaissance Quarterly*, 69 (2016), 903; Kounine, *Imagining the Witch*, p. 114. Of the old regime cases in my sample, only the interrogation of Jan Bailliu under torture was recorded in the first person.

85 FA, *731*, 1514/2. My italics.

86 SABR, *AC-WEST*, 164–446.

87 SABR, *AC-WEST*, 230–1097.

88 SABR, *AC-WEST*, 196–748. The case in Ghent was annulled by the court of cassation and then transferred to the criminal court in Bruges.

89 For Germany, Michael Niehaus and Christian Lück, 'Konfrontationen und Lügenstrafen. Akten zur Geständnisarbeit um 1800', in Jo Reichertz and Manfred Schneider (eds), *Sozialgeschichte des Geständnisses: zum Wandel der Geständniskultur* (Wiesbaden: VS Verlag für Sozialwissenschaften, 2007), pp. 115–41. For France, Frédéric Chauvaud, 'La parole captive: l'interrogatoire judiciaire au XIXe siècle', *Histoire et archives*, 1 (1997), 37–8.

90 At least not in France or the Southern Netherlands; for Germany, see Becker, '"Recht schreiben"', p. 69.

91 Duverger, *Manuel des juges*, vol. 2, p. 466. Cf. Thielen, *Forme et manière*, p. 51.

92 Charles-Jules-Armand Bioche, *Dictionnaire des juges de paix et de police ou manuel théorique et pratique en matière civile, criminelle et administrative* (Paris: Videcoq Fils ainé, 1852), vol. 2, pp. 191–2.

93 Krause, *Witchcraft, Demonology, and Confession*, pp. 36–43.

94 Butler, *Giving an Account*; Krause, *Witchcraft, Demonology, and Confession*, p. 113.

95 Michel Foucault (ed.), *Moi, Pierre Rivière, ayant égorgé ma mère, ma soeur et mon frère… Un cas de parricide au XIXe siècle* (Paris: Julliard, 1973). The genre was not entirely uncommon; see some of the confessions described in Philippe Lejeune, 'Crime et testament. Les autobiographies de criminels au XIXe siècle', in Philippe Lejeune (ed.), *Récits de vie et institutions* (Paris: Centre de Sémiotique Textuelle, 1986), pp. 73–98.

96 SABE, *AC-ANT*, 329; FA, *731*, 1476.

97 Foucault, ed., *Moi, Pierre Rivière*; Bronwyn Davies and Jane Speedy, 'Who was Pierre Rivière? Introduction to the special issue', *Emotion, Space and Society*, 5:4 (2012), 207–15.

2

Making reasonable selves: self-defence, honour and philosophical suicide

The eighteenth century is sometimes called 'the age of reason'; 'reason' being a keyword of the Enlightenment. Kant famously understood Enlightenment as the freedom to use reason publicly against dogmas.[1] Many other Enlightenment thinkers applauded the use of reason to question the doctrines of religion. The light of reason was to dispel the darkness of unreason in all domains.[2] While, as we will see in the following chapters, many (late) Enlightenment authors were no naïve believers in reason and arduously examined its possibilities and limits, reason played an important role, not only and not even necessarily in eighteenth-century intellectual culture, but in wider society, through the institutions that propagated some of the values of Enlightenment thought.[3] The increasing focus of criminal courts on interiority and individuality that was discussed in the previous chapter should not conceal a concurrent prevalence of discourses that suggested the opposite: a universalised, socially oriented self, governed by reason. The eighteenth- and nineteenth-century self was always pluralistic and unstable; it was never singularly inner- or outer-oriented, stable or malleable, whole or fragmented, responsible or dispossessed. Men and women of different social backgrounds put these different discourses into practice according to their different situations and their available cultural resources. Reason, I will show in this chapter, was one of those resources and could play an important role in criminal courts.

Before we go ahead, we should address what 'reason' meant in the eighteenth and nineteenth centuries. It was one of three mental faculties that scholars commonly distinguished in the eighteenth century, the other two being memory and imagination.[4] In the dominant sensationalist psychology of Condillac, reasoning was a mathematical process, taking apart sensations and ideas, comparing them and rearranging them.[5] As such, scholars thought that reason was universal: given the same set of axioms and problems, all who used reason would reach the same conclusions. 'The nature of reason must be the same in all', Mary Wollstonecraft wrote.[6] The reasonable self was therefore not an individualised or inner-oriented self; it was a self in control of itself and oriented towards the world, without much depth.

If many Enlightenment philosophers stressed the importance of feeling for moral behaviour, many also suggested that reasonable behaviour was morally superior. The German philosopher Immanuel Kant most thoroughly explored the matter in his *Groundwork for the Metaphysics of Morals* (1785) and again in his *Critique of Practical Reason* (1788). Kant applied the principle of universalism to morality and concluded that people should 'act so that the maxim of your will can always at the same time hold good as a principle of universal legislation'.[7] People should use reason to determine what to do, and the governing principle of reason should be its universal applicability. On these grounds, Kant condemned suicide, for instance, as it would, if universally applied, lead to the extinction of the human species and of reason and morality.[8] On the same grounds, many *philosophes* denounced sodomy.[9]

Because of this assimilation of morality into reason, reason also became the keyword for many legal and penal reformers in the second half of the eighteenth century: the new criminal justice system they wanted was reasonable, reliable and predictable. The famous Italian criminal justice reformer Cesare Beccaria argued that people who considered committing a crime were to know in advance the penalty they would incur. This penalty, moreover, should be proportionate to the crime in question, so that the disadvantages of the penalty would always be slightly greater than the advantages of committing the crime. The reasonable, calculating individual would then refrain from committing crimes.[10]

Beccaria and his contemporaries certainly did not expect that everyone would use their reason correctly by default; indeed they called for preventive measures, education and deterrence to ensure that people associated abiding the law with pleasure and breaking it with pain – measures predicated not on the principles of reason, but on those of sensationalism.[11] Social circumstances and poor education prevented many from using their reason properly; passions and instincts governed many people's behaviour. Several thinkers argued that women were less reasonable than men.[12] However, they did expect that people who acted reasonably, who analysed and calculated the right parameters, would refrain from committing crimes, and that, therefore, people were to be stimulated to act reasonably. Indeed, as Martin Wiener has shown for early nineteenth-century England, the responsible and rational individual became the guiding vision of criminal justice from the late eighteenth century onwards. Many policymakers believed, moreover, that the best way to *make* people more reasonable and responsible was to 'to hold them, sternly and unblinkingly, responsible for the consequences of their actions'.[13]

In the Southern Netherlands, as in England and elsewhere in Europe, criminal courts encouraged people to practise an autonomous, responsible and reasonable self. Since the late middle ages, following Roman law, criminal courts agreed that people could only be punished for crimes they had willingly committed.[14] Unless evidence to the contrary was presented, the courts assumed this willingness and imbued defendants with individual autonomy and responsibility. If the defendants did not contest this – I will discuss cases where they *did* contest their autonomy and responsibility in the next chapter – they could seek to claim that their actions should still not be punished. The arguments they built were often not new in the eighteenth century. But because of the new appreciation for reason among eighteenth- and nineteenth-century legislators, legal reformers, philosophers and magistrates, they gained a new urgency for criminal justice.

Many of those appearing before courts appropriated the principles (though not the language) of reason to defend themselves. The idea that in an ideal world, men and women were governed by reason led many men and women to consider their acts as reasonable. They stressed not their individuality, deep interiority or loss of self-control, but the universality of their actions and the reasonability of their decisions. They had not acted in a moment of heated passion, but upon reasoned reflection. They claimed autonomy and agency while portraying behaviour that would generally be considered *unreasonable*. These people contended that their killings and thefts, prostitution and suicide attempts were not the result of defective mental faculties, inner dispositions or irrational feelings but, on the contrary, that all reasonable, calculating human beings who found themselves in the same situation would have acted in the same way.

Many of them were unsuccessful. Despite the stress of the criminal court on universal reason, it struggled with its consequences. Courts regularly accepted claims to reason when they were made by elite men, but often contested them when commoners or women made them. While the latter regularly offered socially oriented, universalising discourses, they often found that these were not accepted. Throughout seemingly disparate cases – homicide in self-defence, prostitution out of poverty, killing in the defence of honour and 'philosophical' suicide – a pattern appears, by which criminal justice promoted reason and universality in theory, but had to reconcile it with interiority, individuality and dispossession for most common men and women.

As I discuss the different reasons the courts invited and people offered for their behaviour, I will regularly touch upon the gendered aspects of these reasons. Men and women – or people who were perceived as such – behaved, perceived others and perceived themselves in 'masculine' or 'feminine' ways. Like conceptions of the self, ideas and practices of 'masculinity' and 'femininity' were multiple and sometimes contradictory. Masculine and feminine behaviour and identities could be opposed, but were sometimes also similar. Masculinity and femininity were central to eighteenth- and nineteenth-century criminal justice, but also to the self.[15] As we will see, defendants, witnesses, judges and jurors drew upon a wide range of cultural resources to include and exclude men and women from certain excuses because of their gender.

Reasonable justice, legitimate defence

Killing another human being, the famous *Encyclopédie* noted, was only acceptable in two circumstances: when a soldier killed his enemy during wartime and when an executioner killed a convict. It follows that in all other cases, homicide is unethical, unreasonable and criminal: 'According to divine and human laws, voluntary homicide is a crime meriting death'.[16] Immanuel Kant agreed in his *Metaphysics of Morals* (1797), in which he applied the general principles of the *Critique of Practical Reason* (1788) to more specific matters. All unlawful killing was to be punished by death. As reason dictates that the first duty of human beings to themselves is to *preserve* themselves, and that moral principles should be universal, it follows that homicide would not be reasonable.[17]

Of course, this reasoning could entail paradoxes. What should one do when one's own life was in danger and could only be saved by killing another? For Kant, the matter was clear: people had the right to deprive a wrongful assailant of their life in order to prevent that the assailant would take their life. He recommended moderation in the counterattack, but for Kant this should only be a matter of ethics, not of law. Killing in self-defence should therefore not be punished by law.[18]

The early modern legal system was not as straightforward, however. Throughout the early modern period, as we have seen, urban courts had a quasi-monopoly on criminal justice in the Southern Netherlands and had some flexibility in determining procedures and sentences. Homicide cases were the main exception. The urban criminal courts had few options to convict someone who had committed homicide (and was not insane) to anything but the death penalty. They were to represent the 'rigour of justice'. Just like in France, only the king or his councils could show clemency by pardoning excusable killings, such as those committed by accident, in self-defence or upon a violent provocation. If someone was proven to have committed the material act of homicide, even in self-defence, they generally had to claim their innocence through the clemency of the ruler. In this way, the central government could oversee some criminal procedures and defendants could choose between different authorities to resolve their case in function of their defensive strategies. At the same time, this had as a result that criminal courts were, at least in theory, less concerned with motivations and excuses.[19]

So in 1753, baker's apprentice Gabriel Hosfeldt, living near Binche, related that he had been with a girl in an inn, when another of the inn's guests wanted to claim this girl and to this end started to quarrel with him. Hosfeldt, taking the moral high ground, left the inn, but was followed by the other man, who hit him and knocked him down: 'Finding himself attacked by such a strong and robust aggressor, he believed that his life was about to end, took his knife and stabbed him a few times, of which he has died thirteen days later'. Hosfeldt had then fled the county to avoid an arrest, but since he had only defended his own life, he hoped to receive the Queen's grace. Although the incident could easily be related to Hosfeldt's feelings of jealousy and the love for his girl, he chose to portray his behaviour as disconnected from any interiority and as the result of the application of a universal, detached reason.[20]

Local magistrates (who were always asked for advice) would not confirm the material facts of Hosfeldt's story, so his request was dismissed. Others using a similar narrative were more successful. Jean Martin Froitier applied for grace in 1761 and again claimed that he had been attacked and had hit his assailant on the head to defend his own life. This time, local magistrates were quick to confirm his story, particularly as the victim had a bad reputation and was suspected of two murders. The Privy Council decided that Froitier's case was not really in need of grace, 'as he had in no way exceeded the bounds of a justified defence', but advised giving grace 'as far as necessary'.[21] This continued to be a regular practice until the end of the old regime: people who had committed homicide 'in self-defence and protection of their own body, without malice, aforethought or premeditation' could, if they satisfied a strict set of conditions, particularly that their killing blow had been in proportion to the attack, be acquitted by the courts, but they generally took the route of applying for grace.[22]

Enlightenment critics disapproved of what they considered the arbitrariness of both the courts and the grace procedure. Although the government usually granted or denied grace in accordance with established rules and customs – and not because of the personal compassion of the ruler – reformers denounced the lack of written rules and transparent procedures. Beccaria, among others, argued that judges nor princes were to interpret laws; they were only to decide whether particular actions were conforming to or against the law. This required, of course, the establishment of a new penal code, a code that would be less cruel and take reason as its guiding principle. Once this penal code was in place, grace and clemency were to be abolished: 'Let the executors of the laws be inexorable, but let the legislator be tender, indulgent and humane'.[23]

Beccaria was not particularly concerned with questions of culpability; indeed, his argument was that courts should punish crimes according to the injury done to society, not according to the intention of their authors. He did not consider such cases as accidents or self-defence. When it came to (partially) applying his principles to practice after the French Revolution, legislators did have to consider such questions. In the legalistic system installed in 1791, there was no place for such arbitrariness as grace. Questions of moral culpability were therefore fully integrated in the criminal justice system. Legislators now clearly stipulated that certain homicides were not crimes: if a homicide was an accident, it was no crime; if it had been ordered by the state, it was no crime; if it was 'indispensably commanded by the current need of a legitimate defence of oneself or another', 'there is no crime'.[24]

The keyword was, of course, 'indispensably': if the homicide had only been violently 'provoked', the killer would be convicted to ten years of confinement. The reaction still had to be moderated to the attack, although there were no longer any hard and fast rules to determine this moderation: the legislators left this up to the wisdom of the judges and juries.[25] In all other cases, homicide was punished with at least twenty years of convict labour. Although the code provided youth and old age as mitigating circumstances, there were no provisions for diminished responsibility, such as madness or passion. The legal subject of the new code was an autonomous and rational subject and their behaviour was excusable only if they had acted reasonably. The legislators deemed defending your own or another life the only viable reason to kill someone outside of battle.[26]

The *Code of Offences and Penalties* of 1795 preserved these provisions and was introduced in the Southern Netherlands in the same year. The only notable difference was that, to soften the strict legalistic principles of the penal code, the new code added the possibility to ask juries whether a crime was 'excusable' by some excuse offered by the defendant. If so, the punishment was reduced (to ten years imprisonment for homicide).[27] The courts only rarely asked this question, however. The self-defence argument was immediately one of the most popular strategies defendants used: during the trial, magistrates routinely asked suspects whether they had anything to say to justify themselves. Many seized this opportunity to claim that they had only defended their lives.[28] If juries decided that the homicide had indeed been committed in self-defence, the suspect was set free.

Members of the jury always answered the questions put to them with only a yes or a no; there were no partial excuses; there was no room for arbitrariness. In only one of the cases in my sample did a jury exceed its duty in this respect. In 1799, Marie Therese Boyen was tried in Brussels for killing her former lover, Jean Lambeets. When questioned, she related that the night before the killing, Lambeets had desired to stay over with her, but she had shut her door. The morning after, he had returned, shouting 'bitch, why did you shut your door yesterday evening?' pulled his knife and stabbed her. Boyen ran away, out of her house, but then heard her child cry. She returned inside, took a big stick and started hitting Lambeets to protect her child. She then took her child and ran to the street. Later, she found out that Lambeets had died. When the case came to trial, the jury was asked whether they thought she had acted in legitimate defence of herself and her child. 'Yes', the jury answered, adding that 'it was even an act of heroism'. It is not surprising that this case concerns a woman: men made most claims of legitimate defence; they could access this claim to reason much more easily. Women were not expected to engage in violence, nor to defend themselves so violently. The exceptionality of the case led to an exceptional statement by the jury. A woman defending her child against a man of ill repute sat very well with the jury's gendered ethics, leading them to qualify their verdict. For a woman, protecting her own life and that of her child was the supreme justification for homicide and, indeed, universally reasonable, but at the same time uncommon and unexpected.[29]

Soon after the installation of the new legal system, the French revolutionaries found that their strictly legalistic principles, which allowed only for universal, rational grounds for acquittal, were not workable. In 1802, Napoleon reintroduced grace in the penal system. Grace was, of course, no longer necessary for accidents and simple self-defence, but became a means to take account of all sorts of circumstances that the law did not or not sufficiently recognise, such as verbal provocations, sincere remorse or good behaviour. If the authorities accepted such circumstances as mitigating, the could reduce the sentence.[30] They also frequently gave grace to people who had defended themselves without showing the necessary moderation.[31] Furthermore, the new penal code of 1810 stipulated that 'there is no crime if the suspect was in a state of lunacy at the time of the action' and added minimum and maximum sentences for most crimes, giving the judge some discretion in deciding the severity of the punishment.[32] The experiment with a strictly legalistic justice system that only allowed for rational excuses was over. The justice system and the grace system could (again) pay more attention to individual backgrounds, inner movements and the loss of self-control – as we will amply see in the next chapter.

Of course, the self-defence argument remained popular after these changes. In 1807, Pierre De Leersnyder, finding himself attacked by a group of people, 'feared perishing from their blows, so he believed to have the right to defend himself'. He took a kitchen knife and stabbed his main opponent. The jury agreed with his reasoning and De Leersnyder was set free.[33] Not all were so successful, as an interrogator sceptically asked Pierre Dero, who also pleaded self-defence, whether 'rather than being legitimate defence, he hasn't voluntarily killed Jean Baptiste Devrieze, thus being guilty of murder?' Of course not, Dero claimed, but the jury did not agree in this case. They found that he had been violently provoked, but that he had done more than just defend himself. The judge sentenced him to five years of imprisonment.[34]

Throughout this period, people accepted that self-defence was a natural right and, therefore, a reasonable excuse for homicide. For the law, homicides had to show moderation in their defence, however, and if they could avoid killing their opponent, they had to. As the question of culpability became fully integrated in criminal justice, the law required its subjects to be rational. The preservation of life was the main excuse rational men or women could use after committing crimes. Its extraction from the right of grace and integration in the criminal code was testimony to its universal appreciation.

As such, interactions in criminal court stimulated people to practise a rational self, a self that was calculating, responsible and in control. The law stipulated that killing in self-defence was a reasonable thing to do. Using this law for their own purposes, people thus spoke about their own actions in a universalising way, claiming that they had only killed because it was a universally reasonable thing to do. This had the effect of distancing their behaviour from their deep inner side, from their feelings and even from their social position. In this way, the law stimulated people to accept responsibility for their actions, without implicating their innermost beings.

Obliged to be a public woman

As the moral imperative of self-preservation was so well-accepted, it should not surprise that people also appropriated it for use in less obvious situations. Men most commonly used the argument that they had acted 'reasonably' in defence of their own life. But women, particularly poor women, also laid claim to a similar form of reason. Increasingly, around 1800, women tried for prostitution referred to their poverty to legitimise their choice of trade as reasonable. Of course, prostitutes had previously also generally been poor women, who found few other means to provide for themselves.[35] However, up to the early eighteenth century, in the Southern Netherlands as in most of North-Western Europe, better-off men did not often perceive them as such. With exceptions, of course, they often saw the 'whore' as a woman with an insatiable lust. She was a cunning creature, who lured men to fulfil her own desires and even managed to get some money out of them.

This related to a more general and commonly used image of women as lustful creatures: if men did not restrain them, all women would be whores.[36]

While this image did not entirely disappear, it was complemented with a different image in the course of the eighteenth century. The new view, propagated in many European countries through novels, plays and philosophical and scientific treatises, held that men, rather than women, were the more naturally libidinous sex; and that women were more sensitive, delicate and naturally chaste. Consequently, the causes of prostitution were rethought. Prostitution became more problematic, as prostitutes were now women who defied 'essential' feminine characteristics, while at the same time they became the objects of sympathy, as people assumed that few women would voluntarily choose a life in prostitution. Prostitutes had to be destitute, seduced and exploited. They sacrificed their values out of economic necessity.[37]

Women accused of prostitution were quick to use this new sentimental narrative to their benefit. When they arrested and interrogated suspected prostitutes, judges sometimes showed a (limited) interest in asking why they had been walking the streets. We are particularly well informed of the Brussels case. Prostitutes' most common explanation was that 'they prostituted themselves to survive'.[38] Jeanne Joseph Denis explained after her arrest in 1779, when asked how she provided for herself, that 'she works when she can find work, and when she doesn't, she delivers herself to everyone as a public woman, but she has only started this vile trade after the death of her husband, out of misery'.[39] In 1799, Florence Foullart was asked the same question and replied that 'given the misery in which she is, she is obliged to be a public woman', while her colleague Therese Le Clerc noted that 'given the shortage of work in the circumstances of the times, she is obliged to be a public woman'.[40] Similarly, women who applied for permission to keep a brothel in early nineteenth-century Antwerp frequently reported that poverty had led them to this trade, like Catharina Vaerendonck in 1823, who claimed that she had 'no other means to provide for [her]self and [her] disabled child'.[41]

In effect, these women placed the causes of their stigmatised behaviour outside themselves, outside their body, outside their mind. They argued that everyone in a similar situation would act in the way they did, as it was their only possibility to survive. Their actions were reasonable. Despite the rising sympathy for prostitutes, judges did not easily accept such claims. While they were increasingly sensitive towards poverty in the eighteenth century, judges rarely accepted it as a sufficient excuse for any crime whatsoever. In petitions for grace in homicide cases, supplicants frequently related the state of poverty their family was in upon their arrest, escape or exile, which, if combined with other arguments could be successful. As I will discuss in chapter 4, especially in the 1770s and 1780s it was common to express compassion and sympathy with the poor. At the same time, however, many among the better-off had great contempt for the poor, especially for the able-bodied, 'unde-serving' poor – including prostitutes. Their poverty was seen as irrational, at best a result of insufficient education, at worst the result of plain laziness. If prostitutes were poor, it was probably because they were lazy. Even as com-passion with prostitutes increased, such images remained vivid.[42]

The solution to the problem of prostitution – and to virtually all prob-lems – was 'proper' work. The authorities had to discipline prostitutes in order to save them. This was part of a larger movement towards disciplining the poor. Specifically for prostitutes, in many countries the early nineteenth century saw the erection of private charitable hospitals for 'fallen women', where women lived in a regime of rigid discipline and were to experience the habit of working.[43] In 1824 such an institution was founded in Antwerp, and Brussels followed suit in 1828. Women who wanted to leave prostitu-tion would voluntarily enter the institution, learn the habit of working and then re-enter society. Their stay in the private hospital would 'make them into useful members of the state'.[44]

In the same vein, in 1834, the *Société des sciences médicales et naturelles de Bruxelles* organised a contest to answer the question of what measures governments should take to stop the propagation of syphilis. Synthesising the winning answers, the society wrote a memoir for the Minister of Internal Affairs. The main cause of the spread of syphilis, they contended, was pros-titution. In order to eradicate syphilis, prostitution was to be halted. But they did not argue for stronger punishments or for a larger police force. They agreed that poverty was the main cause of prostitution: 'One must not be mistaken: immorality and corruption of the heart are not always the only causes that have pushed young girls into prostitution'. Often, girls were seduced or in misery, and regretted their decision to enter prostitution every single day. Moreover, many girls were 'dominated by the taste of the age, and want to display luxury'. Because many women were out of work, they resorted to prostitution as their only means to afford expensive apparel. The solution was to provide more workshops for women, so as to avoid idleness and misery, and to provide more shelters such as the ones in Antwerp and Brussels. Workshops, like the shelters, were to 'develop and maintain mod-esty, love for work, order, and all virtuous sentiments' in women.[45] Despite the acknowledgement of poverty as a main cause of prostitution, the *Société* did not accept it as rational, but saw it as a result of an individualised lack of virtue.

In the seventeenth and early eighteenth centuries, people often viewed prostitutes as ordinary, lascivious women who were out of control. They generally related their behaviour to their bodies and to their desires, but they did not usually individualise it: it was a characteristic of their sex. As perceptions of women at least in some circles changed in the course of the eighteenth century, so did the image of the prostitute. Prostitutes themselves presented their behaviour as a result of their poverty. They put the causes of their prostitution outside themselves, arguing that they would not survive if they did not prostitute themselves. As such, they presented prostitution as a rational course of action, not related to their inner self. The authorities, however, could not accept this reasoning, and did find the causes of prostitution in their personal disposition: it was a result of laziness, lack of discipline, luxuriousness and avarice. They agreed that prostitution often related to money and misery but did not accept this as an unavoidable – or acceptable – choice. Whereas men who drew on the discourse of self-defence had their reasonability regularly accepted, women in prostitution found this much harder. Their actions were almost always seen as unreasonable, related to interiority and individual character.

Honourable violence

Self-defence and poverty arguments were viable from the perspective of self-preservation as the first duty of people to themselves. However, some people argued that there was something even more important than self-preservation, more important than life: honour. Kant, for instance, proposed that the death penalty should always be imposed for homicides, except perhaps when honour had led people to commit homicide, as was the case for duels and for infanticide of illegitimate children.[46] To protect their honour, some people thought themselves justified to put their lives on the line.

Honour was an ambiguous concept, so much was already known to contemporaries. It at once signified virtue ('an honourable man'), individual or group reputation, a feeling of self-esteem and a right to respect.[47] The high value put on honour in the eighteenth and nineteenth centuries required that people lived virtuously, or pretended to live virtuously, and defended their reputation against all allegations that they did not. If they 'lost' their honour, people risked 'social death' – being excluded by their peers and, for some even more importantly, their sense of honour (as a sentiment of right to respect) was hurt. The 'code of honour' was highly gendered and intersected with conceptions of masculinity and femininity. Although the language of honour could be adapted for many purposes, and was subject to geographical differences, for men, people often linked honour to courage and trustworthiness. For women, people often used the language of honour to promote chasteness.

Because of its importance throughout society, honour was a common language in which all sorts of conflicts could be resolved in many European

regions. Both elite and common men (and some women) publicly and ostentatiously defended their honour when challenged, for instance, after an
insult. Not every challenge of honour led to violence, of course: there were
many ways to settle conflicts of honour peaceably.[48] But in some situations,
men and some women saw the need to react violently in order to uphold
their honour. In these instances, the defence of honour often took the form
of ritual violence in the form of a duel, fought in accordance with pre-estab-
lished rules. The violence resulting from honour was expected and could be
portrayed as calculated and outer-oriented: people were well-aware of the
performative aspects of honour. But people also *felt* insults to their honour;
they had a sense that they could not let an insult pass without reacting. In
this section, I investigate how people negotiated between these narratives;
how they could portray honour-related violence both as a calculated performance necessary to save their face and as the result of feelings of honour-
ability. My approach contrasts with some other historians, who by stressing
that honour was emotional have sometimes overlooked that it could also be
rational and calculating – something that was not lost on contemporaries.[49]

The history of honour and its role in people's stories before the criminal
courts are a crucial element in the history of the self. As was the case with
the language of self-defence, people could use the language of honour to
disconnect their behaviour from their inner being. They cast their actions
as the necessary result of a widely agreed-upon code of honour; not as connected to their individual nature. They implied and put into practice a strong
social orientation of the self. But honour was, as we will see, not as universal as self-defence. It was more clearly implicated with questions of gender
and social status, and individual feeling was more commonly implied in the
interactions with the court. As a consequence, practices relating to honour
could also work towards a more individualised, interiorised and even dispossessed self. To understand how this worked, we need to take a closer
look at the history of honour and its role in the criminal court.

Historians have shown that during the sixteenth and seventeenth centuries, the code of honour was relatively well integrated across different
social groups. Despite this relative integration, however, most honour-
related violence stayed within the same social groups, and different social
groups fought according to somewhat different rules. The duel of honour,
fought primarily by noblemen and military officers, differed from the popular duel. The differences between both forms increased as the eighteenth
century dawned: elite men did not recognise commoner's claims to honour
and increasingly denied that they could justify their violence with their sense
of honour. While popular fights over honour lost some of their former ritual
characteristics, at the same time, the ritual of the elite duel became more
sophisticated and, in some ways, less violent than before.[50]

The popular duel

Let us attend to popular, less formalised conceptions of honour and violence among men first. Men did not systematically resort to violence when their honour was at stake. Indeed, throughout North-Western Europe historians have observed a decline of honourable violence from the end of the seventeenth century on, especially among the middling sorts.[51] In the first half of the eighteenth century, a greater recourse to civil courts partially compensated this decline in violence: people who had been insulted sometimes sued their opponents and, if successful, could have them publicly revoke their slanderous words. By the second half of the eighteenth century, this practice was also in decline.[52]

While sociability indeed seems to have become more peaceful in the eighteenth-century Southern Netherlands, violent conflicts of honour did not disappear. A typical dispute fought out in terms of honour occurred in Kortrijk in 1740. Michiel Vandenborre, a merchant in flax, had insulted Pieter Malfait, a master mason, at a neighbourhood gathering. Malfait, however, replied that 'it were fine men, who undressed their wives and tied them up in the attic and whipped them'. Vandenborre was furious and challenged Malfait to a fight behind the town walls. Malfait refused and other neighbours intervened. As tradition required, they both drank a beer to reconcile. Later that night, however, Vandenborre was still out for vengeance, for while drinking another glass with Malfait, he stabbed him in the chest and ran off.[53]

Although we do not know if there were any underlying causes for this dispute, Vandenborre and Malfait clearly fought it out in terms of honour. Ritual insults, a challenge to a duel and drinking to reconcile were common elements of disputes of honour, and they were obviously clear to all the participants. The declining success of the rituals is also clear: Malfait could apparently afford to refuse a duel and Vandenborre violated all established rules by – all witnesses agreed – cowardly stabbing Malfait while they were drinking. In numerous other cases in the second half of the eighteenth century, a similar combination of following and breaking established rituals of honour occurred. Quarrels often started with a dispute, for instance about who the better artisan was, about who was to pay for drinks or about who could have a particular spot on the market. Insults ('would you say that I am dishonest?') and violence ensued. If things went badly, they could end in death.[54]

In most of these cases of rather informal duels, suspects of homicide did not portray the defence of their honour as a rational response to a challenge. Indeed, the general idea seems to have been that while they had to react to the challenge, killing their opponent was a bridge too far. There are exceptions, however: in his application for grace in 1755, Jean Giot had the widow of his victim declare that before passing away, her husband had pardoned Giot, 'as he had brought the mortal blow on himself, both by the sharp words and by the insults he had said'. However, the Privy Council found this a most unlikely statement, assumed that Giot had bribed the widow and dismissed his request.[55] In most other cases, therefore, people argued that they had not just acted rationally to defend their honour, but that they had become *angry*. They linked their sense of honour to the feeling of anger to explain why they had resorted to violence. Barthelemi Neutjens, for instance, related in 1753 that he was in his garden when he heard people insulting him, 'burst out in fury', took a stick and hit his insulter.[56] A similar pattern was visible in the case of Vandenborre: witnesses noted that Vandenborre became 'furious' before challenging Malfait. It seems, therefore, that for many common eighteenth-century people, honour was entangled with other feelings.

The early nineteenth century did not witness a decline in the importance of honour or reputation, rather the opposite. The interest of early nineteenth-century courts in reputations increased: references to reputations in witness statements were more frequent in the new regime than in the old.[57] I have also found more explicit mentions of the value of honour. In 1797, for instance, a neighbour found twelve-year-old farmer's boy Louis Derancy 'wholly in tears'. When he asked him why he was crying, Derancy replied that 'they have told him that his brother Jean Baptiste has killed one of the daughters of Jean de Man, and so he has ruined their family's honour and reputation'.[58] Violent fights over insults did not disappear either. In 1822, domestic servant Jean Baptiste Delcon went to a dance party and got into a row with a certain Engelborgh over who could take a particular position in the dance. Engelborgh claimed that he had taken the spot first, but Delcon pushed Engelborgh away, saying 'you scoundrel, just shut up, or I'll throw you against something'. Others came to defend Engelborgh, however, and they threw Delcon out of the inn. When he returned, as a witness observed 'humiliated for having been chased', he provoked everyone, shouting out loudly 'if there is anyone who dares to throw me out, let him step forward!' His honour had been violated, and Delcon needed to re-establish it.[59]

Honourable violence abounded: Pierre Verschuere hit the man who called him a 'ruffian' in 1797, weaver Jean Beckens hit a man who called him a deserter in 1804 and Joannes Taccoen hit the man who called him 'unjust and a scoundrel'. The most peculiar fight over honour – worthy of a *Midsomer Murders* scenario – occurred in Aarschot in 1827. In a brewery called *Den Rooden Leeuw*, Peter Wilms was found severely injured: he was burnt by boiling beer. Before he passed away, he declared that drayman

Hendrik Van Eylen had thrown him in a barrel of beer. Van Eylen had fled, but the police arrested him five days later. He confessed immediately:

> I couldn't say what the origin of the fight was, but he called me a beggar. I told him that his children were beggars too and he challenged me to join him in the garden. Shortly after our work had ended, we left the brewery and Wilms hit me on the chest. I grabbed him and while we held each other, we lay next to a barrel. The barrel was still empty, but boiling beer was running in. By our movements, we reached the barrel, and while I didn't want to push Wilms in, I felt that he was falling. I tried to prevent his fall, but was unable to do so.[60]

A simple fight over honour had ended in a gruesome death.

Notably, in none of these nineteenth-century cases did anyone speak of anger. Disputes of honour seem to have regained a more ritual character, in which passions were less recognised. Just as Katie Barclay has found in early nineteenth-century Ireland, honour required a display of restraint rather than unbounded anger.[61] These disputes were more about showing courage when honour was challenged than about revenge; indeed, as in the case of Van Eylen, they sometimes even seem to have had a playful character. This new approach to honour is also visible in another practice, in which people not only fought to defend their honour after an insult, but also to establish their honour. Pierre De Jonghe, a shepherd in Ingelmunster, was with fellow servants in his master's kitchen in 1815. While the others were just sitting around, he pulled his knife and started to make 'fencing gestures' towards some of them, challenging them to a fight and eventually lethally injuring one of them.[62] Policeman Jan Blomme, in 1830, was playing cards with a merchant in linen, but upon losing the game, challenged his opponent to wrestle.[63] In neither case had the challenger's honour been offended, but they playfully resorted to duels to show their courage.

The elite duel

The more formal and more elite duel followed a slightly different path. As in many European countries, formal duels among the nobility and among military officers were officially prohibited in the Southern Netherlands. The government issued the first ordinance against duelling in 1557, and slightly different versions, specifications and additions in 1589, 1599, 1610, 1616, 1624, 1626, 1628, 1636, 1638, 1658, 1667, 1669, 1671, 1685 and 1701. All of these decrees stipulated that courts should punish duellists and witnesses who did not try to prevent the duel with death, confiscate their possessions and declare them dishonourable. Although the edicts concerned 'all our subjects, of any quality or condition', they especially concerned noblemen and soldiers, who held the 'erroneous, false and mendacious opinion' that they could not undo insults except with a duel and so evaded the justice of the crown. The legislators advised that anyone whose honour was offended should take to the courts to have their opponents punished for their slanderous words.[64]

As the power of the courts became more firmly established in the eighteenth century, the concerns with duelling seem to have waded. Indeed, a military decree in 1706 proposed to pardon soldiers who killed a superior officer in a duel after he had greatly insulted them, for instance by slapping them in the face, 'as honour is estimated higher than life'.[65] In legal practice, moreover, there were hardly any convictions of duellists. In advice regarding a matter of grace in 1779, the officer of justice in Brussels noted that 'because it is extremely difficult to get sufficient proof of a duel, I can find neither in my memory, nor in the archives of my office the existence of a trial for duelling ending with a conviction by the Magistrates of this city'.[66]

As a result, it is difficult to establish how popular the formal duel was in the Southern Netherlands. Ever since the sixteenth century, edicts against duelling lamented the 'many accidents' that happened 'every day' in duels, while contemporary commentaries suggested that, on the contrary, duelling was not very common in the Southern Netherlands, especially in comparison with France.[67] If everything went according to the rules and there were no severe casualties, duels often went unrecorded. The number of known formal duels is therefore very low: in the second half of the eighteenth century, we know of about a dozen duels in the Southern Netherlands.[68] Passing remarks in all sorts of literature suggest, however, that the number of duels and of challenges to a duel was remarkably higher. In his memoirs, the Prince de Ligne (1735–1814), for one, reported taking part in several duels, but also wondered 'how it was possible that I haven't had to fight a hundred duels', as he was always out to make jokes at other people's expense.[69] Many used the language of politeness to 'keep face' while avoiding a dangerous duel.[70] De Ligne cited other noblemen, however, who praised 'the possibility to bring honour to your name' that a duel offered.[71]

Like the popular duel, the formal duel started with an insult or a suggestion of dishonour. A case in point is the duel between Baron Antoine-Joseph de Cassal and Carolus de Valeriola, both law students at the university of Leuven. Cassal had tried to cheat in a card game in 1778. After some mutual insults, Valeriola challenged his opponent to a duel with the sword, which ended with Cassal wounded at his hand, arm and chest.[72] Indeed, not only soldiers and noblemen, but students as well were keen duellists. In 1774, a certain Delbecq and Naveau got into a row after a bet over the correct translation of a sentence into Latin. They decided to resolve their quarrel with a duel. Naveau proposed a swordfight, but Delbecq argued that his opponent would have an unfair advantage over him, as he was not skilled in arms. They then agreed to fight the duel with pistols. They removed their outer garments, took their places five to six steps from each other and shot. Delbecq hit Naveau in the arm, Naveau missed.[73] The case confirms that the duel was not always a test of strength or skill, but mainly of courage.[74]

The formalised duel was not only an activity of the nobility, the military and academics. Men of the middling sorts, generally those aspiring to be included among the elite or with a background in the military, could also propose to settle disputes with a formal duel. This happened in the case of wigmaker Joseph Arnould and medical doctor Joannes Maillart in Brussels in 1779. Arnould and Maillart were drinking in an inn, when they got into an argument over an unspecified matter. They left the inn and went to fight a fist duel in a small alley. Maillart sustained a face injury and they suspended the fight, with Arnould tending to Maillart's wounds. They met again the next day and were overheard formally challenging each other in Latin: 'Visne pugnare hadie vel non?' 'Volo ex toto corde!' ('Do you want to fight today or not?' 'I want to, with my whole heart!') They left the city to find a quiet spot in the countryside. In the official charges against Arnould, the whole duel was dramatically reported, so there must have been witnesses, although their statements have not been preserved. Arnould and Maillart crossed swords and after a few movements back and forth, Arnould stabbed Maillart, who dropped his sword. Maillart cried out 'return me my sword, I'll fight back', but he soon fell down and died a few minutes later. While Arnould cleaned his sword with his handkerchief, he lamented for all bystanders to hear: 'O sadness! What have I done?'

Knowing that he would be prosecuted, Arnould left the city. His father filed a grace request. He claimed not to know a great deal about the matter but asked Her Majesty to consider his great services to the Crown as an artisan of fountains. He claimed, moreover, that his son had been 'forced' to fight Maillart, who had come to fetch him near his house. While he stopped short of making explicit that honour had obliged his son to duel, it was clear what he meant. Fearing the dishonour that would bequeath his family if his son was convicted, he hoped for grace.

The Brussels Officer of Justice, Rapedius de Berg, was ardent in his advice. Arnould could easily have evaded the fight. Moreover, the fight seemed to have been a duel, an additional crime, which was to be punished by hanging, if not in person, then in effigy. However, he added, he left it up to the magistrates to decide whether Arnould and Maillart, not being noblemen or soldiers, could in fact be found guilty of fighting a duel. In any case, he felt that it was important to punish Arnould. His example could perhaps 'cure the mania of swordfights and duels', which were getting fashionable among the 'common class', at the same time that 'the laws, the wisdom of the

Government and a more enlightened education' were allowing the nobility finally to become aware of their 'folly and ridicule'.

The Brussels magistrates agreed: there were no mitigating circumstances, 'all is premeditated and all has been done in cold blood'. Arnould, being a wigmaker, was not even allowed to carry a sword. The argument that he was forced to take part in the duel made no sense, they advised, as, again, he was a wigmaker, not a nobleman or a soldier, which alone 'gave him enough means to refuse this kind of combat'. For the Privy Council, the case clearly concerned a duel, 'which our laws prohibit with reason' and advised to dismiss the request. The Governor followed their advice. When Arnould's wife filed a second request for grace a few months later and the Privy Council offered the same advice, the Governor untypically chose to grant a pardon anyway, given that the supplicant would pay the legal costs.

Now, the Brussels prosecutor faced two problems. First, Arnould's wife was unable to pay the legal costs. Second, he had also litigated against the memory of Maillart, who could be hanged posthumously and whose possessions could be confiscated. However, he thought it would be somewhat 'inconsistent to prosecute the memory of a corpse while his murderer is freed from all investigations'. But, again, who would then pay him? The Privy Council proposed that, in absence of payment, the trial would be continued against both men. While it is unclear what happened with Maillart's memory, the court sentenced Arnould to hanging, given his absence in effigy. The Privy Council, to retain some of the pardon granted, declared that the court should publicly pronounce the sentence, but not execute it, so that 'Arnould and his family were saved of the dishonour that the public attaches not to crimes, but to the execution of their punishments'.[75]

I have reported this case rather extensively because it clearly articulates the prevailing government attitudes to the duel. The case shows that what Robert Nye has called the 'embourgeoisement' of the duel was well underway in the 1770s.[76] While Arnould's father argued that his sense of honour obliged his son to risk his life and accept a duel, the Brussels magistrates were disinclined to allow a common man to use this reasoning. They saw only cold-blooded murder. They rejected Arnould's claim to a particular reasonable, autonomous and socially oriented self for which the defence of honour was indispensable. Not all discourses of male honour were available to every man: just as honour was bound up with gender, it was also bound up with social status. While some men of the middling sorts such as Arnould drew on the same discourses as noblemen, the courts did not easily accept their claims. The Governor, however, must have found some reason in this argument, as he granted grace anyway. In its solution to the non-payment of the legal costs, the Privy Council seemed to assume that the family's honour was indeed what was to be saved. In the end, therefore, they recognised the social orientation of the self, but denied that reason should allow everyone to violently defend their honour. This form of reasonable honour was reserved for men of a particular social status.

Another formal duel among commoners, although not recognised as such, occurred a few years earlier in Brussels, when Guillaume de Smet and a certain Gentil (also called Genty or Janti) crossed swords in 1758. The scene of the duel was an upscale brothel kept by Marie Gouverne. Gentil, who had served in the French army but was now mainly active as a writing tutor for children of the nobility, was reputedly of a 'turbulent humour', especially when he was drunk. He went drinking with some friends and they ended up in Gouverne's brothel. Gouverne offered them a girl, but Gentil was out for something else. He asked to see Guillaume de Smet, Gouverne's pimp. Gouverne said that he was absent and the four men started insulting her. Her ten-year-old son was 'piqued, despite his youth, by Janti's and his companion's discourses', 'expressed his regret at not being older and more powerful to show them his resentment' and went to get De Smet, who was in a nearby inn. De Smet came along and Gentil challenged him to a duel. De Smet accepted and asked his adversary with what weapons he wanted to fight. Gentil chose the sword, they left the brothel and after a short fight, Gentil ended up dead. De Smet went back inside and asked the other three if they wanted to endure the same fate – they did not. He then made his goodbye from Gouverne and left the city.

When the authorities learned what had happened, they arrested Gouverne and tracked down De Smet. Gouverne confessed that she kept a brothel but alleged that 'she had no other means for her and her son's subsistence'. She denied any involvement in the duel, however, and filed a request for grace after three months of imprisonment, during which she had purportedly been promised repeatedly that she would be set free 'soon'. The magistrates of Brussels advised that Gouverne seemed innocent of the homicide, 'except that she had not prevented the combatants of leaving the house, which could be excused by her sex and by the danger of trying to separate two men who were untreatable by anger and drink'. However, given her 'scandalous commerce', they advised against granting grace. Her application was dismissed.

De Smet, meanwhile, had been tracked to Paris, where he had enlisted in the guard. The Paris police arrested him, but they did not reach an agreement on an extradition and set him free again. In 1769, ten years after the incident, De Smet wanted to return to Brussels and his brother applied for grace. He argued that De Smet had 'sadly' killed Gentil 'in self-defence'. As the original officer of justice had passed away and the original investigations could not be found – the magistrates even wrote to the Paris police, as I related in the introduction – the Brussels aldermen took a long time to formulate their advice. (They seem to have been unaware that they had summarised the case ten years earlier in their advice on Gouverne's application for grace.) As people were now interrogated on an affair that had happened more than ten years earlier, the magistrates could only reconstruct the events with difficulty. No decision has been preserved, which indicates that the case was probably dismissed.[77]

While the traditional rational arguments are present in this case – legitimate defence, poverty – honour is not explicitly mentioned. Both De Smet and Gouverne's son clearly participated in the rituals of honour. However, if in the case of Arnould and Maillart there were no references to anger, there were in this case: Gouverne's son felt 'resentment' and De Smet and Gentil were called 'angry'. Although it is perhaps premature to draw conclusions from just two cases, this could relate to the more civilised background and setting of the duel between Arnould and Maillart. The more 'common' the duellists were, the more likely their behaviour seems to have been associated with anger and not with a justifiable sense of honour. The reaction to Gouverne's lack of interference, moreover, points to the intersection of different models of reason and honour with masculinity and femininity. While men often claimed to be reasonable when they had reacted violently, with varying success, women could only be accepted as reasonable for *not* interfering with violence.

Throughout the eighteenth century, a somewhat ambiguous position towards the elite duel was present in law, literature and philosophical treatises: on the one hand, they firmly condemned duels as irrational, immoral and dangerous relicts of an archaic system of private justice.[78] On the other, they often accepted duels as a necessity among soldiers and the nobility to retain their reputation. Beccaria, for one, reasoned that a 'man of honour, deprived of the esteem of others, foresees that he must be reduced either to a solitary existence, insupportable to a social creature, or become the object of perpetual insult; considerations sufficient to overcome the fear of death'. Duelling was part of the repertoire of elite masculinity. He proposed only to punish the individual who gave occasion to the duel by the initial insult, not the one who was obliged to defend his honour.[79] In the Southern Netherlands, legal reformer Goswin de Fierlant agreed that the laws concerning duels were too severe and no longer necessary, as 'this crime has become rare in our country'. Courts should prosecute duels as regular homicides. In this way, there would be no blame on the memory 'of the honest man who had the misfortune of dying in battle, because prejudiced people made him do it in spite of himself, by only leaving him the choice between fighting or being covered in shame and exposed to insults for the rest of his days'.[80] Fierlant, too, agreed that duelling was necessary and reasonable for certain men.

Despite the vocal opposition to duelling in the late eighteenth century, the law was moving towards more leniency in most of continental Europe.[81] When the French legislative assembly discussed the duel in 1790 and 1791, they eventually decided against specific laws on duelling, assuming that the duel could be prosecuted as (attempted) homicide or battery. But once the *Code pénal* was established, opinions diverged. The influential legal scholar Merlin de Douai, for instance, argued that duellists agreed on a private contract and that as long as the duelling code had been followed, they could not be prosecuted, even when the duel ended in death.[82] The Napoleonic penal code did not criminalise the duel either and courts hardly prosecuted any duellists. In 1841, however, a Belgian law on duelling was accepted. In the debates preceding this law, members of parliament characterised the duel as 'barbaric', while at the same time, most agreed that an honourable man could not simply avoid all duels. The new law, rather than punishing duellists more severely, actually sought to treat them differently and more leniently than ordinary homicides.[83] In short, people generally despised the elite duel, but they increasingly accepted it as a necessity for the man of honour. They accepted that putting your life at risk, while not to be done lightly, could be reasonable in light of the 'prejudices' surrounding masculinity, honour and reputation.

Shame and infanticide

When Marie Gouverne applied for grace after the duel between Gentil and De Smet, the Brussels magistrates wrote that she 'could be excused by her sex' for not intervening in the duel. Indeed, most people did not expect women to act violently, not even when someone offended their honour. When she was insulted, her *son* wanted retribution. While some women, primarily among the poor, became violent when someone insulted them, many people disapproved.[84] Violence was, for most, not an acceptable form of femininity. In any case, they could not participate in formal duels. For most women, honour and femininity did not generally depend on their demonstrations of courage, but on their reputation of chastity.

To uphold this reputation of chastity, there was one occasion in which violence was a part of a woman's cultural repertoire: when they gave birth outside marriage. Again, this could be portrayed as a reasonable thing to do. Kant argued that 'no decree can remove the mother's shame when it becomes known that she gave birth without being married' and understood that some women therefore killed their illegitimate children.[85] Beccaria agreed, claiming that a woman pregnant of an illegitimate child faced a cruel dilemma: 'The alternative is, either her own infamy, or the death of a being who is incapable of feeling the loss of life. How can she avoid prefer-ring the last to the inevitable misery of herself and her unhappy infant!'[86] Neither Kant nor Beccaria argued that these women should escape pun-ishment completely, but rather that they should be punished more moder-ately. Beccaria in particular called for preventive measures to 'protect weak women' against male seduction.

From these arguments, it would seem that women accused of the infan-ticide of an illegitimate child could use the same strategies as men accused of duelling. But things were rather more complex. Provisions against infan-ticide in the ancien régime varied between courts. In the seventeenth cen-tury, courts sometimes found infanticides guilty of witchcraft as well and punished them severely: we know of cases of women who were burned, buried alive or drowned.[87] Such drastic punishments had disappeared by the eighteenth century. Death by hanging or beheading was the regular punish-ment for infanticide, though the number of convictions was very low.[88] One of the reasons for this was the great difficulty in proving child murder. In France and England, special statutes had been issued concerning infanticide, specifying that a woman who hid her pregnancy and lost her child could be condemned to death.[89] In the Southern Netherlands, however, full proof remained necessary to convict a woman of infanticide. If the woman did not confess, and there had been no witnesses to the delivery, such proof was difficult to achieve. On several occasions in the late eighteenth century, the Privy Council reproved local courts that convicted women on the basis of meagre evidence.[90]

When women were tried on suspicion of infanticide, they used a variety of defensive strategies. Most popular was the claim that their child had been stillborn. If they had not made their pregnancy public beforehand, they often alleged that they had themselves been unaware of it. One woman purported that she had passed out during labour and could not relate the fate of her fruit, another that she had lost the child while on the privy.[91] In none of these cases did the women confess to having killed their child on purpose, and they never referred to the shame of illegitimate childbirth. Of the ten infanticide cases I studied from before 1795, only three led to a conviction. One woman was whipped and exiled; another was sentenced to beheading but pardoned; the third was sentenced to whipping in effigy and banishment but also pardoned.[92] In their arguments for granting pardon, the Privy Council did not refer to shame, but only to insufficient proof and the 'excessive rigour of the sentence'. Infanticides received sympathy as vic-tims, not as rational or honourable beings. As in many of the previous cases we have seen, reason turned out to be much less accessible to women than it was to men.

In the French Revolutionary Penal Code, there were no specific provisions for infanticide. Courts had to treat it as regular homicide. As such, it was punishable by death if premeditation could be proven. From 1810 onwards, premeditation was no longer even required for a death sentence: it sufficed if a woman had *intended* to kill her infant.[93] While this differed little from the older regulations, the new system of proof – requiring only the 'conviction intime' of the juries – allowed for a far greater number of cases to be brought to court.

While some continued to use the former strategies of defence, other women now also referred to shame. Even if they denied having killed their child, women often said that they had hidden their pregnancy, had not asked for help during labour or had not reported the birth of the child, 'out of shame' or 'to preserve her honour'. Interrogators often followed up, suggesting that they had killed the child in a further attempt 'to hide their shame'.[94] When they did confess, honour and shame often played an important role in their justifications. In 1802, twenty-year-old servant Catharina Van Erck stood accused of killing her new-born child. In her second interrogation, she confessed that the child had been born alive and that she had thrown it in the river. In her next interrogation, she denied this again, claiming that she thought that the child was stillborn. Still, when asked for her motives for killing her infant, she professed that 'she was desperate because her lover didn't want to marry her, and her honour couldn't suffer giving light to a child that was disowned by its father. In that moment she didn't know what she did, but she doesn't believe that the child was still alive when she threw it in the river'.[95] Another servant, Isabelle Desmet, argued in 1815 that her child was stillborn, but that she had thrown it in the river 'with the intention to preserve her reputation and to be able to retain her position'.[96] In 1820, servant Cecile Broucke argued that she had secretly buried her illegitimate child, which had died an hour after birth, 'in the hope of forever erasing the proof of her weakness and dishonour'.[97]

In these narratives, there is an element of calculation: these women acted in the way they did because they estimated that the consequences for their reputation would be disastrous. They portrayed acting to protect their honour as something reasonable to do. But almost all women accused of infanticide mixed this sense of reason, calculation and autonomy with a sense of dispossession: they did not know what they were doing. More than men invoking the protection of their reputation, they portrayed themselves as victims. This sat well with many juries: they often found women accused of infanticide innocent while there was plenty of incriminating evidence, and even when they actually confessed. A woman, it seemed, could not easily

claim reason, and many women therefore drew on other discourses to justify their actions.

Honour and the self

To conclude this section on honourable violence, it seems that both men
and women could and did use honour as a reasonable argument to commit
a crime, but in different ways. Men, especially elite men, could use honour
to justify killing in man-to-man combat, while women could use it to justify
the killing of illegitimate offspring. While courts accepted that people who
fought and killed to protect their reputation to some extent did so calcu-
latingly, they also found that this was only a partial excuse. People who
referred to honour could sometimes count on the sympathy of judges and
juries, but most observers agreed that their behaviour was only the result
of the 'prejudices' surrounding honour. In a more enlightened or civilised
society, such prejudices should disappear and with them the honourable
killings.[98]

Nevertheless, it seems that the arguments of honour became more important, not less, in the new regime, which was seemingly based on enlightened
principles. Indeed, my findings confirm those of Robert Nye and Ute Frevert
concerning the duel in nineteenth-century France and Germany, and those of
William Reddy concerning the role of honour in post-revolutionary France.
In the early nineteenth century, Reddy has argued, people did not only perceive honour and its pendant, shame, as feelings, which were increasingly
the realm of women. Men's quest for honour became a 'civilized, rational,
impersonal kind of endeavour'.[99] Robert Nye confirms that from the late
eighteenth century on, the duel became integrated in a bourgeois sociability characterised by asceticism and emotional self-control.[100] Duelling codes
limited emotional display before, during and after the duel and governed
violence and male social interaction in a 'civilised' way.[101] Still, honour also
remained a 'felt' matter, which could be practised in a 'purified' or 'stylised'
manner through the duel. Honour and the duel, to some extent, undid the
increasing opposition of reason and feeling, of 'head' and 'heart'.[102]

If Nye, Frevert and Reddy focus on honour as a means of bridging thinking and feeling for men, this was not, however, an exclusively male affair.
In the early nineteenth century, women accused of infanticide also referred
to honour and shame as determining factors in their behaviour. More than
in the case of men, these 'rational feelings' were often joined with narratives of dispossession. They portrayed themselves as victims of the system
of honour, while men generally took a more active part in the defence of
their honour. Honourable violence was an acceptable part of the cultural

repertoire of masculinity, at least for some men and in some circumstances. It was rarely an acceptable course of action for women.

Referring to honour in court entailed practising a socially oriented self. Through practices of honour, people showed that they were primarily concerned with their place in the world. They cast their behaviour as actions that others in their position would also portray, thus detaching them from their individuality. But the courts often steered people – when they were not elite men – towards a more individualised and less calculating self. People who had committed honour-related violence were, in their view, often misguided. The valuation of honour in general went along with its dismissal in many individual cases.

The sense of an ending

Death seemed to challenge the role of reason in criminal justice. Punishments were increasingly proportional to crimes, so that they would deter people from committing those crimes. The thief would not steal if she knew that she would become poorer. An offended man would not kill his foe if he knew he would be killed in turn. However, death was the limit to this reasonable justice system. Reasonable people who faced a choice between committing a capital crime and certain death would choose crime; reasonable people who faced a choice between committing a capital crime and something worse than death, like dishonour, would also choose to commit the crime. The ultimate challenge to reasonable justice, then, was suicide. 'The laws are obeyed through fear of punishment, but death destroys all sensibility', Beccaria wrote. 'What motive then can restrain the desperate hand of suicide?'[103]

Beccaria and most other penal reformers in late eighteenth-century Europe argued against punishing suicides. This was not, however, because they found suicide reasonable, rather to the contrary. Suicide was 'an action which so strongly revolts the desire of self-preservation that nature has given to all living beings', that Goswin de Fierlant favoured assuming that all suicides were (suddenly) insane.[104] Most magistrates and many philosophers and common people subscribed to the same narrative, which I will analyse in more detail in the next chapter. A small number of philosophers – and a small number of suicides – framed suicide differently. They did not see suicide as a morally reprehensible crime only committed by the insane, but as a free, rational decision. Killing oneself was not self-murder, but voluntary death. The discourses surrounding suicide therefore lead us to consider one last instance of practising a reasonable, calculating self in relation to criminal justice.

Portraying suicide as a rational action was not entirely novel. Radical eighteenth-century thinkers about suicide often drew inspiration from antiquity, especially from stoics such as Cato and Seneca, and from Montaigne's reflections on suicide.[105] Never before, however, had the defence of suicide as a legitimate choice been so arduously discussed.[106] Around 1755, David Hume finished an essay in which he refuted traditional arguments against suicide, contending that when one has little to offer to society anymore, when one becomes a burden to oneself and to society, suicide becomes not only rational, but even laudable.[107] Hume retracted his essay following early controversial reactions, but a clandestine French edition circulated in the 1770s. Similarly, in his *Système de la nature* (1770), Holbach (who was probably also responsible for the translation of Hume's essay) defended the right to suicide, as 'death is the only remedy to despair'. People who committed suicide were not necessarily insane: when they suffered so much that nothing could make them happy again, suicide was reasonable and moral.[108] Other *philosophes*, such as Montesquieu, Rousseau and Voltaire, took a more moderate position, defending the right to suicide only in a limited number of cases.[109]

On Christmas Day in 1773, two young soldiers took their own lives at an inn in Paris and left a 'philosophical testament', explaining that they had 'experienced all pleasures, even those of obliging our fellow men' and that they were now sick of their existence and wished to part it.[110] Their act caused quite the stir. Conservative writers were quick to blame Enlightenment philosophy. They started to speak of 'suicide philosophique': the number of suicides was rising, they argued, because people were reading Enlightenment defences of suicide. The *philosophes* defended themselves against such allegations: 'It is not maxims which determine men to take such a violent resolution', wrote Holbach, 'It is a temperament embittered by sorrows, a constitutional defect, a breakdown of the machine; it is necessity'.[111] While Holbach and others defended suicide as moral and rational in the abstract, they found that most suicides in practice were not.[112]

After the young soldiers' suicides, other suicides of elite men were occasionally labelled 'philosophical', although many of them more explicitly referenced early romantic ideas – a copy of *Werther* next to their corpse – than Enlightened arguments about reasonable suicide.[113] In the Southern Netherlands, however, there was at least one suicide that could certainly be (but was not) labelled 'philosophical'. This was the suicide of Sébastien Joseph Antoine Cupis de Camargo, the day before Christmas in 1772 – almost to the day a year before the two soldiers ended their lives in Paris.

Camargo, a member of a minor aristocratic family, was tried in 1772 for misbehaviour and an attack on the mayor of Leuven. As was common to avoid transferring noblemen to prison, the magistrates confined him in a Brussels monastery while he awaited his trial. There he completed a tract which virulently attacked religion, strongly inspired by Voltaire, Holbach and other radical Enlightenment thinkers. In his final essay, Camargo wrote a defence of suicide. Having already established that 'all is only matter', it followed naturally that man was free to kill himself. It was not a sin against God, nor was it an offence against society, he argued. Since we did not agree to enter this life, we should be allowed to choose to leave it. 'Searching the good and avoiding the bad is the law of nature. He who kills himself only does this because life in his eyes is bad; he therefore only follows the law of nature, the primitive law, the only universal law, the law that society cannot proscribe'. Death was not something to be afraid of, as everyone had to die. It could be a welcome release from suffering; 'nothing is more comfortable than leaving life'. Suicide, Camargo argued, was the universal and reasonable self in action.

At the end of his manuscript, Camargo added a note to those who found it: 'Weary of suffering captivity I have decided to take my own life and I am about to execute this resolution. I would have executed it six weeks ago, had I not wanted to finish this book; I believe it is worthy of print and recommend it to those who acquire it'. On 24 December 1772, he was found dead in his room, having hanged himself with a piece of linen. His wish for his manuscript to be published remained in vain, however. The report of his suicide did not mention his manuscript, nor did the press. The text was preserved, although it is unclear by whom. It was only published more than two hundred years after his death. Unlike the two French soldiers, Camargo did not have a (in)famous afterlife as a philosophical suicide.[114]

Philosophical suicide was a concept that was only applied to educated, elite men. Some elite women, however, such as Mary Wollstonecraft, drew on similar discourses in their portrayal of suicide.[115] Some ordinary people did as well. Several suicides who left a note or survived their attempt explained their deed in quasi-rational terms, generally referring to their misery, poverty and debts. In 1765, a pregnant woman tried to hang herself but was saved by vigilant neighbours. She declared that 'she had done it out of despair because of debts she had contracted unbeknownst to her husband, who was poor like her'.[116] There was often also a sense of honour in their suicide attempts: they wanted to avoid the shame of having their failures revealed. Jan Baptist Gillis, in Antwerp in 1776, announced some days before his suicide that 'he would rather jump in the Scheldt river than have to beg for his bread'.[117] Melchior Antoine Quittelier, a former plumber who wrote a suicide note in 1778, explained that 'as I have not been able to find work in any city nor in any regiment [...] and I did not want to become a thief, I have preferred a different fate'. In the same note, however, he also alleged that 'I have lost my good sense, for I am sure that if I had the same spirit now in this misery as when I was affluent, this would not have happened'.[118] He combined rational consideration and loss of the self in his

note. Finally, again in Brussels, in 1805, a police report noted that Jacques
Chatenier had killed himself because of 'the embarrassment of being behind
on the payment of his house by a year and a half, for which he was being
prosecuted'.[119] Honour, again, seemed to prevail over self-preservation. For
some men, it was possible to portray suicide as a reasonable result of following accepted codes of masculinity.

This was certainly not the kind of rationality – a preoccupation with honour and shame – that most *philosophes* had in mind. Many (even Camargo)
explicitly condemned suicide when one was in debt or still had obligations
to fulfil. Later authors, such as Kant, argued that suicide was fundamentally
contrary not only to one's duties to others, but also to pure morality. 'To anni-
hilate the subject of morality in one's own person is to root out the existence
of morality itself from the world, as far as one can, even though morality is an
end in itself'. Moral subjects could not be allowed to destroy their own morality; reason could not allow its own annihilation.[120] Suicide was one of the
contradictions of the reasonability of the Enlightenment: on the one hand, it
could be justified as moral and reasonable, while on the other, it was contrary
to the essential duties to oneself and to others.[121] The solution to this conun-
drum lay in presenting suicide as the opposite of reason. Suicide increasingly
became the realm of irrational feeling and dispossession.

It is perhaps somewhat strange to consider suicide or even the practices
surrounding it – such as writing a note, announcing one's intentions or
explaining an attempt – as a practice of the self, as the self in question
was not to be much longer. But these practices were of course also directed
towards others: by interpreting their self in a particular way, suicides influenced the expectations and opinions of those surrounding them. The movement to interpret suicide as a rational act, an act that was the result of a
careful and dispassionate analysis of the advantages and disadvantages of
continuing to live, stimulated people to think of themselves as rational people too; to cast their decisions – however unrelated to suicide – in the same
light of a calculating self and not in the light of a deep inner being. It encouraged people to interpret their most questionable actions as wilful decisions
and not as a loss of self-control.

Complicating interiority

The importance of responsibility and reasonability in criminal justice was
increasing in the late eighteenth and early nineteenth centuries. As we have
seen in chapter 1, and as I will elaborate in chapter 5, the question of who
had committed crimes and why became increasingly acute. Traditional
assumptions of crime as the result of a natural inclination toward sin were

faltering. Instead came a view that people were or should be 'rational' by default: they were out after their own interests. The criminal justice system after the French Revolution sought to make sure that punishments would negate all the benefits people could reap from committing crimes.

But even before this new system had been installed, reason became a problem for criminal justice. Many people who asserted their responsibility before eighteenth- and early nineteenth-century criminal justice – and even more in the early nineteenth century than in the eighteenth – also claimed that they had acted reasonably. They had (however quickly) calculated the benefits and drawbacks of a particular course of action and concluded that their crime was the best possible option, not just for themselves, but for anyone who would be in their situation. They generally used two arguments. The first was that they had acted to preserve their own or another's life, the second that they had acted to preserve something even more important than their life: their honour. They could use these arguments to justify crimes as diverse as homicide, prostitution, theft, duelling, infanticide and suicide. Both arguments were problematic for the philosophy of criminal justice. Because the law could never, so criminal justice reformers assumed, give harsher punishments than death, they presented a challenge to the justice system that was intent on making crime irrational. The arguments also provided a moral problem, for surely a criminal justice system could not require people to forsake their own life, or worse, their honour?

The criminal courts did not find a neat, consistent solution to these problems. They dealt with them in differing ways. They accepted the argument of self-preservation as viable when it was a response to an immediate danger, a physical attack to one's life. As such, legislators even integrated it in the criminal justice system after the French Revolution, although the courts still needed to evaluate the proportionality of the counterattack. These same courts did not accept long-term threats to life, for instance poverty and material need, as rational arguments for committing crime, be it prostitution, theft or infanticide. Instead, they cast poverty itself as irrational, a moral failure.

The courts dealt with the argument of the preservation of honour in a similarly ambiguous way. In no case did they accept honour as a formal justification for committing crimes. But in everyday practice, they often showed leniency towards elite men who fought to defend their honour. The formalised duel was even, after the French Revolution, *de facto* legalised. More informal fights over honour – often typified as mere 'brawls' – were not so easily dismissed: the courts did not recognise common people's honour and their fights were therefore less reasonable. When women referred to their honour in cases of infanticide, courts were even less inclined to accept this as 'reasonable'. If the courts sometimes met them with compassion, this was because of their poor state, not because of their reasonable actions.

All these solutions may have been very specific, but the pattern is clear. Enlightenment ideas of rationality permeated the new criminal justice system after the French Revolution. But although men and women of all social origins used reasonable arguments to defend themselves, the courts only accepted them if they came from men, and preferably if they came from elite men. This is perhaps unsurprising. Many of the leading philosophers of reason and many of the legislators in revolutionary France explicitly argued that only elite men were capable of properly using reason. Mary Wollstonecraft forcefully argued against these ideas in her *Vindication of the Rights of Woman* (1792). Women, too, she claimed, should be trained to use their reason; they should be treated as reasonable.[122] Like Wollstonecraft, many women and common men claimed reason from below. While they found ways to integrate reason in their defences, criminal courts, like many of Wollstonecraft's male readers, usually denied these as possibilities. Their behaviour was more often connected to their individual passions, character or mental state. They had not acted in a universal rational way. Reason strongly intersected with gender and social position. As a result, the highest members of society were often the least individualised and interiorised, as they could refer to the general reasonability of their actions, while its lowliest characters had to be unreasonable, individualised and emotional.[123]

In chapter 1, we have seen how the criminal justice system came to increasingly attend to the inner self and how practices of interiority rose to prominence in the early nineteenth century. In this chapter, we have witnessed the promotion of a socially oriented self. The integration of self-defence in the criminal code and the ambiguity surrounding the duel of honour invited people to appropriate reason for their own defences. They took responsibility for their actions but suggested that they were not really particular to themselves, for everyone would portray them. They declined their individuality and neglected any deep, inner dispositions. Even when the courts – or people in their environment – denied their claims to reason, the self that they practised in the interpretations they offered to the court was in part a socially oriented self. The early nineteenth century was not characterised by a straightforward turn inward. The importance of a quasi-universal reason and a socially oriented system of honour complemented and complicated practices of individualised interiority.

Notes

1 Immanuel Kant, 'Beantwortung der Frage: Was ist Aufklärung?', *Berlinische Monatsschrift*, 4:12 (1784), 481–94.
2 E.g. Thomas Paine, *The Age of Reason: Being an Investigation of True and Fabulous Theology* (Paris: Barrois, 1794). In the Southern Netherlands, see for

instance Jozef De Wolf, *Den geest der reden* (Amsterdam [Ghent]: Wed. Boklar, 1777).

3 On the interest in reason and its limits, see Jessica Riskin, *Science in the Age of Sensibility: The Sentimental Empiricists of the French Enlightenment* (Chicago, IL: University of Chicago Press, 2002), chap. 2; Philipp Blom, *A Wicked Company: The Forgotten Radicalism of the European Enlightenment* (New York, NY: Basic Books, 2010), pp. 204, 248.

4 Goldstein, *The Post-Revolutionary Self*, p. 30.

5 Lorraine Daston, 'Enlightenment calculations', *Critical Inquiry*, 21:1 (1994), 184–91.

6 Mary Wollstonecraft, *A Vindication of the Rights of Woman*, ed. Eileen Hunt Botting (New Haven, CT: Yale University Press, 2014), p. 80.

7 Immanuel Kant, *Critique of Practical Reason*, trans. Thomas Kingsmill Abbott (London: Longmans, 1873), pt. 1, bk. 1, chap. 1, section 7.

8 Immanuel Kant, *The Metaphysics of Morals*, ed. and trans. Mary Gregor (Cambridge: Cambridge University Press, 1991), p. 219.

9 Jeffrey Merrick, 'Sodomy, suicide, and the limits of legal reform in eighteenth-century France', *Studies in Eighteenth-Century Culture*, 46 (2017), 189.

10 Cesare Beccaria, *An Essay on Crimes and Punishments* (London: Newbery, 1767), chap. 6; Pieter Spierenburg, 'The rise of criminology in its historical context', in Paul Knepper and Anja Johansen (eds), *The Oxford Handbook of the History of Crime and Criminal Justice* (Oxford: Oxford University Press, 2016), p. 376.

11 Beirne, *Inventing Criminology*, pp. 11–64.

12 Rob Boddice, *A History of Feelings* (London: Reaktion Books, 2019), pp. 115–16.

13 Martin J. Wiener, *Reconstructing the Criminal: Culture, Law, and Policy in England, 1830–1914* (Cambridge: Cambridge University Press, 1990), pp. 11–12.

14 Though negligence was also punishable in some cases. On the integration of Roman legal ideas about criminal intent in continental European criminal justice, see Pohl-Zucker, *Making Manslaughter*, pp. 30–42; Monballyu, *Six Centuries*, pp. 70–3.

15 Barclay, *Men on Trial*, pp. 1–9; Hoegaerts, *Masculinity and Nationhood*, pp. 5–6; Tine Van Osselaer, *The Pious Sex: Catholic Constructions of Masculinity and Femininity in Belgium, c. 1800–1940* (Leuven: Leuven University Press, 2013), p. 13.

16 Antoine-Gaspard Boucher d'Argis, 'Homicide', in Denis Diderot and Jean le Rond d'Alembert (eds), *Encyclopédie, ou Dictionnaire raisonné des sciences, des arts et des métiers* (Paris: Briasson, 1751–1772), vol. 8, p. 250–3. https:// encyclopedie.uchicago.edu.

17 Kant, *The Metaphysics of Morals*, pp. 142, 218.

18 Kant, *The Metaphysics of Morals*, p. 60.

19 On the grace procedure, Marjan Vrolijk, *Recht door gratie: gratie bij doodslagen en andere delicten in Vlaanderen, Holland en Zeeland (1531–1567)* (Hilversum: Verloren, 2004); Kevin Pirotte, 'Les grâces du Vendredi saint et le

gouvernement autrichien dans les Pays-Bas sous Marie-Thérèse (1740–1780): procédure, pouvoir central et normes judiciaires face à l'homicide' (master's dissertation, University of Louvain, 2013). On the resulting legal pluralism and the possibilities this offered for defendants, Van Dijck, 'Towards an economic interpretation'. On France, Reynald Abad, *La grâce du roi: les lettres de clémence de Grande Chancellerie au XVIIIe siècle* (Paris: Presses de l'université Paris-Sorbonne, 2011). On the early modern grace system in general, Quentin Verreycken, 'The power to pardon in late medieval and early modern Europe: New perspectives in the history of crime and criminal justice', *History Compass*, 17:6 (2019). On different degrees of culpability for homicide and acceptable excuses in early modern Germany (and Europe), Pohl-Zucker, *Making Manslaughter*.

20 NA, *PCAP-C*, 620/A, Gabriel Hosfeldt (1753).
21 NA, *PCAP-C*, 587/B, Jean Martin Froitier (1761).
22 NA, *PCAP-C*, 631/A, Jean De Ro (1771).
23 Beccaria, *An Essay on Crimes*, chap. 46.
24 *Code pénal du 25 septembre–6 octobre 1791*, pt. 2, title 2, section 1, art. 1–6 and 9.
25 'Défense', in Philippe-Antoine Merlin (ed.), *Répertoire universel et raisonné de jurisprudence* (4th ed., Paris: Garnery, 1812–1825), vol. 3, pp. 384–5.
26 However, the question that was meant to establish whether the crime had not been an accident was formulated to inquire whether the homicide had been 'voluntary', which could be interpreted more broadly if necessary.
27 *Code des délits et des peines du 3 brumaire, an 4 [25 October 1795], contenant les Lois relatives à l'instruction des affaires criminelles*, art. 646. See also Allen, *Les tribunaux criminels*, pp. 110–11.
28 E.g. SABE, AC-ANT, 72 (1798); SABR, AC-WEST, 128–128 (1798); SABR, AC-WEST, 120–107 (1798); NA2, AC-BRA, 255–455 (1802), NA2, AC-BRA, 329–983 (1806).
29 NA2, AC-BRA, 255–500.
30 Ruller, *Genade voor recht*; Bert Vanhulle, '"Uitmunten door vlijt": Gratie in het gevangeniswezen tijdens het Verenigd Koninkrijk der Nederlanden (1815–1830)', in Dirk Heirbaut, Xavier Rousseaux and Alain Wijffels (eds), *Histoire du droit et de la justice: Une nouvelle génération de recherches / Justitie- en rechtsgeschiedenis: Een nieuwe onderzoeksgeneratie* (Louvain-la-Neuve: Presses universitaires de Louvain, 2009), pp. 411–22; Edwige de Boer, 'Les registres de la grâce', *Sociétés & Représentations*, 36 (2013), 251–65.
31 Dareau, 'Défense', p. 385.
32 *Code pénal de 1810*, art. 64.
33 SABR, AC-WEST, 201–802.
34 NA2, AC-BRA, 457–1921.
35 On the living conditions of women in prostitution in the Austrian Netherlands, see Maja Mechant, 'Hoeren, pauwen ende ondeughende doghters. De levenslopen van vrouwen in de Brugse prostitutie (1750–1790)' (PhD dissertation, University of Ghent, 2018), chaps. 7–8.

36 Jos Monballyu and Nanouche Heeren, 'Prostitutie en vrouwenhandel in de Nieuwe Tijd', in Lieve De Mecheleer (ed.), *Van badhuis tot eroscentrum. Prostitutie en vrouwenhandel van de middeleeuwen tot heden* (Brussels: Algemeen rijksarchief, 1995), p. 24; Lotte van de Pol, *Het Amsterdams hoerdom. Prostitutie in de zeventiende en achttiende eeuw* (Amsterdam: Wereldbibliotheek, 1996), pp. 172–3; Gowing, *Common Bodies*, pp. 109–10; Laura J. Rosenthal, *Infamous Commerce: Prostitution in Eighteenth-Century British Literature and Culture* (Ithaca, NY: Cornell University Press, 2006), pp. 2–4; Faramerz Dabhoiwala, *The Origins of Sex: A History of the First Sexual Revolution* (Oxford: Oxford University Press, 2012), pp. 141–2.

37 Pol, *Het Amsterdams hoerdom*, pp. 175–7; Randolph Trumbach, *Sex and the Gender Revolution. Volume One: Heterosexuality and the Third Gender in Enlightenment London* (London: University of Chicago Press, 1998), p. 169; Rosenthal, *Infamous Commerce*, p. 4; Dabhoiwala, *The Origins of Sex*, pp. 142–4 and 154. For qualifications, see Jessica Steinberg, 'For lust or gain: perceptions of prostitutes in eighteenth-century London', *Journal of Gender Studies*, 26 (2017), 702–13.

38 CAB, *HA Trials*, 9170.

39 CAB, *HA Trials*, 9170.

40 NA2, AC-BRA, 272–557.

41 FA, *Modern City Archives (MA)*, 525/1, Letter of 20/11/1823. Sarah Auspert has found similar discourses in early-nineteenth-century Namur: Sarah Auspert, 'La prostitution à Namur sous le régime français (1795–1813)', in Sarah Auspert, Philippe Bagard and Vincent Bruch (eds), *Namur de la conquête française à Waterloo (1792–1815). Armées, société, ordre public et urbanisme* (Namur: Société royale Sambre et Meuse, 2015), p. 139.

42 Pol, *Het Amsterdams hoerdom*, pp. 177–8; Dabhoiwala, *The Origins of Sex*, p. 158; Jessica Steinberg, 'She was "a comon night walker abusing him & being of ill behaviour": Violence and Prostitution in Eighteenth-Century London', *Canadian Journal of History*, 50:2 (2015), 243.

43 Dabhoiwala, *The Origins of Sex*, pp. 266–9.

44 CAB, *Administrative Archives: Police (ADM-POL)*, 283, Letter of 12/8/1828.

45 Commission permanente du congrès médicale de Belgique, *Exposé des causes les plus fréquentes de la propagation de la maladie vénérienne et des moyens à y opposer* (Brussels: Etablissement Encyclographique, 1836), pp. 58–62.

46 Kant, *The Metaphysics of Morals*, pp. 144–5.

47 Jean François Saint-Lambert, 'Honneur', in Diderot and d'Alembert, *Encyclopédie*, vol. 8, pp. 288–90.

48 Allyson F. Creasman, 'Fighting words: anger, insult, and "self-help" in early modern German law', *Journal of Social History*, 51:2 (2017), 272–3.

49 E.g. Jonas Liliequist, 'From honour to virtue: The shifting social logics of masculinity and honour in early modern Sweden', in Carolyn Strange, R. B. Cribb and Christopher E. Forth (eds), *Honour, Violence and Emotions in History* (London: Bloomsbury, 2014), pp. 45–67; Creasman, 'Fighting words'.

50 J. A. Sharpe, *Defamation and Sexual Slander in Early Modern England: The Church Courts at York* (York: Borthwick Insitute of Historical Research,

1980); Martin Dinges, *Der Maurermeister und der Finanzrichter: Ehre, Geld und soziale Kontrolle im Paris des 18. Jahrhunderts* (Göttingen: Vandenhoeck & Ruprecht, 1994), p. 138; Gerd Schwerhoff, 'Early modern violence and the honour code: from social integration to social distinction?', *Crime, Histoire & Sociétés / Crime, History & Societies*, 17:2 (2013), 37–41; Joachim Eibach, 'Violence and masculinity', in Paul Knepper and Anja Johansen (eds), *The Oxford Handbook of the History of Crime and Criminal Justice* (Oxford: Oxford University Press, 2016), pp. 239–41.

51 Robert Shoemaker, 'Male honour and the decline of public violence in eighteenth-century London', *Social History*, 26 (2001), 190–208; Pieter Spierenburg, *A History of Murder: Personal Violence in Europe from the Middle Ages to the Present* (Cambridge: Polity, 2008), pp. 66–110; Liliequist, 'From honour to virtue', pp. 52–62.

52 Elwin Hofman, 'An obligation of conscience. Gossip as social control in an eighteenth-century Flemish town', *European Review of History*, 21:5 (2014), 661.

53 SAK, *OCAK*, 14177. I also discuss this case in Hofman, 'An obligation of conscience', 658.

54 The cases I refer to are SAK, *OCAK*, 10790 (Pierre Coelembier, 1765); NA, *PCAP-C*, 597/B (Leonard Caprace 1780); CAB, *HA Trials*, 6920 (Jacob Ceulemans 1781); SAK, *OCAK*, 3842/2 (Willem Carpentier 1782). Most cases are even less formal than the popular knife fights Spierenburg found in early eighteenth-century Amsterdam: Pieter Spierenburg, 'Knife fighting and popular codes of honor in early modern Amsterdam', in Pieter Spierenburg (ed.), *Men and Violence: Gender, Honor, and Rituals in Modern Europe and America* (Columbus, OH: Ohio State University Press, 1998), pp. 103–27.

55 NA, *PCAP-C*, 620/A (Jean Giot 1755).

56 NA, *PCAP-C*, 620/B (Barthelemi Neutjens 1753).

57 In homicide cases, the number of excerpts I tagged as 'reputation' or 'honour' increased from 53 between 1750 and 1789 (108 cases; 49 references per 100 cases) to 169 between 1790 and 1829 (247 cases; 68 references per 100 cases).

58 SABR, *AC-WEST*, 117–91.

59 NA2, *AC-BRA*, 510–1963.

60 NA2, *AC-BRA*, 593–1232.

61 Barclay, *Men on Trial*, pp. 165–6.

62 SABR, *AC-WEST*, 276–326.

63 SABR, *AC-WEST*, 410–1553.

64 Dries Raeymaekers, '"Pour fuyr le nom de vilayn et meschant." Het duel in de Zuidelijke Nederlanden: aspecten van eer en oneer in de Nieuwe Tijd' (licentiate's dissertation, KU Leuven, 2004), pp. 52–66; Dries Raeymaekers, '"Grosses querelles & haines mortelles". De centrale overheid versus het duel om eer in de Zuidelijke Nederlanden (1550–1650)', *Tijdschrift voor Geschiedenis*, 120:3 (2007), 316–31.

65 Raeymaekers, 'Pour fuyr le nom', p. 61.

66 NA, *PCAP-C*, 587/A (Joseph Arnould 1779).

67 Raeymaekers, 'Grosses querelles', 322–9.

68 Raeymaekers, 'Pour fuyr le nom', attachment 1. In addition to the cases summed up by Raeymaekers, without specifically searching for duelling cases, I encountered one other case, related both in the archives of the Brussels court and in the archives of the Privy Council: CAB, *HA Trials*, 10449; NA, *PCAP-C*, 587/A (Marie Gouverne 1760).

69 Charles Joseph de Ligne, *Fragments de l'histoire de ma vie*, ed. Jeroom Vercruysse (Paris: Champion, 2000), vol. 1, p. 85.

70 Cf. Stephen Banks, *A Polite Exchange of Bullets: The Duel and the English Gentleman, 1750–1850* (Woodbridge: Boydell Press, 2010), pp. 43–4.

71 Ligne, *Fragments de l'histoire*, vol. 1, p. 143.

72 Raeymaekers, 'Pour fuyr le nom', pp. 118–21.

73 Raeymaekers, 'Pour fuyr le nom', pp. 114–16.

74 Ute Frevert, *Men of Honour: A Social and Cultural History of the Duel* (Cambridge: Polity, 1995), pp. 150–77; Robert B. Shoemaker, 'The taming of the duel: masculinity, honour and ritual violence in London, 1660–1800', *The Historical Journal*, 45:3 (2002), 536.

75 CAB, *HA Trials*, 882; NA, *PCAP-C*, 597/A (Joseph Arnould 1779–1781).

76 Robert A. Nye, *Masculinity and Male Codes of Honor in Modern France* (New York, NY: Oxford University Press, 1993), p. 133.

77 NA, *PCAP-C*, 587/A (Marie Gouverne 1790); CAB, *HA Trials*, 10449.

78 For a broader overview of the Enlightenment criticisms and defences of duelling, see Frevert, *Men of Honour*, pp. 17–27.

79 Beccaria, *An Essay on Crimes*, chap. 10.

80 Fierlant, 'Premières idées', fo. 1026v.

81 The English case seems to have been somewhat different, as there was no clear 'embourgeoisement' of the duel, which was increasingly discredited and became far less popular by the early nineteenth century. See Shoemaker, 'The taming of the duel'; Banks, *A Polite Exchange*; Donna T. Andrew, *Aristocratic Vice: The Attack on Duelling, Suicide, Adultery, and Gambling in Eighteenth-Century England* (New Haven, CT: Yale University Press, 2013).

82 François Guillet, *La mort en face: histoire du duel de la Révolution à nos jours* (Paris: Aubier, 2008), pp. 135–42.

83 Josephine Hoegaerts, '"L'homme du monde est obligé de se battre". Duel-vertogen en -praktijken in en rond het Belgische parlement, 1830–1900', *Tijdschrift voor Geschiedenis*, 124:2 (2011), 193–6.

84 On violent women and their motives, see Manon van der Heijden, *Misdadige vrouwen. Criminaliteit en rechtspraak in Holland 1600–1800* (Amsterdam: Prometheus – Bert Bakker, 2014), pp. 110–35.

85 Kant, *The Metaphysics of Morals*, pp. 144–5.

86 Beccaria, *An Essay on Crimes*, chap. 31. For the broader context of this movement, see Daniela Tinková, 'Protéger ou punir? Les voies de la décriminalisation de l'infanticide en France et dans le domaine des Habsbourg (XVIIIe–XIXe siècles)', *Crime, Histoire & Sociétés / Crime, History & Societies*, 9:2 (2005), paras. 29–30; Kerstin Michalik, 'The development of the discourse on

infanticide in the late eighteenth century and the new legal standardization of the offense in the nineteenth century', in Ulrike Gleixner and Marion W. Gray (eds), *Gender in Transition: Discourse and Practice in German-Speaking Europe, 1750–1830* (Ann Arbor: University of Michigan Press, 2006), pp. 53–6.

87 René Leboutte, 'Offense against family order: infanticide in Belgium from the fifteenth through the early twentieth centuries', *Journal of the History of Sexuality*, 2 (1991), 165.

88 In Ghent, for instance, no one was prosecuted for infanticide throughout the seventeenth and eighteenth centuries: Anne-Marie Roets, '"Rudessen, dieften ende andere crimen". Misdadigheid te Gent in de zeventiende en achttiende eeuw: een kwantitatieve en kwalitatieve analyse' (PhD dissertation, University of Ghent, 1987), p. 186. In Brussels, Fernand Vanhemelryck found 11 women convicted of infanticide between 1404 and 1789: Fernand Vanhemelryck, *De criminaliteit in de ammanie van Brussel van de late middeleeuwen tot het einde van het Ancien Régime (1404–1789)* (Brussels: Koninklijke academie voor wetenschappen, letteren en schone kunsten van België, 1981), p. 309.

89 Dana Rabin, 'Bodies of evidence, states of mind: infanticide, emotion and sensibility in eighteenth-century England', in Mark Jackson (ed.), *Infanticide: Historical Perspectives on Child Murder and Concealment, 1550–2000* (Aldershot: Ashgate, 2002), pp. 74–5; Tinková, 'Protéger ou punir', para. 9.

90 NA, *PCAP-C*, 575.

91 NA, *PCAP-C*, 620/A (Marie Geeraerts 1753); FA, *V*, 110 (Anna Catharina Van den Rijn 1774).

92 FA, *V*, 110 (Anna Catherina Van den Rijn 1774); NA, *PCAP-C*, 575 (Marguerite Masson 1774; Marguerite Jacquet 1793).

93 Tinková, 'Protéger ou punir', 55–8.

94 SABR, *AC-WEST*, 168–486.

95 NA2, *AC-BRA*, 304–661.

96 SABR, *AC-WEST*, 277–336.

97 SABR, *AC-WEST*, 320–723.

98 Some historians have suggested that, indeed, shame became a less common emotion as the world 'modernised'. For a grand overview, see Peter N. Stearns, *Shame: A Brief History* (Urbana, IL: University of Illinois Press, 2017).

99 William M. Reddy, *The Invisible Code: Honor and Sentiment in Postrevolutionary France, 1814–1848* (Berkeley, CA: University of California Press, 1997), p. 228.

100 Nye, *Masculinity*, p. 217.

101 Robert A. Nye, 'How the duel of honour promoted civility and attenuated violence in western Europe', in Carolyn Strange, R. B. Cribb and Christopher E. Forth (eds), *Honour, Violence and Emotions in History* (London: Bloomsbury, 2014), pp. 183–202.

102 Frevert, *Men of Honour*, p. 150.

103 Beccaria, *An Essay on Crimes*, chap. 32.

104 Fierlant, 'Premières idées', fo. 1027v.

105 John McManners, *Death and the Enlightenment: Changing Attitudes to Death among Christians and Unbelievers in Eighteenth-Century France* (Oxford: Clarendon, 1981), p. 411.

106 Lester G. Crocker, 'The discussion of suicide in the eighteenth century', *Journal of the History of Ideas*, 13:1 (1952), 47–72.

107 David Hume, *Essays on Suicide and the Immortality of the Soul* (London: Thoemmes Press, 1783), pp. 19–23.

108 Holbach cited in Dominique Godineau, *S'abréger les jours: le suicide en France au XVIIIe siècle* (Paris: Colin, 2012), p. 153.

109 Georges Minois, *Histoire du suicide. La société occidentale face à la mort volontaire* (Paris: Fayard, 1995), pp. 265–74; Zilla Gabrielle Cahn, *Suicide in French Thought from Montesquieu to Cioran* (New York: Peter Lang, 1998), pp. 51–93.

110 McManners, *Death and the Enlightenment*, p. 431; Godineau, *S'abréger les jours*, pp. 151–2.

111 Holbach cited in McManners, *Death and the Enlightenment*, p. 433.

112 Jeffrey R. Watt, *Choosing Death: Suicide and Calvinism in Early Modern Geneva* (Kirksville, MO: Truman State University Press, 2001), p. 120.

113 McManners, *Death and the Enlightenment*, pp. 431–2; Godineau, *S'abréger les jours*, pp. 153–4.

114 Sébastien Joseph Antoine Cupis de Camargo, *Lettres de Cang-ti, grand mandarin de la Chine, recueillies par Mylord Shaftesbury* (Paris: Champion, 2009). Quotes pp. 455–467.

115 Boddice, *A History of Feelings*, pp. 118–24.

116 NA, *PCAP-C*, 575.

117 FA, V, 112 (Jan Baptiste Gillis 1776).

118 CAB, *HA Trials*, 10364.

119 CAB, *ADM-POL*, 438 (Jacques Chatenier 1805).

120 Kant, *The Metaphysics of Morals*, p. 219.

121 Cf. Andreas Bähr, 'Condemning oneself to death. The semantics of suicide in self-narratives of the German enlightenment', in Claudia Ulbrich, Kaspar von Greyerz and Lorenz Heiligensetzer (eds), *Mapping the 'I': Research on Self-Narratives in Germany and Switzerland* (Leiden: Brill, 2015), pp. 166–89.

122 Wollstonecraft, *A Vindication*.

123 Cf. Foucault, *Discipline and Punish*, pp. 191–4.

3

Losing your self: magic, madness and other ways of losing control

Unlike the suspects we encountered in the last chapter, many people in the eighteenth- and nineteenth-century courts did not claim that they were reasonable. Their self was not responsible and stable, it was not socially oriented. They denied responsibility for their crimes. Even if they confessed that they had committed the material crime, they claimed that they could not be held accountable, because they had lost their reason and had not been in control of themselves – thus they had not *been* themselves.

According to early medieval Germanic law, actions could be punished regardless of the intentions of the person who committed them. From the thirteenth century onwards, however, criminal courts all over Europe start to adopt the Roman and Canon law principle that an action had to be committed *willingly* in order to be punishable. Conversely, the attempt to commit a crime could henceforth also be punished and 'premeditation' became in some cases an aggravating factor.[1] As a result, someone who was not 'compos sui' (in control of himself) or not 'sana mentis' (sound of mind), was, as one lawyer argued in Antwerp in 1772, 'doli capax non', not capable of malice.[2]

The will and the mind, what in English common law has been called the 'mens rea', the 'guilty mind', could therefore become of interest to the criminal courts to assess the 'culpability' of the suspect.[3] The degree to which criminal courts could or would do this in practice was often limited: as we have seen in the previous chapter, courts often silently assumed the intention of the defendant. Courts did not consider intentionality in general, but only a variety of specific excuses and justifications. Even so, this opened a space for defendants to make claims about their state of mind. In Zurich, claims about 'diminished intent' seem to have increased in the seventeenth century.[4] In eighteenth-century English courts, the language of mental excuses increased from the 1730s and 1740s onward.[5] Similarly, many suspects in the eighteenth- and nineteenth-century Southern Netherlands professed that they had some kind of 'true' or at least 'regular' self that could be 'displaced' by something else – by drunkenness or passion, for instance, or by more incisive events such as demonic possession or temporary insanity.[6] Hence, they claimed, they were not fully responsible for their crimes.

From the mid- to late-eighteenth century, I will show in this chapter, the strategies people used to claim the displacement of the self were relatively diverse. Selves in the criminal courts were relatively malleable and permeable; it was quite easy to 'lose' your self under the influence of drink or emotion. These possibilities became more limited by the early nineteenth century. While in the late eighteenth century, people often assumed that the disturbance of the self came from outside, in the early nineteenth century, especially judges and doctors, but common witness as well, increasingly thought that it came from within. Temporary insanity was increasingly medicalised. The courts more explicitly linked drunkenness and strong emotions to inherent character flaws and increasingly saw claims of demonic possession as a sign of insanity. As a result, they saw many instances of displacement of the self as part of the self.

A drink too many

By far the most common argument for the loss of self-control throughout the period was drunkenness. Countless people – mostly men, of all social statuses – argued before the courts that they or others had not been able to use reason or to control their actions because they were drunk. A witness said in 1782 that when Stephanus Janssens grabbed the witness' penis in an inn, Janssens 'was so drunk that he didn't know what he was doing'.[7] Claude de Bernaerde alleged in 1789 that when he was picking a fight with some people, again in an inn, 'it was the booze that made him talk'.[8] Jean Kersbilck, in 1802, when asked for a justification for a homicide in a fight, said that 'he was so drunk that he did not have presence of mind during the row', adding that he did not even remember having hit anyone.[9] In 1823, finally, Antonius Bernaerts vandalised a brothel and abused a woman in it. He claimed 'that he does not know what he has done, since he was robbed of his senses as a result of excessive drinking'.[10]

Defining drunkenness as the loss of reason was a common theme in eighteenth-century Europe. Drunkenness, the *Encyclopédie* noted, 'is a breach of natural law, which orders us to preserve our reason'. It is 'a stupid, coarse and brutal vice, which troubles the faculties of the mind'.[11] Moralists agreed: drinking 'without measure makes us lose Reason and makes us equal to unreasonable animals', wrote J.A.F. Pauwels in 1778 in a lamentation on drink.[12] 'Drunkenness', preached Ferdinand Vander Sloten to his parish in 1791, 'is a voluntary excess in drink, to the extent that one is robbed of the use of his reason and wit. [...] The drunkard suffocates the light of his reason in drink'.[13] Being drunk was a practice of unreason.

To understand the implications of these discourses for the self, it is useful to remember that these notions fitted within a longstanding battle against drinking and drunkenness. This battle was, in the first instance, waged by Christian moralists. Theologically, drunkenness was a capital sin precisely because people lost their reason, which God had given humans to distinguish them from animals. By becoming drunk, people forsook their divine purpose.[14] Practically, moralists condemned drinking for two main reasons: first, because the inn was a competitor for the church as the place to be on a Sunday morning; second, because they found that drinking led to other sinful, unholy behaviour, such as unchasteness and neglect of duties.[15] Since the sixteenth century, preachers, teachers and confessors regularly orated against drinking, a tradition which continued relatively unaltered in the eighteenth and nineteenth centuries. They did not eschew brutal images: in a popular schoolbook, Petrus Vanden Bossche, for instance, referred to an example from Augustin of a drunk who killed his father, mugged his mother and tried to rape his sister.[16]

The Church was perhaps less consistent in practice than in discourse – complaints about drunken priests and friars abounded up to the seventeenth century, and renegade capuchin Pieter Vervisch confirmed them at the end of the eighteenth century.[17] Still, urban and central governments held an even more ambiguous position. In the Southern Netherlands as in many European countries, the central government issued the first edicts to reduce drunkenness – or, more precisely, the disorders that they thought to result from drunkenness – in the sixteenth century and mainly aimed at reducing the number of public houses, reducing their opening hours and reducing the number of people who frequented them.[18] However, as governments' finances were in large part dependent on taxes on the production of beer and jenever (a type of gin), they were not particularly insistent on diminishing alcohol consumption, nor were they particularly harsh on public drunkenness.[19]

In the 1770s, however, a different – though by no means novel – view gained popularity. In a movement similar to the British 'gin craze', several city governments started complaining that jenever abuse among common people had dire economic consequences.[20] The problem was especially the habitual drunkard. 'The abuses worsen every day', the aldermen of Kortrijk wrote to the central government in 1781, 'to the extent that working men are not only wasting their family's means of subsistence, but weakening the human species every day. If no solution is found, it is to be feared that within some twenty years, our guilds and manufactures will not find any more labourers, thus ruining the town'.[21]

Common people's conceptions of drunkenness were also hardly always positive, even if people sometimes perceived being able to drink much without losing (all) control as masculine and honourable. People often regarded men who were consistently drunk poorly, though much depended on the circumstances. Female drunkenness was more consistently nega- tively commented upon. Drinking excessively was not an accepted femi- nine discourse.[22] For all, drinking moderately was a proper social activity.[23] Drinking immoderately was either portrayed as a sign of bad character, or explained as a sort of coping mechanism. When judges asked Peter De Man in 1765 why he was drunk so often, he explained that it was 'sometimes out of chagrin, and sometimes for diversion, like everyone else. Out of chagrin because he was losing everything'.[24] In 1804, tailor Therese van Lerberghe testified of a couple that 'she has remarked a few times that the wife was drunk, which she presumes is a result of the chagrin her husband gives her, because he, in contrast, was very often drunk'.[25] In 1829, finally, Constant Pringiers' wife was having an affair. A witness testified that 'since then, out of sorrow, he has abandoned himself to drinking'.[26]

The conception of drunkenness as the loss of reason implied a specific anthropology of drunkenness. A common theme among moralists was that drinking *transformed* men and women, generally into animals.[27] When you are drunk, Ferdinand Loys advised youths in 1772, 'your condition changes, you change from human into beast'.[28] The drunk, Ferdinand Vander Sloten preached,

> has imitated the unreasonable animals, and has become like them. [...] Good God! What a gruesome monster is a drunken man! [...] He behaves like a roaring lion, like a savage bull, like an all-devouring wolf.[29]

In less charged terms, even Immanuel Kant noted that 'a man who is drunk is like a mere animal'.[30] They thus interpreted drunken behaviour as some- thing that was external to the self: because they lost their reason, people were not themselves when they were drunk; they were like animals.

Many people were said to have a 'sober' self and a 'drunk' self. Jacob Mol's wife was 'often drunk and then she was as vicious as a hellish devil'.[31] In 1765, Joanne Vandenberghe complained to her neighbour that her husband was drunk, 'and then he is always wholly facetious'.[32] Gerard Deboysere confessed in 1802 that 'when he has drunk he is nasty'.[33] A wit- ness in the case against Jacob Ceulemans in 1781 observed that drunken characters differed. He said that he 'had seen that Ceulemans, when drunk, was wholly merry and pleasant of mind and didn't even curse', while his victim 'when drunk was a vile person, looking for fights'.[34]

There was an alternative approach to drunkenness as well. In a sev- enteenth-century character sketch of the drunkard, the Antwerp author Richard Verstegen noted that: 'When he is fully drunk / one can turn his inside out / and see what he has hidden in his heart'.[35] When people were drunk, Verstegen suggested, they revealed their true self. Indeed, many eighteenth-century moralists also warned that 'wine brings all into the light' and that 'a drunken mouth speaks from the heart. A drunkard keeps nothing inside; as he empties his stomach, he likewise empties his heart'.[36] Such sentiments were not popular in the depositions before criminal courts. While drunks were perhaps looser with secrets, the idea that drunkenness revealed your true self was clearly less popular than the idea that it transformed you into someone else.[37]

The idea of a transformation was, of course, problematic for the law. As we have seen in the previous chapter, the law operated on the principle that its subjects were reasonable and responsible. As people lost their reason when they were drunk, could they be held fully responsible for crimes committed in drunkenness? Lawmakers and legal commentators disagreed. In 1531, for instance, Charles V issued a decree stipulating that drunkenness was no excuse in homicide cases but on the contrary required a heavier punishment. While they might not be fully conscious of what they were doing when drunk, people were responsible for being drunk in the first place. His ordinance was re-issued several times in the sixteenth and early seventeenth centuries, but seems to have been ignored by most courts.[38] Only a few years before Charles' ordinance, the influential legal commentator Filips Wielant had advised that serious drunkenness, when not habitual, was a sufficient ground for grace or even for excluding punishment.[39]

This ambiguity in European legal thought continued in the eighteenth and nineteenth centuries. In his *Premières idées*, Goswin de Fierlant offered a nuanced consideration of the matter. Drunkenness was no sufficient ground for dismissing a trial, but could be considered as an extenuating circumstance. 'I hold for certain that although the vapours of drink [...] trouble the head and make us act with precipitation and without making the reflections we would make with a cool head [...], their impressions do not go as far as depriving us of reason altogether, as long as they still allow us to act'. He continued that while drunk offenders were perhaps less guilty, 'public order does not allow that laws exempt [them] from all punishment'.[40] Merlin de Douai, an influential commentator on the Revolutionary and Napoleonic penal codes, was stricter, arguing that 'drunkenness may not extinguish nor even extenuate the punishment of a crime. He who voluntarily drinks so much as to trouble his reason, renders himself responsible for all the consequences of his drunkenness'.[41] Pellegrino Rossi, another influential legal scholar, proposed in 1829 that drunken offenders should be punished for the imprudence of being drunk, but not for the specific acts they had committed. However, he left it up to the conscience of the juries to decide whether drunkenness was simply an excuse, or a justification of a crime.[42]

As a result of these inconsistent opinions, how courts dealt with drunken offenders was up to individual judges and juries. People in criminal courts talked about drunkenness mainly on four occasions. First, to portray someone negatively, as a habitual drunk. Second, they referred to drunkenness to justify incomplete memories of a particular event. Norbert Tomas, when asked in 1778 whether he had stabbed Jan Haverslag, replied that 'he did not know, given his drunkenness'.[43] Similarly, when the magistrate asked Jan Van Thuyne, a farmer, in 1823 whether he had had a dispute, he said that 'he doesn't know, because he was very drunk'.[44] Drunkenness gave suspects the option to choose a middle way between confessing and denying. A third use of drunkenness was to retract an accusation or confession. Again in the Tomas case, Anna Casens wanted to change her deposition, claiming that 'she didn't know what she was saying or doing because of her alteration [a feeling of shock, after seeing the corpse] and moreover that she had exceptionally drunk a lot of jenever'.[45]

Finally, and most interestingly for the history of the self, some people referred to drunkenness in order to deny responsibility. Francis Paridaens clearly articulated this reasoning in 1828. Paridaens had stabbed Lodewijk Van Speybroek, after a fight over debts late at night in an inn. When Paridaens was arrested, he told the village constable 'one sometimes does things with a drunken mouth, which one has to pay when sober'. After initially denying the stabbing, he finally confessed that he had stabbed Van Speybroek, who owed him money while he himself was in misery. 'That night, being drunk and all these circumstances coming to his mind, and remembering that Van Speybroek had assaulted him four years earlier, he didn't possess himself anymore'. Indeed, he later added, 'he has the greatest regret over what has happened in his drunkenness, which would otherwise not have occurred'.[46] Drunkenness was an external influence that led to a loss of self-control, Van Speybroek claimed, and that led him to portray behaviour that his true, sober and reasonable self would not. The consumption of alcohol destabilised his self.[47]

While such stories were abundant in both the eighteenth and early nineteenth centuries, the claim of a displaced self was complicated after around 1800. People increasingly perceived drunkenness, and especially habitual drunkenness, as a moral problem that was inherent to the self rather than an external displacement of the self.[48] While this had to some extent already been the case in the eighteenth century, it was only in the early nineteenth century that many witnesses and prosecutors started to comment on drunkenness in this way. This was particularly, but not exclusively the case for poor people. The prosecutor said of Henry Janssens in 1800, for instance, that 'as a result of his passion for drink, he abandoned his work immediately after having earned some money'.[49] Of Jean Verbrugge, his employer said in

1819 that he was 'a good worker, but he has a decided penchant for drink'.[50] In 1822, Hendrik Spijns, a merchant accused of killing his wife, alleged that she had brought her death to herself by drinking. He had observed shortly after marrying her 'that she abandoned herself to drink [*zich overgaf aan den drank*]; at first only a little bit, but slowly her urge for drink increased ever more, to the extent that whenever they had any money, she was very drunk'.[51] In all these comments, people connected habitual drunkenness to passions, penchants and urges: habitual drunkenness became, in the early nineteenth century, a part of the self.[52]

Because courts did not motivate their sentences, it is difficult to assess how, in the end, drunkenness affected the verdict. Most courts do not seem to have been lenient, at least not in homicide cases. Norbert Tomas, for instance, was convicted to perpetual banishment. People like Tomas could apply for grace, however. When drunkenness was not habitual and the other circumstances were also favourable, the central government could give grace, as it did in the Tomas case.[53] Pierre Antoine Devos was in a similar case in 1751. He had committed an 'accident' while in 'youth, anger and drink'. Although his request was initially dismissed, he was eventually able to receive grace after a new application in 1754.[54] After the installation of the new justice system, the drunkenness defence was even less effective, while it remained common, since juries were not inclined to find a drunk homicide entirely innocent and judges had little space for arbitrariness in determining the punishment. The courts convicted both Francis Paridaens and Jan Van Thuyne to branding and a life of hard labour.[55] While people commonly perceived drunkenness as a transformation of the self and the (partial) loss of reason and judgment, its effect in criminal court was, at least for serious offences, limited. Drunks were, after all, responsible for getting drunk.

This first means of denying responsibility was the most common and least incisive way to do so. Men and women of all social statuses used it, but particularly men, as it more easily tied in with certain perceptions of masculinity. People who were drunk were unconscious of what they did and they were therefore not the same person. An external substance led to a less stable and dispossessed self.[56] In the eighteenth and nineteenth centuries, drunkenness was a practice to destabilise the self, to make it permeable. But especially in the early nineteenth century, this perception was complemented with a different view. People increasingly related drunkenness to a bad character; they saw it as the result of an individual lack of self-control. They connected drunkenness to passions, penchants and urges. As a consequence, drunkenness was no longer simply an external displacement of the self, but also inherent to the self, a part of the self. This view would again change later in the nineteenth century. While drunkenness remained connected to the self, physicians increasingly portrayed it as a form of mental illness rather than a lack of self-control. Habitual drunkenness would become 'dipsomania', it would become 'alcoholism'.[57]

Violent passions

One of the problems with drunkenness – one of the reasons why it had value as an excuse – was that it resulted in people not being able to control their 'passions' anymore. Drunkenness and 'passionate', emotional behaviour were often cited together. Pierre Antoine Devos, in 1754, reported that he was 'taken by anger and by drink' during an argument and then struck his opponent.[58] Of Pierre Vanderstocken, the Privy Council concluded in 1792 that during a row, 'in the heat [dans la chaleur] and a bit inebriated' he stabbed his opponent.[59] Like drunkenness, heat and anger suggested that people were not entirely in control of themselves.

Passions, the *Encyclopédie* noted, are:

> penchants, inclinations, desires & aversions, pushed to a certain degree of vivacity, joint with a confused sensation of pleasure or pain, occasioned or accompanied by some irregular movement of blood and animal spirits.

Passions 'go up to depriving us of the use of liberty, a state in which the mind is in some way rendered passive; hence the name of passions'.[60] Although some of the passions would today be referred to as emotions – a concept that did not yet have its current meaning in the eighteenth century – passions were also different. They included not only 'feelings', but also desires and motives.[61] People used the word 'passion' especially when referring to violent commotions of the mind – commotions that could, as the *Encyclopédie* indicated, take away reason and autonomy.[62]

In 1759, Adriaen Leysen applied for grace for the homicide of innkeeper Jan Van Gompel. Van Gompel's brother had insulted him, they had argued and when Leysen tried to leave, Van Gompel grabbed him and started hitting him, 'because of which the supplicant, being in anger and no longer possessing his reason, grabbed some sort of wood or club, with which supplicant has hit the innkeeper, his aggressor, because of his great anger'.[63] Similarly, Augustine Henaux, when asked whether she had threatened to kill her mother-in-law, said she did not recall, observing 'that when one is angry, one says things one ought not to say'. Hermina Van Welbergen, in 1824, reportedly asked a friend to put away a bread-knife, for 'one cannot know what one would use it for when in anger'.[64] Passions, especially anger and fury, took away reason and disturbed the regular self.

The idea behind being overcome by passion was that people had not been able to reflect on their actions. Theodore Toulouse articulated this particularly well in 1803. Toulouse found himself insulted and attacked and 'then he took his knife out of his pocket to defend himself, and having opened it without reflection and in a fit of anger, he stabbed her in the throat with the said knife [...], having in this way sadly wounded the said Louise Persyn, against his intention and of which he repents'.[65] Indeed, many people testified of regret after they had acted in a fit of anger. After Nijt van der Neusen had pushed his wife into the mud while 'in full anger and while grinding his teeth like a raging man', 'he seemed to regret having done this'.[66] In 1795, Joseph André, when asked if he had anything to report in his defence, said that 'he has done it in a moment of anger and that he has immediately had regret and remorse of conscience'.[67] Jean Joseph Ladon, finally, after having hit his father in 1805, told his sister that he regretted his act, 'saying that vivacity had brought him to these excesses'.[68] They practised regret to distance their actions from their 'true' self. They suggested that had they been their ordinary, reasonable self, had they had the time to overthink their actions, they would not have acted in the same way.[69]

In general, people were expected to control their passions as much as their drinking. Passions were, in the Christian tradition, dangerous movements of the soul, leading to all sorts of sins.[70] A whole literature developed, aiming to get people to control or 'master' their passions.[71] This campaign intensified especially in the early nineteenth century: anger control became a central concern in the burgeoning family advice literature.[72] The project was quite successful, because like habitual drunks, people who were often passionate were sometimes negatively commented upon. They were 'choleric' or 'hot-tempered'. In 1787, for instance, Pieter Van der Plancke was found 'so choleric and unrestrained' that people publicly mocked him with the nickname 'Pierre the rude'.[73] Beneath the imperative of self-control lay a view of passions inspired by humourism.[74] Passionate behaviour was associated with heat and excess in yellow bile ('kholè' in Greek, hence the use of the words 'colère'/'colere' and 'cholerique'/'choleriek' in French and Dutch). The metaphor of 'hot blood' was common: people stressed that they had not acted 'in cold blood', but in a moment of 'heat'.[75] People were to use the power of their will to conquer the imbalances of the humours.

When using passion as an explanation for their behaviour, people therefore stressed that it was not simply a lack of control on their part. They indicated that their victim had provoked them so severely that anyone would lose self-control. Often, men did not respond to challenges to their honour with reason, as in the cases in the previous chapter, but with anger. Antoine Deleporte, for instance, reported in 1764 that he had hit a girl because of her 'excessive and piquant provocations, which inflame the blood and so cause vivacity in the most patient of persons'.[76] Ambroise Vrancx applied for grace in 1771, after having lethally wounded his stepmother. First, he established that the woman in question was an 'evil woman', who was abusing his father and who had attacked him first. Then, he claimed that he had hit her while 'he was in a natural emotion, resulting from the outrages his father had received'. Indeed, the magistrates of Grez advised that:

> if one considers on the one hand that it is a son who argues for his father, against a stepmother for whom one generally only has sentiments of hatred, this extreme opposition of sentiment may have produced in him a passion that is difficult to conquer and that has conducted him to this crime.[77]

With their continuous provocations, people incited passions that could no longer be controlled. Defendants stressed that this was not an individual flaw, but that no-one would be able to bear such insults.

Like the argument of drunkenness, the arguments of anger and passion were highly gendered and class specific. Being able to control your passions was often portrayed as a masculine trait. Nevertheless, being angry could be portrayed as masculine too: men could and should be angry when they were insulted or when an injustice was taking place. Anger intersected with their feelings of male honour.[78] The argument of anger was, however, especially in the early nineteenth century, often more associated with men of a lower social status. Whereas the portrayal of 'just' anger had been common for all men in the fifteenth and sixteenth centuries, it had become more difficult to reconcile elite, polite masculinity with anger.[79] For women, in contrast, it was always difficult to portray anger as a positive feminine trait. Unlike men, women rarely used it as an excuse.

For legal scholars, the excuse of passion was similar to that of drunkenness. Some jurists even explicitly compared the two, observing that while drinkers and angry people were perhaps unable to fully control their actions, they were fully responsible for becoming drunk or angry.[80] Goswin de Fierlant suggested that, as in the case of drunkenness, as long as passions still allowed one to act, they had not deprived him of reason entirely, so the passionate delinquent should still be prosecuted. He suggested giving a less severe punishment.[81] Foreign legal commentators, such as Daniel Jousse in France, similarly suggested that passions, when they prohibited cool-headed reflection, were grounds to diminish punishments.[82] After the French Revolution, anger and other passions were no longer acceptable as excuses, except when they were the result of violent physical provocations.[83] After 1802, convicts could again refer to their passions when applying for grace, although this does not seem to have been common.[84]

As with drunkenness, it is difficult to assess how effective referring to anger or passion was in the courts. While some local courts were clement towards passionate behaviour in their advice to the Privy Council, the latter never considered anger or passion sufficient grounds for grace; even if they recommended grace in cases where the supplicant had referred to passions, they did not mention it in their advice. Thus Ambroise Vrancx, who killed his stepmother and was favourably commended by the local magistrates, was found unfit for grace by the Privy Council. Nevertheless, the governor granted him pardon – without, of course, motivating this course of action.[85] The difference with earlier periods – when anger was by far the most common grounds for grace – could hardly be greater.[86] The increasing stress on controlling passions left less room for clemency.

Thus far, I have mainly attended to the passion of anger. Today, when considering crime and passion, the so-called 'crime of passion' is what comes to mind most immediately: killing out of love or jealousy. While this was certainly not the most common instance in which people referred to passions, a concept similar to that of crime of passion did exist. Some foreign legal commentators, such as Jousse and Muyart de Vouglans, attended to love as an excuse for crime, and proposed that it was similar to anger (people could be 'blinded by love'), although it was generally not applicable for serious crimes.[87] In the Southern Netherlands, the only provision for 'crimes of passion' was that traditionally, ancien régime justice allowed a husband to kill a man he found having intercourse with his wife, given that the lover was not a nobleman (the reverse – a wife killing her adulterous husband's concubine – was not legal). That this did not (explicitly) have to do with impulses of love or jealousy, but rather with honour, propriety and entitlement, is apparent by the fact that the married woman's father had the same right.[88] While eighteenth-century legal scholars did not mention this right, it was still referred to in an advice of the Privy Council concerning a grace application in 1760. The Privy Council qualified the murder of a man who was raping (!) Pierre Van Quickelbergh's wife as 'a simple homicide committed by a husband because of a just resentment against the adulterer of his wife, who has been found in the act of consuming the insult and shame of the husband'.[89]

In the French Revolutionary penal system this provision was abolished, but it was re-introduced in the Napoleonic penal code. The murder committed by a husband on his adulterous wife and her accomplice when he caught them *in flagrante delicto* in their marital home was excusable, meaning it would be punished only with imprisonment of one to five years.[90] The changes in the formulation of this excuse are notable – no longer was the father given a right kill and only when he caught them in the act was the husband allowed to act. (Women, however, were still not allowed to act against an adulterous husband. A violent response to infidelity was apparently not an acceptable part of the repertoires of femininity.) Far more than the former provisions, this code suggested something similar to our current conception of uncontrollable impulse. Legal scholar Pellegrino Rossi treated love and jealousy under the same heading as anger in 1829, but he was more lenient toward anger, if provoked, than toward love and jealousy, passions which he felt people should control.[91] Later in the nineteenth century, many European criminal codes began to attend more explicitly to crimes committed in fury.[92]

In the case of Pierre Calland in 1814, jealousy and anger played an important part. Someone had told Calland that his wife had been dancing with a certain Pierre Vyncke, 'which has brought a jealousy in his heart and a hatred toward the latter'. A few days later, he was in an inn with his wife, with Vyncke also present. While he went to the loo, he heard Vyncke talking with his wife, 'and he believed that they promised to commit infidelities'. He reproached his wife, who said 'you always think more than there is'. He went to the loo again, heard them talking again and then 'being strongly angered' he pulled his knife and stabbed Vyncke. In his final interrogation, Calland stated once more that 'he was accused of having killed a man. He has done it in the moment that he wanted to enjoy his wife'. The court found Calland guilty of manslaughter – not of premeditated murder, but also not of excusable homicide – and convicted him to perpetual forced labour and branding.[93]

Suspects often called upon passions – violent emotions – to distance their actions from themselves. They had acted without being able to reflect, in the heat of the moment, while they could not reason properly. Their regular self had been disturbed: like drunkenness, practices of anger, jealousy and other passions destabilised the self. But also like drunkenness, referring to passions only had a limited effect on the verdicts in criminal courts, especially in the early nineteenth century. If people should abstain from too much drinking, they should also be able to control their passions. Like drunkenness as well, passions of anger, jealousy and love were primarily (though not exclusively) invoked by men, increasingly men of a lower social status. Women rarely claimed to have acted 'in a fury' – this form of disturbance of the self was not a trope women could easily draw upon, as violent outrage was not a form of femininity acceptable to the law. By the early nineteenth century, the excuse of passion was becoming less successful for everyone, although some continued to invoke it. As controlling passions had become increasingly adamant, passionate behaviour was mainly becoming a flaw rather than an excuse.

Sense and sensibility and witchcraft

Like drunkenness and passion, magic, demons and the devil could influence people's selves. Belief in such supernatural interventions is generally associated with the period before the eighteenth century. Scholars of the early modern self have used it to stress that the self was fluid and permeable. 'The line drawn around the self was not firmly closed', wrote Nathalie Zemon Davis. 'One could get inside other people and receive other people within oneself', through possession, bewitchment, exorcism or even taking the body of Christ.[94] Spirits, John Martin observed, could take possession of the body, while the soul could leave the body. Exorcists had the task to ensure that people could 're-posses' themselves, that their experience was again their own. While not everyone believed that such journeys of spirits and souls were possible, most people in sixteenth- and early seventeenth-century Europe did.[95]

Although influential early modern legal commentators like Filips Wielant and Joos de Damhouder did not specifically attend to possession or bewitchment – unlike drunkenness, passion and madness – the general principle that there could be no crime without the will to commit crime suggested that demoniacs and those under the influence of magic could not be held responsible for their actions. Indeed, theologians and legal scholars generally agreed that the only person who could be held responsible in these cases – besides the devil – was the witch.[96] The Spanish Benedictine Benito Feijoo, writing in the mid-eighteenth century, even considered fake possession one of the greatest threats to criminal justice, for it would allow people to commit all sorts of terrible crimes without being punished.[97] However, as far as I know, no suspect in the Southern Netherlands successfully claimed before a criminal court to have been possessed or bewitched. Getting people to commit serious crimes seems to have been beyond the powers of most witches.

If they did not extensively comment upon the legal position of the demoniac or the bewitched, legal scholars made the position of the witch quite clear. 'Sorcery, divination, wizardry and incantations are punished with fire', Wielant wrote, for witchcraft is 'against faith and the ordinance of our mother the Holy Church'.[98] The ensuing witch hunt all over Europe is well-known. In the Southern Netherlands, between 1450 and 1685, at least 2800 witches were executed.[99] By the late seventeenth century, however, the great witch hunt was over. Under increasing central supervision and in light of gruesome abuses, criminal courts became more careful when dealing with witches. The Church felt sufficiently powerful to afford ignoring superstitious practices, most of which had gone underground after the great witch hunts, and the civil authorities shifted their attention towards other forms of disorder.[100] While courts still prosecuted practitioners of magic in the eighteenth and nineteenth centuries, they treated them not as diabolic creatures, but as crooks, and accordingly punished them more mildly, often with fines.[101]

The end of the witch trials did not signal the end of supernatural beliefs and practices. Certainly, there were sceptics, and their numbers increased in the eighteenth century. Particularly among elites who associated with the Enlightenment, many thought that supernatural events were if not impossible, then at least very rare. Being sceptical of witchcraft was 'fashionable' among cosmopolitan elites.[102] Nevertheless, for many people, even for many educated people, witchcraft remained a reality, a method to influence and explain the world.[103] In eighteenth-century Sweden, for instance, Jacqueline van Gent has found that magical practices remained common. For many, the conception of self remained porous. Mind and body were not neatly separated and the self was mostly relational. Stories of self-transcendence, soul journeys and love magic reveal that the self was not an autonomous, rational subject. People's behaviour and thoughts could be influenced by supernatural means.[104]

In the Southern Netherlands as well, magic remained a part of the everyday life of a large part of the populace. There were magical healers and exorcists, love potions for sale and wizards who could help find lost objects.[105] Preachers warned their parishioners of witches who could fly or transform into animals – though they also stressed that many phenomena that seemed supernatural, in fact had natural explanations.[106] In the cities, fortune tellers predicted the future and helped people with all sorts of small problems. The fortune tellers were often themselves not very fortunate: witnesses said that a certain Bellotje in Antwerp was a poor woman who worked both in prostitution and as a fortune teller.[107] In 1809, Jeanne Gallet was prosecuted for murder after she had sold an abortive powder which had allegedly poisoned a woman. When interrogated, she confessed that she had 'read the cards for more than two hundred girls' in Leuven, but denied ever having sold any powders or potions. The court convicted her to death nonetheless.[108]

Violent reactions to practitioners of magic were not uncommon. Throughout the eighteenth and nineteenth centuries, cases have been reported of people harassing, attacking and even burning suspected witches, mainly women but occasionally also men.[109] In 1821, Mathias Tirion killed his wife, whom he suspected of being a witch, as he had told several neighbours (who did not believe him). After he had killed her, a witness overheard him murmuring 'it was only a witch, she had to die'. Although the court would find Tirion insane, he clearly borrowed from a known cultural repertoire of dealing with witches.[110]

The reactions of the authorities were not entirely straightforward. In 1760, the Privy Council received a grace application from the neighbours of Mrs. De Gage in Ghent, for her son Philippe, sixteen years old, who had committed a gruesome murder on a nine-year-old child. Philippe was playing a game with some other children in the neighbourhood. The nine-year-old boy was wearing a blindfold. Philippe approached him, claiming that his eyes were not entirely covered, and then stabbed him in the throat. The neighbours suggested that De Gage was insane. However, in their advice, the magistrates of Ghent argued that he had planned this murder in advance, 'on the suggestion of the devil, or by an evil spirit'. This was proven 'by his own declaration, for he has voluntarily confessed that he has committed this crime on the suggestion of the devil'. The Privy Council did not retain this devilish intervention in their advice, but also concluded that the murder was premeditated. Only the governor decided that the case was worthy of grace, because of the youth of the perpetrator, and commuted the death sentence to life imprisonment. It is striking, however, that the Ghent magistrates so eagerly agreed that the devil could give people suggestions.[111]

In most cases, however, and certainly as the century progressed, authorities resolutely denied supernatural influences. When in 1772 some children were thought to be possessed in Namur and an exorcism was performed, the chairman of the Privy Council made his opinion amply clear: he wrote of 'weak and superstitious minds', 'ignorance', and 'pretended witchcraft or demonic possession'. The Chancellor in Vienna concluded that 'it is most essential that in the lands of Namur and Luxembourg, they take to the task of uprooting the ridiculous prejudice that the small people retain regarding sorcery'.[112] In most criminal cases where witchcraft was mentioned, magistrates took a sceptical and often patronising position, expressing disbelief at the 'credulity' of people. Especially in the early nineteenth century, they were often supported by a part of the witnesses, who were also sceptical of magic. Neighbours did not believe that Tirion's wife was a witch, and a friend of Jeanne Gallet's victim allegedly 'wondered about the weakness and credulity of her companion'.

The influence of most magic on the self was limited. Clairvoyance, which was the most common form of magic, did not immediately affect selves – though it did suggest a deterministic worldview. The supernatural influence on the self is clearer in the case of Philippe De Gage, whose actions the devil influenced. Still, De Gage was believed to have retained his free will at least to some extent, or he would not have been punished. The transformation of the self was most clear in cases of demonic possession. In 1771, for instance, Judocus De Vriese had taken a spade and killed the publican of the inn where he was staying in Ingelmunster. When asked for his motives, he said that that he had none, but that he was 'called by demons' to kill the publican. The magistrates investigated how much De Vriese had drunk that day, but they did not find much. The local priest, however, testified that De Vriese had come to him several weeks before, claiming that 'he was possessed by demons and damned'. Judges and witnesses agreed, in the end, that De Vriese had been mad. He was to be locked away.[113]

Another, violent case illustrates the relationship between self, magic and insanity around 1800. In 1801, Elisabeth Van Moer, eight years old, ran home crying. She had been cutting herbs in the woods near Grimbergen with her sister Barbe, aged twelve, and her little brother François, aged two.[114] Suddenly, Gilles Van Eeckhout came running towards them, 'entirely naked'. Van Eeckhout hit Barbe, took her knife, pushed her to the ground and started cutting off her head. Elisabeth ran away, and told her older brother what had happened. He ran to the scene immediately, only to find his little sister's corpse, all bloody, her head separated from her body.

After beheading Barbe, Van Eeckhout tried to attack another girl, but upon hearing people coming he ran away to a church. In the vestibule, he used the knife to cut off his genitals. Bleeding heavily, he hid in a shed, where bystanders locked him up until the justice of the peace came and interrogated him. When asked why he had mutilated himself, he said that 'he had killed the daughter of Guillaume Van Moer and would tell us the reasons'. After receiving medical attention, he was transported to Nivelles, where he was interrogated by the director of the jury. Van Eeckhout was a forty-year-old married man, who used to be a forester, but had lost his job about a year earlier. He claimed not to remember anything of killing a girl, but agreed that it was possible that he had done it, for 'he thought it was his own wife in the forest'.

Q: 'Why did he want to do this to his own wife?'
A. 'Because he knows that it is she who has, together with the provost of Nieuwenrode, bewitched him, taking his senses, making him run around like a beast'.
[...]
Q. 'Why has he mutilated himself?'
A. 'Because he didn't have his senses anymore and it seemed that he had to do that and that it was so determined and fixed'.
Q. 'How has he lost his senses?'
A. 'By witchcraft, by a flying spirit and by the co-operation of the provost of Nieuwenrode'.
Q. 'How does he know that he has lost his senses?'
A. 'Because he wouldn't have done that, if he hadn't lost his senses'.
Q. 'What did he feel when he had lost his senses?'
A. 'He felt fear and pain in his head and in his legs, arms and male parts, and sometimes two to three hundred people were pursuing him with rifles, forks and sticks and wanted to take his life'.

Van Eeckhout suggested that his wife had bewitched him and that, as a result, he had not been himself. Magic had led to the loss of the self. He had acted the way he did because it had felt like he had to. Interestingly, he explained that his analysis of his own bewitchment was the result of the fact that he would not have acted in this way if he had had his 'senses' at

122 *Trials of the self*

the time. Van Eeckhout declared that his self had been displaced by magic because he had acted in a way not in line with his regular self. The belief in magic thus allowed people to practise and explain an unstable, permeable and dispossessed self.

Witnesses who had helped to lock Van Eeckhout up in the shed were in doubt. Some witnesses, like fifty-one-year-old hunter Quentin Pollaert, thought that he was 'like disturbed, or in dementia'. Sixty-year-old gardener Joannes Peeter, however, upon seeing Eeckhout grinding his teeth, eating his own blood, roaring like a beast and making horrible faces, 'believed that he was possessed by the devil or bewitched'. While Van Eeckhout's interrogators displayed great interest in his bewitchment and never told him that it was impossible, they were more interested in his mental state and, as in the case of De Vriese, also inquired about his jenever use. Eventually, they had Van Eeckhout examined by three physicians. They concluded that he suffered from a 'periodical mania' and should be confined in a hospital for the insane. Indeed, the magistrates decided that as Van Eeckhout did not have his full mental capacities, he could not be tried. He was transferred to a hospital, where he passed away a few months later.[115] The case is revealing of the changing approach to the displacement of the self: no longer was it commonly accepted that the self could be displaced from the outside, by witchcraft. Rather, the cause of the displacement was sought inside the self: it was insanity.

This is madness

Drunkenness, passion, bewitchment. All three offered, to different extents, the possibility of transformation, of not being yourself. People who were drunk, emotional or bewitched lost (a part of) their ability to reason, to reflect and to control their actions. In some cases, their state was explicitly compared to another state of dispossession – the state of madness. In 1794, for instance, a verdict related that Pierre Carette 'habitually forgot himself in drink, so to say periodically lost his mind'.[116] Jacob Mol, as I discussed in the introductory chapter, argued that he had struck his wife in a moment of anger, and that he was therefore not 'sound of mind'.[117] And many witnesses considered Gilles Van Eeckhout, as we have just seen, not to be possessed, but simply insane. Discussing insanity in the courts often provided an occasion for probing the mind and self of the suspect.

People had a good reason for equating these different conditions with insanity, as insanity was the main argument in establishing a lack of intention and therefore a lack of culpability. Courts should not punish those who were 'in mad frenzy' during their crime, Wielant wrote in the sixteenth century, later specifying that 'the mad who are mad of great madness' ('dulle die dul zyn van grooter dullicheyt') are excused of homicide, 'for they do not know what they are doing'.[118] All over Europe, eighteenth-century legal scholars agreed that courts should not punish crimes committed in a state of insanity. 'No one can be prosecuted for whatever action committed during a state of alienation of the mind', Goswin de Fierlant wrote, 'because this state, rendering him incapable of malice or bad intention, renders him incapable of committing any crime, offence or excess'.[119]

After the French Revolution, this position remained the same. The penal code of 1791 had not specifically mentioned insanity, but as juries and judges had to consider whether a particular action had been committed voluntarily, they could set the insane free in this way.[120] The lack of an explicit mention of insanity was, however, sometimes problematic in practice, as I will discuss below. After much debate, then, Article 64 of the Napoleonic penal code of 1810 unambiguously declared that 'there is neither crime nor offence if the suspect was in a state of dementia at the time of the action'.[121]

An important change between the old and the new regime was that there were no longer any other states of mind that people could invoke to deny responsibility. Drunkenness and passionate behaviour had not been included in the codes after 1791, and possession or bewitchment was, at least officially, no longer accepted as possible. It should perhaps not surprise then, that in the course of the nineteenth century, people presented all three not only as states similar to insanity, but as forms of insanity – as dipsomania, as moral insanity or as hysteria.

The problem was therefore not whether insanity was grounds for acquittal – everyone agreed on that. The problem was also not what to do with the violent or dangerous insane – most eighteenth- and nineteenth-century legal thinkers agreed that they should be locked up by juridical order, or (though the popularity of this opinion was declining) left to the care of their family.[122] The problem was rather to determine definitions of insanity and what degrees of insanity were sufficient to excuse a defendant.[123] Criminal policymakers were concerned that too loose a definition would allow criminals to go unpunished. In 1771, the public prosecutor in the case of Judocus De Vriese argued that he should not be excused, 'not even on the pretext that at the time he was in a frenzy or fury', for 'if this was to be believed, and he was to be absolved on this pretext, you and many others would be able to commit such homicides without danger or fear of being punished'.[124]

The *Encyclopédie* distinguished two entries on madness ('folie'): madness in a general, moral sense and madness in a stricter, medical sense. In the general sense, the *Encyclopédie* distinguished madness from 'imbecility' and 'weakness': losing reason without knowing it, because one has no ideas, is being *imbecile*. Losing reason knowingly, but with regret because one is a slave of a violent passion, is *weakness*. But losing reason with the firm persuasion that one is following it, that is what is called *madness*.[125] In its medical sense, madness was 'a lesion in animal functions', 'an illness of the mind', 'a sort of aberration of reason, a depravation of the thinking faculty'.[126]

Thinking about insanity was characterised by many distinctions. Commonly, as in the *Encyclopédie*, scholars distinguished four types of mental illness: *mania*, which disturbs reason and makes people act in ridiculous ways without motive; *melancholia*, which is a fixation linked to sadness; *dementia*, when there is no longer any reason at all; and *idiocy* or *imbecility*, a permanent lack of reason. People only considered the first two of these to be treatable (in some cases), generally with bloodletting or purgation. Although some physicians added new diseases (such as Pinel's hypochondria, Esquirol's monomania) and new treatments (such as Tuke's moral treatment, Mesmer's magnetism), the basic taxonomy of insanity remained the same as it had been since late antiquity.[127] Physicians and philosophers alternated between considering insanity a physical disease or a disease of the mind or the will, or something in between.[128]

Of all forms of insanity, idiocy was the least problematic from a legal point of view. 'Louis is a boy of simple mind, who plays and jests with the small children in the streets', the Lord of Steinbach wrote in 1760 in a supplement to a grace application by Louis Felten's parents. He was 'imbecile of mind', the magistrates concurred, and had in his simplicity accidentally shot a gun which he was cleaning. Felten immediately received grace.[129] These 'simple people' were recognised as such by their communities and because their condition was long-term, establishing their mental state was often relatively straightforward. In some cases, however, it was difficult to establish whether a defendant was indeed 'idiotic' – and therefore innocent – or just a bit 'slow'.

The other three classical forms of insanity – mania, melancholia and dementia – often proved to be more ambiguous. Long-term sufferers of one of these disorders could be well-known as such and therefore relatively unproblematic, like the 'idiots', especially if they suffered from some violent and easily visible mania or rage. More subtle forms of insanity, like 'a mild delirium', were harder to judge.[130] Even more difficult to assess were those who suffered from 'intermittent' or 'partial' insanity. Joanna Catharina Janssens' counsel, for instance, argued in 1757 that 'one can compare the defendant with a lunatic, who has good and bad intervals'.[131] Medical innovations of the early nineteenth century, such as the concept of 'monomania' and especially of 'homicidal monomania', further complicated matters. In cases of monomania, the will was diseased independently of intelligence; the monomaniac's crime could be their only symptom, which made it a very

problematic concept for the law.[132] Some people in Belgium were familiar with the concept of homicidal monomania, and some even accepted
it, most notably penal reformer Edouard Ducpétiaux, who referred to the
concept in his treatises against capital punishment in 1827. But the courts
were not convinced of such new and dangerous medical ideas, at least not
before 1830. Indeed, Ducpétiaux himself noted the resistance of public
prosecutors to the concept.[133] I have not encountered cases where people
specifically offered a diagnosis of monomania (or any other 'new' form of
insanity).[134]

In the eighteenth century, Goswin de Fierlant offered a set of guidelines
to determine whether an offender was insane. As a rule, courts had to consider the history of the offender: they should presume that someone who
had never been insane had not been insane during his crime, unless proven
otherwise; and that someone who had a history of insanity had been insane
during his crime, unless proven otherwise. Fierlant also advised that courts
should presume that those with a history of intermittent insanity were
insane at the time of their crime, unless proven otherwise. To prove insanity
in the present, Fierlant recommended calling upon doctors; to prove insanity in the past, the court should hear witnesses.[135]

Consulting medical men was not a consistent practice in the late eighteenth century, but hearing people from the environment of the accused to
establish their mental condition was common. Witnesses of all ranks testified
about insanity, often with great confidence. They regularly referred to external signs of madness. A common observation was that the defendant 'spoke
more crazy than wise reasons, and when she corrected her, she became even
more crazy'.[136] A woman in 1787 testified that her husband showed 'signs
of a wandering and unhealthy mind in his reasons and discourses'.[137] People
also interpreted strange bodily movements – raging, stamping, grinding
teeth, wild eyes, spasms – as signs of insanity.[138]

Laypeople continued to testify about insanity in the new regime, but
their statements were more frequently corroborated by expert testimony
on the one hand, and by the courts' own investigations on the other.[139]
This signalled a decline in the trust in common people's abilities to assess
mental states. Two cases may elucidate these practices. First, the case of
Henry Steenbeek in 1804. When the village secretary of Sint-Joris-Weert
near Leuven reported that Steenbeek had killed his stepfather, he immediately added that 'his mind has long been disturbed and only madness
has made him commit this excess'. The director of the jury heard witnesses, who claimed that 'everyone in the village says that he is mad',
while some had witnessed themselves 'that Steenbeek pulled faces and
laughed in church'. Sometimes, he did not reply to questions and only
laughed.

Steenbeek had fled, but was arrested and interrogated by the director of the jury. When asked about several details concerning the murder, he denied everything. A month later, the president of the criminal tribunal interrogated him again. After several introductory questions, the interrogation became more personal. Because they suspected insanity, the magistrates adapted their techniques to establish the mental capacities of the suspect. They asked about his feelings for his parents and about his relationship with his stepfather, and reported his unusual behaviour in response to these questions. Finally, they asked him to sum up the Ten Commandments, and noted that he omitted the commandment prohibiting killing. 'When we asked him why, he has not answered and seemed so profoundly affected, just like every time we spoke him of his stepfather, which has led us to suspect that this individual is out of his mind'.[140] His answers and his peculiar, unreasonable behaviour led them to conclude that he was insane. The self that was unable to make moral judgments and to reason was not a proper self.

A somewhat similar interrogation occurred in the case of Yves Delva in 1814. Delva, a thirty-two-year-old oil-crusher, had killed his brother in Wervik near Kortrijk, but again, a neighbour testified that 'this young man is of a difficult trade, he is extremely irascible, he occasionally has attacks of fury, which has made the neighbourhood suspect that he is perhaps a maniac'. Another neighbour, Eugenie Franchomme, a weaver of only twenty-six, portrayed great expertise in insanity, claiming that:

> without being completely mad or imbecile, he has nevertheless a more or less deranged mind, his intellectual faculties are only incompletely developed. He is in general silent and only answers to questions with yes or no, very often he answers the same question both with yes and no. He is above all very irascible and inclined to go to extremities against those who object to him; finally, he passes publicly for what one calls half mad, or half imbecile.

Unlike Steenbeek, Delva immediately confessed his crime when the magistrate interrogated him. After reconstructing the crime, the judge of instruction again pushed further. The magistrates asked Delva simple questions, questions about his feelings and about his own appreciation of what was happening. Like Steenbeek, they asked about his relationships with family members and about his wish to return home. Moreover, they seemed to try to ascertain his moral capacities, asking, for instance, 'Does it not seem to him that the brother who takes his brother's life deserves a great punishment?' In both Steenbeek's and Delva's interrogations, the judges attempted to establish the defendant's sanity or insanity by inquiring about their feelings, desires and sense of morality. Although they did not altogether ignore the body, their focus was clearly on the mind. Although they did not ignore intellectual capacities, they were clearly more interested in moral and feeling faculties. For the courts assessing insanity, whether defendants were capable of discerning good and evil was of the essence.[141]

In both cases, the court also called for experts. Such a move was not exactly novel. Already in the seventeenth century, courts sometimes asked medical men for expert testimony on madness.[142] Goswin de Fierlant, as we have seen, put great faith in the abilities of physicians to decide whether someone was insane. He proposed that the court only took its own decision when doctors were undecided.[143] Indeed, the courts often worked together with medical doctors to determine insanity.[144] In the case of Peter Claukens, who killed his infant in 1772, the court called upon no less than five of Antwerp's city doctors to determine whether he was insane.[145] In other cases, however, the courts did not find medical testimony necessary to declare someone insane. In 1768, upon hearing testimony by employers and colleagues, judges found Willem de Naeyer insane at his trial for rape.[146]

In the new regime, courts called upon doctors to decide on insanity more commonly than before, although there were still cases where they were absent. In the case of Mathias Tirion in 1821, for instance, one physician testified about his earlier acquaintance with Tirion, but no doctors examined Tirion's current mental state, while the jury still decided that he was insane.[147] In the French debates over the article on insanity in the 1810 *Code pénal*, several intervenors doubted physicians' abilities to adequately distinguish real from feigned insanity. The general tenor of the debates was, however, that they were at least the most qualified to do so – they were accepted as experts of the mind.[148] This legal position and the resulting calls upon doctors in criminal trials, as Joel Eigen has argued for England, stimulated and shaped the development of psychiatry later in the nineteenth century.[149]

In the case of Henry Steenbeek, three physicians wrote a medical report, which remained altogether inconclusive: the doctors suggested that he was not insane, but all recommended taking further information. No sentence has been preserved.[150] For Yves Delva, upon six visits, doctors and surgeons estimated that 'the intellectual faculties, which constitute the moral and reasonable man, have not entirely developed and he is in a state of near imbecility and very harmful to society'. The jury decided that Delva was insane and therefore innocent, but he was sent to the court of the first instance to determine whether he should be locked up.[151]

Although doctors presented themselves and were to some extent accepted as experts, who possessed knowledge that other people did not have, their methods and conceptions of insanity did, up to 1830, not greatly differ from laypeople. More than the courts, they attended to (outer) bodily movements, but they also used the method of interrogation to determine the suspect's sanity. Their conclusions focused on (inner) intellectual faculties, the ability to reason and moral awareness. Although they preferred a 'stable' diagnosis of sanity or insanity, they left room for periodical insanity, an insanity which temporarily displaced the regular, reasonable and moral self.

Madness was a way to make sense of the most irrational crimes when there were no external influences – the perpetrator was not drunk, not in anger, not bewitched. Of course, there might have been an external influence that triggered madness – misery, loss of employment, loss of a child, disappointment in love – but other people going through the same experiences did not lose their right mind. The causes of losing the self were within oneself. Madness could therefore explain what could not be explained. It was a means for communities to make sense of senseless crimes, and a means for people to make sense of their own irrational and immoral behaviour. Madness was a way to take the self away from the self.

The history of suicide is revelatory of the history of insanity and the self. In the previous chapter, I have discussed how people sometimes spoke about and practised suicide as a rational act. Far more commonly, people saw suicide as the most *irrational* action one could take – indeed, so irrational that by the late eighteenth century, many people considered the act of suicide by itself sufficient evidence that one was mad. This was not entirely new: already in the sixteenth and seventeenth centuries, people sometimes suggested madness as an explanation for suicide, often mixed with narratives of demonic temptations.[152] By the mid-eighteenth century, however, criminal courts in many western European countries accepted that insanity was at play in most cases of suicide.[153] As official belief in demonic inspiration declined and accepting suicide as a rational act was uncomfortable, insanity provided a convenient answer. Suicide could be morally condemned, while it was decriminalised in practice.[154]

In the Southern Netherlands, suicides were generally found insane after 1750. In an advice in 1782, the Privy Council decided that 'every suicide carries a certain delusion of the mind, or at least it should be held as such when in doubt'.[155] Indeed, in suicide cases, authorities were far more inclined to accept insanity than in other cases. They even accepted controversial, partial forms of insanity. 'Does experience not prove that madness often strikes like lightning?' Goswin de Fierlant rhetorically asked.

> There are momentary frenzies, there are those which only concern a single object, with an individual reasoning and behaving sensibly in all other respects, so why not suppose that an action which so strongly revolts the desire of self-preservation that nature has given to all living beings [...] has been committed in a state of delirium?[156]

This was indeed a common practice in suicide cases. Not only authorities, but witnesses too often offered insanity or at least some form of mental torment as an explanation for suicide.[157] It is unsurprising that the question was definitively resolved with the decriminalisation of suicide after the French Revolution. Suicide was so contrary to the reified natural law of self-preservation that it had become useless to punish violators – they had to be mad.

A similar evolution took place with respect to infanticide, though later and less pronounced. Again, in the previous chapter, I discussed how infanticide was sometimes rationalised with references to shame or misery. A complementary account of infanticide rendered the crime a consequence of temporary insanity after childbirth. Already in the eighteenth century, people knew that upon giving birth, some mothers displayed strange behaviour. In England, the country for which this has been studied most extensively, after 1750, infanticide trials started to focus on the defendant's mental condition. For some doctors, the act of infanticide was itself a sign of insanity, caused by weakness after childbirth combined with fear and shame. By 1820, doctors described the concept of 'puerperal insanity' extensively for the first time, a form of insanity that occurred immediately after childbirth. It was first referred to in an English criminal trial in 1822 and became a dominant strategy of defence in the nineteenth century.[158]

Like other novel medical concepts, people did not explicitly refer to the concept of 'puerperal insanity' in trials in the Southern Netherlands before 1830.[159] However, beginning in the early nineteenth century, many women accused of infanticide referred to a particular state of mind after giving childbirth, a state which did not allow them to control their own actions. When asked if she had anything to say for herself concerning the murder of her new-born child, Rosalie Berghe declared in 1807 that 'she did not have presence of mind and that she did not think about what she was doing'. Although the interrogator argued that she had 'the greatest presence of mind', as she had been able to hide her child, the jury decided that Berghe had not killed her child, despite all evidence and a confession. This solution allowed them to bypass the lack of a specific question concerning the defendant's mental state.[160]

The 'language of mental distress' – to borrow Dana Rabin's phrase – was not always so well accepted. In 1820, the Assize Court of West-Flanders judged three separate infanticides, and each woman claimed that 'she did not know what she was doing' at the time, in almost the exact same words. One of them was found innocent, a second was found to have been imprudent and sentenced to two years of imprisonment and a fine, while the third was sentenced to death, not even receiving grace.[161] It is difficult to ascertain the motives of the different juries to reach these verdicts. It is clear, however, that the idea of a state of temporary insanity after childbirth was known and popularly used. Like suicide, infanticide was by the early nineteenth century found to be so contrary to nature – I will return to this idea in chapter 5 – that contemporaries were more easily inclined to consider signs of temporary insanity.

In general, therefore, insanity was primarily an issue either when defendants had a history of known insanity, or when their crime itself was so unnatural, so irrational, so incomprehensible that no sane person would commit it. The principle thus partially replaced the influence of the devil. Actions qualifying for its criteria were historically variable – suicide mainly from the late eighteenth century onwards, infanticide mainly from the early nineteenth century. Especially in cases where extreme cruelty without motive was involved, the question of insanity occurred. 'If we accept that one has to be delirious or furious to kill oneself, may I not suppose these same causes for those homicides that make nature tremble?' asked Ducpétiaux. 'A ruined man who believes himself to be very rich, or a beggar who imagines himself a king are called madmen, they do not know what they say or do: but the man who kills his beloved wife is thought to be reasonable, just like the mother who stabs her children, or the daughter who poisons her parents!' Ducpétiaux seemed to suggest that all horrible crimes were committed by madmen, who could not be held fully responsible.[162]

After this reasoning, he quickly regressed, stating that insanity should always be medically diagnosed to prevent that 'one would make of each assassin a monomaniac'. In practice, authorities were also reluctant to openly declare that people who were simply too cruel were innocent, in the nineteenth century as in the eighteenth. But Ducpétiaux's argument held some truth. The criminal justice system in the early nineteenth century required that crimes be understandable to judges and juries. The post-revolutionary society and its criminal justice system were, as we have seen, founded upon ideas of rationality and responsibility. If people did not act in a way that conformed to commonly accepted rationality, insanity was a neat explanation. The origins of crime, particularly of violent, irrational, senseless crime, were put outside of society and within the person. There may have been circumstances inducing insanity, but the ultimate cause lay within the perpetrators themselves. Insanity removed people's guilt and responsibility, but with it their agency.

The self and the not-self

From this chapter and the previous, a picture is emerging. In their stories before the criminal courts, people in the second half of the eighteenth century practised a self that was implicitly reasonable and responsible. A lack of these characteristics was easily explainable with references to external influences. They could argue that they had temporarily lost control over themselves, that they had 'not been themselves', because of drink, because of the heat of the moment or because of supernatural interference. With these stories, people practised a self that could be displaced. When they were drunk, they claimed, they could not reason properly and thus were not themselves. When they acted in the heat of the moment, they did not reflect on their actions and were not themselves. When they were bewitched or possessed, someone else was in control of their actions. These stories suggest that throughout this period, there was a sense that people had a 'true' or 'proper' self, but that this self could be eclipsed. This proper self was reasonable, morally good and in control of its actions. The stories suggested that it was relatively stable, but also easily permeable: external influences could displace the self and cause it to lose control, morality and reason.

In the new legal system installed in 1790s, the responsible and reasonable self was reified. More than before, the need for reason was made explicit in the courts. Stories of external displacement were discredited. Courts increasingly denied the occurrence of magic (at least officially), while they cast drunkenness and passionate behaviour as moral flaws, which could no longer count as extenuating circumstances. They were no longer mere external influences displacing the self, but were becoming the result of inherent characteristics of the self. This evolution was not complete: people continued to offer drunkenness and passion as excuses, but they were not so easily accepted to diminish responsibility in the courts.

Instead, the criminal courts shifted their attention from the external influences on the self offered by the defendants to the internal sources of displacements that could only be assessed by others. Insanity became an increasing concern in cases where rationality was lacking; and it became an incentive for criminal courts to scrutinise defendants' selves. Of course, insanity was hardly a new concept, and indeed, while proto-psychiatric discourse launched many new syndromes, the basic nosology of madness remained quite similar to that of bygone centuries. The novelty of the late eighteenth and early nineteenth centuries lay in the increased reference to specific, short-term forms of insanity.[163] The concept of monomania was perhaps only a reflection of this larger preoccupation with momentary displacements of the self. While there could be an external trigger, the cause of this displacement was mainly interior, within the self itself. This does not mean, however, that, in the period up to 1830, madness was interpreted as a part of the essential self. The concept of the 'born killer', for instance, would only gain currency later in the nineteenth century.[164] Insanity – or at least some forms of insanity – was a displacement of the self, even while it came from within.

The arguments for displacement of the self were often related to gender and social status. Drunkenness and violent passions were mainly male excuses, and mostly the excuses of men from lower social groups. Although women occasionally referred to them, it was usually seen as a sign of bad character; men of a higher social standing more regularly claimed that they had acted reasonably. Bewitchment could happen to everyone, but I have only found cases of men who claimed or were thought to be bewitched or possessed. Insanity was the most democratic: people argued for men and women of all social standings that they could be insane. In the discourses of the courts, the male self could be displaced in more diverse ways than the female self and the lower-class self more easily than that of better-off people. Men from the lower social orders were therefore most acutely confronted with the internalisation of the displaced self, as their claims of external displacement were increasingly rejected.

Dana Rabin has argued that the language of mental states and pleas of diminished responsibility were increasingly common in English courts from the mid-eighteenth century on. The possibility of 'displacement' allowed for a malleable self: the drunk or passionate self could coexist with a moral and reasonable self.[165] This chapter has shown that, despite the very different legal context, a similar evolution was taking place on the continent. Through the criminal courts, the evolution affected people of all social statuses. By the early nineteenth century, however, a malleable self was yielding its way to a more stable one, as the different external influences on the self were increasingly discredited, while insanity – which was thought to come from within – became the main argument for irresponsibility. In this process, the self became a more urgent topic of discussion and practices of the self proliferated in the criminal courts.

Notes

1 André Laingui, *La responsabilité pénale dans l'ancien droit (XVIe–XVIIIe siècle)* (Paris: Pichon et Durand-Auzias, 1970), pp. 176–8; Monballyu, *Six Centuries*, pp. 70–86; Pohl-Zucker, *Making Manslaughter*, pp. 30–42.

2 FA, V, 108 (Petrus Claukens 1772).

3 Elizabeth Papp Kamali, *Felony and the Guilty Mind in Medieval England* (Cambridge: Cambridge University Press, 2019); Thomas A. Green, 'Societal concepts of criminal liability for homicide in mediaeval England', *Speculum*, 47:4 (1972), 669–94.

4 Pohl-Zucker, *Making Manslaughter*, chap. 5.

5 Rabin, *Identity, Crime, and Legal Responsibility*, p. 107; Thomas A. Green, 'The jury and criminal responsibility in Anglo-American history', *Criminal Law and Philosophy*, 9:3 (2015), 423–42.

6 I borrow the terminology of 'displacement' from Dana Y. Rabin, 'Searching for the self in eighteenth-century English criminal trials, 1730–1800', *Eighteenth-Century Life*, 27:1 (2003), 85–106; Rabin, *Identity, Crime, and Legal Responsibility*.

7 FA, *V*, 116 (Stephanus Janssens 1782).

8 SAK, *OCAK*, 5771.

9 SABR, *AC-WEST*, 159–417.

10 SABE, *Court of the First Instance of Antwerp*, 171 (Antonius Bernaerts 1823).

11 Louis Jaucourt, 'Ivrognerie', in Diderot and d'Alembert, *Encyclopédie*, vol. 9, p. 83.

12 Jan Antoon Frans Pauwels, *Rechtveerdig klagt-dicht, ofte Generaele redenvoeringe van verschyde staeten, conditien en persoonen, gedaen aen den uytvinder van den drank en bevelhebber over den-zelven Bacchus, rakende het misbruyk en ongevallen hier door veroorzaekt* (Antwerp: J. P. de Cort, 1778), p. 5.

13 Ferdinandus Josephus Vander Sloten, *Sermoonen op de zondagen des jaers* (Antwerp: Bincken, 1805), vol. 4, pp. 128–30. Similar sentiments in Antonius Hennequin, *Nieuw-jaers-giften ofte Sermoonen op nieuw-jaers-dag. Sermoonen voor d'eerste communicanten* (Antwerp: Hubert Bincken, 1772), vol. 1, p. 98.

14 Marcel Bernos, '"Yvrognerie": où commence le péché?', *Rives méditerranéennes*, 22 (2005), paras 4–5.

15 Hugo Soly, 'Kroeglopen in Brabant en Vlaanderen, 16de–18de eeuw', *Spiegel Historiael*, 18 (1983), 573–4; Thomas Edward Brennan, *Public Drinking and Popular Culture in Eighteenth-Century Paris* (Princeton, NJ: Princeton University Press, 1988), pp. 198–9.

16 Petrus Vanden Bossche, *Den katholyken pedagoge, ofte Christelyken onderwyzer in den catechismus* (Ghent: Jan Meyer, 1767), pp. 613–14.

17 Soly, 'Kroeglopen', 574; P. F. D. Vervisch, *Wonderbaer en rugtbaer leven van den ex-pater Auxilius van Moorslede, alias Pieter-Francis-Dominiq Vervisch* (Maastricht: Wauter Dronkers, 1791), vol. 2, pp. 70–2.

18 Soly, 'Kroeglopen', 572–3; B. Ann Tlusty, *Bacchus and Civic Order: The Culture of Drink in Early Modern Germany* (Charlottesville, VA: University Press of Virginia, 2001), chap. 5.

19 Raymond Van Uytven, 'De drankcultuur in de Zuidelijke Nederlanden tot de XVIIIde eeuw', in *Drinken in het verleden* (Leuven: Stadsbestuur Leuven, 1973), p. 19.

20 On the gin craze, see Jessica Warner, *Craze: Gin and Debauchery in an Age of Reason* (London: Profile, 2003); Hitchcock and Shoemaker, *London Lives*, pp. 168–80. On the 'mercantilist' approach to drunkenness, see also Brennan, *Public Drinking and Popular Culture in Eighteenth-Century Paris*, pp. 193–205.

21 Cited in Arthur Cosemans, 'Alcoholisme en drankbestrijding in vroeger eeuwen', *Handelingen van de Zuid-Nederlandse Maatschappij voor Taal- en Letterkunde en Geschiedenis*, 10 (1956), 117–18.

22 B. Ann Tlusty, 'Crossing gender boudaries: women as drunkards in early modern Augsburg', in Sibylle Backman *et al.* (eds), *Ehrkonzepte in der Frühen Neuzeit. Identitäten und Abgrenzungen* (Berlin: Akademie Verlag, 1998), pp. 185–98; Tlusty, *Bacchus and Civic Order*, pp. 115–46; A. Lynn Martin, *Alcohol, Sex, and Gender in Late Medieval and Early Modern Europe* (Basingstoke: Palgrave, 2001); Benjamin Roberts, 'Drinking like a man: the

paradox of excessive drinking for seventeenth-century Dutch youths', *Journal of Family History*, 29:3 (2004), 244.

23 Anne-Laure Van Bruaene and Sarah Van Bouchaute, 'Rederijkers, Kannenkijkers: Drinking and Drunkenness in the Sixteenth and Seventeenth-Century Low Countries', *Early Modern Low Countries*, 1:1 (2017), 24.

24 SAK, *OCAK*, 14643.

25 SABR, *AC-WEST*, 172–521.

26 SABR, *AC-WEST*, 398–1460.

27 Véronique Nahoum-Grappe, 'Le boire et l'ivresse dans la pensée sociale sous l'ancien régime en France (XVIe–XVIIIe siècles)', in *Histoire et alcool* (Paris: L'Harmattan, 1999), pp. 76–7; James Nicholls, *The Politics of Alcohol: A History of the Drink Question in England* (Manchester: Manchester University Press, 2009), p. 68; Mark Hailwood, '"It puts good reason into brains": Popular understandings of the effects of alcohol in seventeenth-century England', *Brewery History*, 150 (2013), 48–9; Cathy Shrank, 'Beastly metamorphoses: losing control in early modern literary culture', in Jonathan Herring *et al.* (eds), *Intoxication and Society: Problematic Pleasures of Drugs and Alcohol* (Basingstoke: Palgrave Macmillan, 2013), p. 196.

28 Ferdinandus Loys, *Den nieuwen spiegel der jongheyd, of gulden A.B.C.* (Ghent: Judocus Begyn, 1772), p. 30. Compare Petrus Verheyen, *Ziele-spys ofte christelyke leeringe* (Antwerp: Hubertus Bincken, 1764), vol. 5, p. 185; Pauwels, *Rechtveerdeig klagt-dicht*, p. 28.

29 Vander Sloten, *Sermoonen*, vol. 4, p. 130.

30 Kant, *The Metaphysics of Morals*, p. 222.

31 FA, *V*, 103 (Jacob Mol 1750).

32 SAK, *OCAK*, 14643.

33 SABR, *AC-WEST*, 164–446.

34 CAB, *HA Trials*, 6920.

35 Cited in Willem Ogier, *De gulsigheydt, speel-ghewys vertoont op de kamer vanden Olyf-tack den 18. october anno 1639. binnen Antwerpen*, ed. Willem Van Eeghem (Antwerp: De Sikkel, 1921), p. xi.

36 Pauwels, *Rechtveerdeig klagt-dicht*, p. 85; Verheyen, *Ziele-spys*, vol. 5, pp. 189–90.

37 I elaborate on ideas of character and true nature in chapter 5.

38 Raoul Van Der Made, 'L'influence de l'ivresse sur la culpabilité (XVIe & XVIIe siècles)', *Tijdschrift voor Rechtsgeschiedenis / Revue d'Histoire du Droit / The Legal History Review*, 20:1 (1939), 74–6.

39 Filips Wielant, *Corte instructie in materie criminele*, ed. Jos Monballyu (Brussels: Koninklijke academie voor wetenschappen, letteren en schone kunsten van België, 1995), ed. 1, chap. 102; ed. 2, chaps. 58 and 85.

40 Fierlant, 'Premières idées', fo. 493r.

41 'Intention', in Philippe-Antoine Merlin (ed.), *Répertoire universel et raisonné de jurisprudence*, 4th ed. (Paris: Garnery, 1812–1825), vol. 6, p. 418.

42 Pellegrino Rossi, *Traité de droit pénal* (Brussels: Société typographique belge, 1850), vol. 2, pp. 7–11.

43 FA, *V*, 113 (Norbert Tomas 1778).

44 SABR, *AC-WEST*, 353–1054.

45 FA, *V*, 113 (Norbert Tomas 1778).

46 SABR, *AC-WEST*, 396–1440.

47 Cf. Dana Rabin, 'Drunkenness and responsibility for crime in the eighteenth century', *Journal of British Studies*, 44:3 (2005), 471 and 476–7.

48 Peter Scholliers, 'The medical discourse and the drunkard's stereotyping in Belgium, 1840–1919', in Alexander Fenton (ed.), *Order and Disorder. The Health Implications of Eating and Drinking in the Nineteenth and Twentieth Centuries* (East Linton: Tuckwell Press, 2000), p. 228.

49 NA2, *AC-BRA*, 1609.

50 SABR, *AC-WEST*, 310–620.

51 SABR, *AC-WEST*, 349–1014.

52 I discuss the terminology of passions, penchants and urges in chapter 5.

53 FA, *V*, 164, pp. 24–6 and index.

54 NA, *PCAP-C*, 620/A (Pierre Antoine Devos, 1751–1754).

55 SABR, *AC-WEST*, 353–1054, 396–1440.

56 Cf. Locke, *An Essay Concerning Human Understanding*, bk. II, chap. 27, para. 22.

57 Gerry Johnstone, 'From vice to disease? The concepts of dipsomania and inebriety, 1860–1908', *Social & Legal Studies*, 5:1 (1996) 37-56; Mariana Valverde, *Diseases of the Will: Alcohol and the Dilemmas of Freedom* (New York: Cambridge University Press, 1998).

58 NA, *PCAP-C*, 620/A (Pierre Antoine Devos 1754).

59 NA, *PCAP-C*, 606/B (Pierre Vanderstocken 1792).

60 'Passions', in Diderot and d'Alembert, *Encyclopédie*, vol. 12, p. 142.

61 Thomas Dixon, *From Passions to Emotions: The Creation of a Secular Psychological Category* (Cambridge: Cambridge University Press, 2003), p. 18.

62 Dixon, *From Passions to Emotions*, p. 62.

63 NA, *PCAP-C*, 587/A (Adriaen Leysen 1759).

64 SABE, *AC-ANT*, 1340.

65 SABR, *AC-WEST*, 164–449.

66 FA, *V*, 103 (Nijt van der Neusen 1752).

67 SABR, *AC-WEST*, 101–7.

68 SABR, *AC-WEST*, 184–640.

69 See also the discussion of remorse in chapter 1.

70 Dixon, *From Passions to Emotions*, p. 18.

71 Carol Z. Stearns, '"Lord help me walk humbly": Anger and sadness in England and America, 1570–1750', in Peter N. Stearns and Carol Z. Stearns (eds), *Emotion and Social Change: Toward a New Psychohistory* (New York, NY: Holmes and Meier, 1988), pp. 44–5; Susan Broomhall, 'Feeling the wynds. Media representation of affective practices in urban Scotland in the first half of the nineteenth century', in Susan Broomhall (ed.), *Spaces for Feeling: Emotions and Sociabilities in Britain, 1650–1850* (Abingdon: Routledge, 2015), p. 217.

72 Carol Zisowitz Stearns and Peter N. Stearns, *Anger: The Struggle for Emotional Control in America's History* (Chicago, IL: University of Chicago Press, 1986), p. 36.

73 SAK, *OCAK*, 15131.

74 Ulinka Rublack, 'Fluxes: the early modern body and the emotions', *History Workshop Journal*, 53 (2002), 1–16.

75 NA, *PCAP-C*, 631/A (Pierre Schepemans 1764).

76 SAK, *OCAK*, 8293.

77 NA, *PCAP-C*, 643/B (Ambroise Vrancx 1771).

78 Creasman, 'Fighting words'; Karl A. E. Enenkel and Anita Traninger, 'Introduction: discourses of anger in the early modern period', in Karl A. E. Enenkel and Anita Traninger (eds), *Discourses of Anger in the Early Modern Period* (Leiden: Brill, 2015), pp. 16–45.

79 Kamali, *Felony and the Guilty Mind*, pp. 93–163; Nathalie Zemon Davis, *Fiction in the Archives. Pardon Tales and Their Tellers in Sixteenth-Century France* (Stanford, CA: Stanford University Press, 1987), pp. 36–42; Dawn Keetley, 'From anger to jealousy: explaining domestic homicide in antebellum America', *Journal of Social History*, 42:2 (2008), 275–6; Barclay, *Men on Trial*, pp. 165–6.

80 Creasman, 'Fighting words', 6. Creasman refers to a 1654 legal opinion in Freiburg.

81 Fierlant, 'Premières idées', fo. 493r.

82 Jousse, *Traité de la justice*, vol. 2, pp. 614–15. Cf. Laingui, *La responsabilité pénale*, pp. 215–17.

83 Ute Frevert, 'Honour and/or/as passion: historical trajectories of legal defenses', *Rechtsgeschichte – Legal History* 22 (2014), p. 246.

84 Sibo van Ruller does not mention it in his study of grace in the nineteenth-century Netherlands: Ruller, *Genade voor recht*.

85 NA, *PCAP-C*, 631/B (Ambroise Vrancx 1772).

86 Aude Musin and Michel Nassiet, 'Les récits de rémission dans la longue durée. Le cas de l'Anjou du XVe au XVIIIe siècle', *Revue d'histoire moderne et contemporaine*, 57:4 (2010), 57; Pirotte, 'Les grâces du Vendredi saint', p. 75.

87 Laingui, *La responsabilité pénale*, pp. 217–18.

88 Wielant, *Corte instructie*, ed. 2, chap. 90. Cf. Laingui, *La responsabilité pénale*, pp. 303–14; Frevert, 'Honour and/or/as passion', 246.

89 NA, *PCAP-C*, 587/A (Pierre Van Quickelbergh 1760). It is unclear why the council chose to refer to this principle while it was of course also acceptable for a husband to kill while defending his wife against rape.

90 *Code pénal de 1810*, art. 324.

91 Rossi, *Traité de droit pénal*, vol. 2, pp. 11–16.

92 Frevert, 'Honour and/or/as passion', 248–9.

93 SABR, *AC-WEST*, 262–213.

94 Nathalie Zemon Davis, 'Boundaries and the sense of self in sixteenth-century France', in Thomas C. Heller and Morton Sosna (eds), *Reconstructing Individualism: Autonomy, Individuality and the Self in Western Thought* (Stanford, CA: Stanford University Press, 1986), pp. 55–6.

95 Martin, *Myths of Renaissance Individualism*, pp. 84–100.

96 Brian P. Levack, *The Devil within: Possession & Exorcism in the Christian West* (New Haven, CT: Yale University Press, 2013), pp. 196–7. Owen Williams

discusses a sixteenth-century English case of someone who successfully used this defence: Owen Williams, 'Exorcising madness in late Elizabethan England: "The seduction of Arthington" and the criminal culpability of demoniacs', *Journal of British Studies*, 47:1 (2008), 30–52.

97 María Tausiet, 'From illusion to disenchantment: Feijoo versus the "falsely possessed" in eighteenth-century Spain', in Owen Davies and Willem de Blécourt (eds), *Beyond the Witch Trials: Witchcraft and Magic in Enlightenment Europe* (Manchester: Manchester University Press, 2004), pp. 45–60.

98 Wielant, *Corte instructie*, ed. 2, chaps. 61 and 74.

99 Dries Vanysacker and Erik Aerts, 'Hekserijbestraffing met twee snelheden. Peilen naar geografische verschillen in de Zuidelijke Nederlanden', in Michiel Decaluwe, Véronique Lambert and Dirk Heirbaut (eds), *Inter amicos: liber amicorum Monique van Melkebeek* (Brussels: Koninklijke Vlaamse academie van België voor wetenschappen en kunsten, 2011), p. 322.

100 Edward Bever, 'Witchcraft prosecutions and the decline of magic', *Journal of Interdisciplinary History*, 40:2 (2009), 263–93; Brian P. Levack, 'The decline and end of witchcraft prosecutions', in *Witchcraft and Magic in Europe: The Eighteenth and Nineteenth Centuries* (London: Athlone, 1999), pp. 1–93; Marie-Sylvie Dupont-Bouchat, 'Sorcellerie et superstition: l'attitude de l'Eglise dans les Pays-Bas, XVIe–XVIIIe siècle', in Hervé Hasquin (ed.), *Magie, sorcellerie, parapsychologie* (Brussels: Editions de l'Université de Bruxelles, 1984), p. 83.

101 C. Douxchamps-Lefevre, 'A propos de la sorcellerie dans le Namurois au 18e siècle – le procès à charge de Joseph Saucin, manant de Spy (1762–1763)', in Marie-Sylvie Dupont-Bouchat (ed.), *La sorcellerie dans les Pays-Bas sous l'Ancien Regime: aspects juridiques, institutionnels et sociaux. De hekserij in de Nederlanden onder het Ancien Regime: juridische, institutionele en sociale aspecten* (Heule: UGA, 1987), pp. 71–7; Michel Porret, *Sur la scène du crime: pratique pénale, enquête et expertises judiciaires à Genève (XVIIIe–XIXe siècle)* (Montréal: Presses de l'Université de Montréal, 2008), pp. 30–47.

102 Roy Porter, 'Witchcraft and magic in enlightenment, romantic and liberal thought', in *Witchcraft and Magic in Europe: The Eighteenth and Nineteenth Centuries* (London: Athlone, 1999), pp. 191–282; Dries Vanysacker, 'Enlightenment and witchcraft. The dangers of denying the existence of the devil', *Hexenforschung*, 114 (2016), 25–33; Bever, 'Witchcraft prosecutions', 283–5.

103 Marijke Gijswijt-Hofstra, 'Witchcraft after the witch-trials', in *Witchcraft and Magic in Europe: The Eighteenth and Nineteenth Centuries* (London: Athlone, 1999), pp. 95–188.

104 Jacqueline van Gent, *Magic, Body and the Self in Eighteenth-Century Sweden* (Leiden: Brill, 2009), chap. 2.

105 Marie-Sylvie Dupont-Bouchat, 'Le diable apprivoisée. La sorcellerie revisitée: magie et sorcellerie au XIXe siècle', in Robert Muchembled (ed.), *Magie et sorcellerie en Europe du Moyen Age à nos jours* (Paris: Colin, 1994), pp. 235–66.

106 Christine Van De Steene, *Satan en zijn trawanten volgens de achttiende-eeuwse predikatie* (Aartrijke: Decock, 1991), pp. 88–94.

107 FA, *V*, 126 (Isabella van den Broeck *et al.* 1792).

108 NA2, *AC-BRA*, 353–1197.

109 See e.g. NA, *PCAP-C,* 620/B (Pierre Lambion *et al.* 1751–1753). O. Colson, 'La sorcellerie au pays wallon. Etat actuel de la croyance', *Wallonia*, 6 (1898), 55–64; Dupont-Bouchat, 'Le diable apprivoisée'; Gijswijt-Hofstra, 'Witchcraft after the witch-trials', pp. 115–16.

110 SABE, *AC-ANT*, 1228.

111 NA, *PCAP-C,* 587/A (Philippe De Gage 1760).

112 Hervé Hasquin, 'A propos d'exorcisme au siècle des Lumières. Les réactions d'un fonctionnaire "éclairé"', in Hervé Hasquin (ed.), *Magie, sorcellerie, parapsychologie* (Brussels: Editions de l'Université de Bruxelles, 1984), pp. 102–3.

113 SAK, *OCAK*, 8092.

114 I discuss this case and the history of witchcraft in the Southern Netherlands somewhat more extensively in Elwin Hofman, 'Heksenwaan. De nadagen van magie in de Zuidelijke Nederlanden', *Historica*, 40:2 (2017), 19–24.

115 NA2, *AC-BRA*, 304–680 and 177. Van Eeckhout's death is mentioned in State Archives, Leuven, *Registrar's Office of Humbeek*; marriage certificate of Elisabetha Van Eeckhout and Jacobus Herremans, 7 February 1826.

116 SAK, *OCAK*, 15281.

117 FA, *V*, 103 (Jacob Mol 1750).

118 Wielant, *Corte instructie*, ed. 2, chaps. 58 and 85.

119 Fierlant, 'Premières idées', fo. 483v. Cf. Joel Peter Eigen, *Witnessing Insanity: Madness and Mad-Doctors in the English Court* (New Haven, CT: Yale University Press, 1995), chap. 2.

120 Laurence Guignard, *Juger la folie: la folie criminelle devant les Assises au XIXe siècle* (Paris: Presses universitaires de France, 2010), pp. 37–8.

121 *Code pénal de 1810*, art. 64. Cf. Laurence Guignard, 'La genèse de l'article 64 du code pénal', *Criminocorpus. Revue d'Histoire de la justice, des crimes et des peines* (22 April 2016).

122 Laingui, *La responsabilité pénale*, pp. 195–7; Fierlant, 'Premières idées', fo. 487v.

123 Eigen, *Witnessing Insanity*, p. 55.

124 SAK, *OCAK*, 8092.

125 André Lefebvre, 'Folie (Morale)', in Diderot and d'Alembert, *Encyclopédie*, vol. 7, pp. 42–43.

126 Arnulphe d'Aumont, 'Folie (Medecine)', in Diderot and d'Alembert, *Encyclopédie*, vol. 7, p. 44.

127 Michel Foucault, *History of Madness* (New York, NY: Routledge, 2006), pp. 201–2; Dora B. Weiner, 'The madman in the light of reason: Enlightenment psychiatry. Part I: Custody, therapy, theory and the need for reform', in Edwin R. Wallace and John Gach (eds), *History of Psychiatry and Medical Psychology* (New York, NY: Springer, 2008), p. 267.

128 Weiner, 'The madman I', pp. 268–9.

129 NA, *PCAP-C,* 587/A (Louis Felten 1760).

130 Fierlant, 'Premières idées', fo. 490r-v.

131 SAK, *OCAK*, 6676.

132 On (homicidal) monomania and its challenges for the law, see Jan Goldstein, *Console and Classify: The French Psychiatric Profession in the Nineteenth Century* (Cambridge: Cambridge University Press, 1987), pp. 162–78; Sibo van Ruller, 'De territoriumstrijd tussen juristen en psychiaters in de negentiende eeuw', in F. Koenraadt (ed.), *Ziek of schuldig? Twee eeuwen forensische psychiatrie en psychologie* (Arnhem: Gouda Quint, 1991), pp. 23–33; Frédéric Chauvaud, 'Le prétoire, la monomanie et l'expertise judiciaire: la difficile naissance des "experts de l'âme" (1791–1832)', in Philippe Artières and Emmanuel Da Silva (eds), *Michel Foucault et la médecine: lectures et usages* (Paris: Kimé, 2001), pp. 213–30; Guignard, *Juger la folie*, pp. 80–4.

133 Edouard Ducpétiaux, *De la peine de mort* (Brussels: H. Tarlier, 1827), pp. 90–4; Edouard Ducpétiaux, *De la justice de répression et particulièrement de l'inutilité et des effets pernicieux de la peine de mort* (Brussels: Cautaerts, 1827), pp. 22–3.

134 Although it may be that some lawyers plead monomania, as I have not investigated pleas but only diagnoses in the case files.

135 Fierlant, 'Premières idées', fo. 490r.

136 SAK, *OCAK*, 10780.

137 SAK, *OCAK*, 15131.

138 Cf. Romy Gouverneur, 'La perception et la prise en charge des insensés dans le Namurois au XVIIIe siècle', in Sarah Auspert, Isabelle Parmentier and Xavier Rousseaux (eds), *Buveurs, voleuses, insensés et prisonniers à Namur au XVIIIe: déviance, justice et régulation sociale au temps des Lumières* (Namur: Presses Universitaires de Namur, 2012), pp. 83–113, pp. 88–93.

139 A similar evolution occurred in the English courts around 1800: Eigen, *Witnessing Insanity*, p. 136.

140 NA2, *AC-BRA*, 1734.

141 SABR, *AC-WEST*, 263–227. Eigen, *Witnessing Insanity*, p. 33; Joel Peter Eigen, *Mad-Doctors in the Dock: Defending the Diagnosis, 1760–1913* (Baltimore, MD: Johns Hopkins University Press, 2016), p. 1.

142 E.g. Romain Parmentier, 'Dans l'ombre d'un pendu: justice et mentalités autour du suicide à la fin du XVIIe siècle', *Dix-septième siècle*, 271 (2016), 322–4.

143 Fierlant, 'Premières idées', fos. 490r–91.

144 Cf. Julie Doyon, 'Les enjeux médico-judiciaires de la folie parricide au XVIIIe siècle', *Crime, Histoire & Sociétés / Crime, History & Societies*, 15:1 (2011), 5–27.

145 FA, V, 108 (Peter Claukens 1772).

146 FA, V, 107 (Willem de Naeyer 1768).

147 SABE, *AC-ANT*, 1228.

148 Guignard, 'La genèse', para. 15.

149 Eigen, *Mad-Doctors in the Dock*, p. 168.

150 NA2, *AC-BRA*, 1734.

151 SABR, *AC-WEST*, 263–227.

152 Sonja Deschrijver, 'From sin to insanity? Suicide trials in the Spanish Netherlands, sixteenth and seventeenth Centuries', *Sixteenth Century Journal*, 42:4 (2011),

981–1002; Parmentier, 'Dans l'ombre d'un pendu'. Cf. also Alexander Kästner, *Tödliche Geschichte(n): Selbsttötungen in Kursachsen im Spannungsfeld von Normen und Praktiken (1547–1815)* (Konstanz: Universitätsverlag Konstanz, 2012).

153 See e.g. the contributions to Jeffrey R. Watt (ed.), *From Sin to Insanity: Suicide in Early Modern Europe* (Ithaca, NY: Cornell University Press, 2004).
154 Andreas Bähr, 'Between "self-murder" and "suicide": the modern etymology of self-killing', *Journal of Social History*, 46:3 (2013), 624.
155 NA, *PCAP-C*, 575. See also Monballyu, 'De decriminalisering van zelfdoding', 450–9.
156 Fierlant, 'Premières idées', fo. 1027v.
157 E.g. FA, *V*, 106 (Elisabeth Pauwels 1765); CAB, *HA Trials*, 10364 (Quittelier 1778); CAB, *HA Trials*, 8213 (Fioccardo 1781), NA, *PCAP-C*, 575 (Simon 1792).
158 Rabin, *Identity, Crime, and Legal Responsibility*, pp. 101–2; Hilary Marland, 'Getting away with murder? Puerperal insantiy, infanticide and the defence plea', in Mark Jackson (ed.), *Infanticide: Historical Perspectives on Child Murder and Concealment, 1550–2000* (Aldershot: Ashgate, 2002), pp. 173–4; Dana Rabin, '"For the shame of the world, and fear of her mother's anger": Emotion and child murder in England and Scotland in the long eighteenth century', in Carolyn Strange, Robert Cribb and Christopher E. Forth (eds), *Honour, Violence and Emotions in History* (London: Bloomsbury, 2014), p. 80.
159 Likewise, the first explicit reference to puerperal insanity in a criminal trial in the (Northern) Netherlands occurred only in 1911: Willemijn Ruberg, 'Travelling knowledge and forensic medicine: infanticide, body and mind in the Netherlands, 1811–1911', *Medical History*, 57:3 (2013), 361.
160 SABR, *AC-WEST*, 200–784.
161 SABR, *AC-WEST*, 320–723, 323–758 and 323–747.
162 Ducpétiaux, *De la justice de répression*, pp. 21–4.
163 Cf. Eigen, *Witnessing Insanity*, pp. 179–80.
164 Guignard, *Juger la folie*, pp. 265–8.
165 Rabin, 'Searching for the self', 100–1.

4

The tears of a killer: practising sentimentalism and romanticism in criminal court

The Enlightened man was not only a man of reason and responsibility. The Enlightened man was also a man of feeling. In the course of the eighteenth century, English, French, German and American thinkers began to consider what we call emotions in a new way. Their novel approach to feeling lay at the core of the Enlightenment project to study human nature. Beginning in the early eighteenth century, English and Scottish philosophers such as the Earl of Shaftesbury, David Hume and Adam Smith, searching for a new principle to build a peaceful and moral society, developed a theory of 'moral sentiments'. Feelings of sympathy for others, they argued, formed the basis of conceptions of good and evil and would prevent total chaos in a society driven by self-interest. Their ideas strongly influenced French and German philosophers, who, like Jean-Jacques Rousseau, came to stress the virtues of pity as a natural and universal emotion.[1]

From the 1740s on, adaptations of these ideas spread through novels, plays and periodicals. Sentimentalist novels successfully invited their readers to sympathise with characters who dragged themselves from one heartbreaking incident to another, while literary magazines recommended a certain 'sensibility' to their readers.[2] Sensibility lost many of its intellectual aspects and became a cult of visible emotional expression. Soon, displaying a general sensibility became a common feature of letters, speeches, sermons, memoirs and personal diaries all over Europe. Tears, in particular, developed into an important means to show that one was a sensitive man or woman, concerned about the fate of his or her fellow human beings – for this reason, the eighteenth century has been dubbed 'the weeping century'. Only by the end of the century, the sentimental style began to be seriously criticised.[3]

Some studies have suggested that sensibility was crucial for the formation of an inner self. Scholars such as Roy Porter and Lynn Hunt have argued that the culture of sensibility promoted a greater sense of interiority. The great stress on feeling in novels and letters required that people practised an inner core from which these feelings came forth.[4] Other scholars, particularly Dror Wahrman and Sarah Knott, have disputed this view. They have argued that with its stress on outer sensations and fellow feeling, the culture of sensibility did not promote a sense of interiority, but rather an outward orientation. The feelings that were central to sensibility did not originate deep inside the self, but from exterior impressions. Interiority was not brought about by sensibility or the sentimental novel. The self propagated by sensibility was socially constituted and socially oriented.[5]

I propose that sensibility worked to promote both social and inner orientations. On the one hand, it was occupied with outward expression, especially through the use of tears, and with others, by the importance placed on sympathy. On the other, however, there was a distinct idea that these feelings were personal and interior. With this argument, I follow Nicole Eustace's study of emotions in the American Revolution. The ideals of sensibility might have been directed towards feeling for others, but they were equally working towards a more individualised and interior self. 'Achieving fellow feeling without personal feeling proved to be an impossible action', Eustace has noted. Therefore, '[t]he more sympathy was emphasised, the more profound the collective inward turn became'.[6] As such, the culture of sensibility laid the basis for the romantic culture of the early nineteenth century, in which less emphasis was put on feeling for others and public expression of emotions, and more on personal, deep feelings that were mainly practised in private. Sensibility provided a path towards a more individualised and more interiorised self that would radicalise in the early nineteenth century.

In this chapter, I investigate the cultures of sensibility and romanticism from the perspective of the criminal courts and assess its influence on the self.[7] Much of the historiography of sensibility has focused on sources of the upper middling sorts; this literature has hence concluded that sensibility was mainly an affair of the upcoming, consumerist urbanites.[8] I hope to balance this picture and show that people from lower social groups also took part in this culture.

I should make a short caveat about the terminology of 'emotions'. I have already discussed emotions occasionally throughout this book: in chapters 1 and 3, I have shown that emotions played an important role in the investigations of the court (practices of remorse, signs of guilt) and in the excuses of the defendants (losing self-control because of strong passions). But the term 'emotion' is problematic. While the word was known in the eighteenth century, it did not carry the same meaning as today, referring mostly to a sense of agitation.[9] Sympathy would generally not be considered as an emotion, while weeping could signify much more than only emotionality or sentimentality. Some scholars distinguished between 'passions' and 'affections' and 'sentiments'.[10] Nevertheless, I will use the term 'emotion' (and related terms such as 'feeling') as shorthand to refer to the variety of experiences and sensations that would today be characterised as emotions, without suggesting that they were or should be understood as all somehow similar to each other. I approach these emotions as practices, in the sense that Monique Scheer has proposed, and in a way similar to my approach to the self: practices of naming particular conditions, practices to evoke certain sensations, practices of portraying and interpreting bodily movements, practices to regulate other people's emotions. These practices did not simply 'reflect' inner feelings: emotions only emerged in their doing and saying.[11]

Angry men

'Pour la triste ville où je suis, c'est le séjour de l'ignorance, de la pesanteur, des ennuis, de la stupide indifférence'.[12] In 1740, Voltaire not only bemoaned Brussels' supposed lack of intellectual activity, but also its emotional culture. Brussels was a 'sad city' of gravitas, of boredom, of indifference. Indeed, he implied, no traces were found of the delicate *sensibilité* that people in Paris were beginning to value so highly. Although Voltaire, longing to return to his friends in France, was perhaps not the most neutral observer, before 1760, the increased display of emotions on the Parisian stages, for instance in the 'comédies larmoyantes', hardly resonated in the Southern Netherlands.[13] In the criminal court cases I analysed from between 1750 and 1770, I have also found no traces of the cult of sensibility.

Illustrative of the emotional culture in criminal trials is the case of Jacob Mol in 1750, which I discussed in the introduction. Asked why he had stabbed his wife, Mol told judges that it was 'because he had been in fury and huge anger'. Mol's parents petitioned for grace and the Antwerp judges were asked for their advice. They agreed that Mol had committed his crime in a rage. 'If the wickedness of a woman may excuse such an excess of rage', they observed, several witnesses had confirmed that Ketelaer was 'a veritable fury'. All things considered, the judges recommended, the case was suitable for receiving grace, as it had not been a premeditated crime, but 'a sudden rage', provoked by the victim's insults. Their advice was followed and Mol received grace on Good Friday.[14]

The emotional practices in Mol's case are typical for many cases of violent behaviour between 1750 and 1770. Anger is one of the most frequently mentioned emotions in the trial records I studied, particularly in homicide cases.[15] In the previous chapter, I have shown how this squared with ideas of irresponsibility and 'passion'. Here, I am more interested in how anger figured in people's stories as an everyday emotion. People generally said that someone was angry after an insult or accusation, upon which they started shouting or became violent. The fact that clerks recorded this as such shows that suspects, witnesses and magistrates agreed that anger was an emotion which was expected and understandable in these situations. They did not necessarily *accept* it, however, as they generally commented negatively upon anger. It always figured as an excess that people should have been able to control.

As I discussed in the previous chapter, for men, this excess was sometimes acceptable to the court, when their honour had been challenged. For women, in contrast, it was always an indication of their poor character. Men of all social statuses were sometimes said to be angry, but only a few women were called angry, and they were all of the lowest descent. While witnesses in the case against Mol indicated that both Mol and Ketelaer were continually cursing and fighting, witnesses only said that Ketelaer was 'an evil serpent of a bitch' and 'as vicious as a hellish devil'.[16] In the context of a trial, anger could only be understood as appropriate for people in a dominant position – anger was connected to power. As a result, in a legal context dominated by men, anger was not a part of the culturally acceptable repertoire of femininity. Women angry with their husbands were seen as out of line.[17]

For people not in a superior position, negative situations often resulted in reports of emotional practices similar to anger, but more passive. Although there was a great variety in these practices, I will group them as 'sadness', which I use as a generic description for more passive practices that were interpreted as related to regret, dissatisfaction, complaint and disappointment.[18] Trial records reveal both sad men and sad women, but the emotion was again most often reported among men. After Francis Verlinden had shot one of his hunting mates in 1752, he was 'inconsolable', witnesses testified, 'very upset and lamenting about the incident'.[19] Similarly, after Pierre van de Wiele had shot a man near Kortrijk in 1757, he claimed to be 'deploring the fatal moment day and night', as it had been an accident.[20] Both applied for grace, but only Verlinden was successful, as he had more clearly established that the victim had been a close friend and that his grief was therefore sincere. This illustrates that the court also evaluated emotional practices: naming emotions did not suffice; the circumstances had to be right.

When these and other men were sad, they made this clear through their facial expression, by sighing, lamenting or keeping silent, but not – or at least clerks never reported this – by weeping. This corresponds with a common historiographical theme that in this period and in a secular context, people did not consider weeping to be masculine, regardless of social status. Crying was only an accepted practice of masculinity in specific situations, for instance, at the death of a child or partner, and even then, men should avoid excess.[21] After he had accidentally fired his gun, numerous witnesses testified that Francis Verlinden was 'moaning heavily' and 'lamenting heavily' for days after the event, but no-one said that he had wept.[22] Similarly, after Peter Coelembier had killed a man in a pub fight in Kuurne, near Kortrijk, witnesses observed him 'pitying himself with great melancholy for having done an accident' and 'moaning and calling on God and his saints for solace'.[23] But the records did not report that he wept. This may indicate that these men had not wept or it may indicate that they *had* wept, but that witnesses had not reported this. Or it may even indicate that clerks had chosen not to write this down. In any case, it signals that male weeping was found inappropriate in these circumstances.

The only incidences of weeping reported before the 1770s concern women weeping after someone close had died. Desperate after yet another argument with his wife Catharina Devinck in 1752, Nijt van der Neusen had committed suicide. After Devinck found him, witnesses saw her 'in shock, lamenting and weeping so much'.[24] In 1759, neighbours were woken at night when they heard a young woman crying. When they came to see what was going on, they found that her father had stabbed her brother and run away.[25] In both cases, the shock of discovering the death of a close relative allowed a woman to weep. The records studied never reported that men in similar situations were crying. Weeping was more easily accepted as a practice of femininity.

The self that was practised in the emotional culture of the 1750s and 1760s was mostly outward-oriented. People became angry or sad because of external events; or because their own actions had unintended consequences. While self-pity and sadness suggest some sort of interiority and self-reflection, this provoked little explicit articulation.

Weeping for the killer

In 1771, upon hearing that Jean-Jacques Rousseau would be prosecuted in France, Prince Charles-Joseph de Ligne wrote a letter inviting Rousseau to join him on his estate in Beloeil in the Southern Netherlands: 'People cannot read in my country; you won't be admired nor persecuted'.[26] When Ligne met Rousseau afterwards and the latter said that he preferred to stay in Paris, Ligne replied, as he later recalled, 'with tears in his eyes', 'Be happy, sir. Be happy despite yourself'.[27]

Rousseau stood for the public and intense expression of feeling. His popularity in France coincided with the height of the cult of sensibility. In sentimental novels and bourgeois dramas, French citizens were confronted with an abundance of moral dilemmas and with characters shedding copious tears.[28] As argued by scholars of sentimentalism, such as Frank Baasner and William Reddy, this led to a 'trivialisation' (perhaps we should more neutrally call it a 'transformation') of sentimentalism in the 1770s and 1780s. Sentimentalism lost its intellectual aspects and the visible expression of sentiment became fashionable in all layers of society.[29] While earlier, men were not often supposed to weep, in this new emotional culture, things were changing: the 'man of feeling' was allowed to show his sensitivity, and even weep in public.[30]

Despite Ligne's disdainful remarks about the country's literacy, recent French literary products, including sentimentalist ones, were by the 1770s well distributed in the Southern Netherlands, even if original productions of sentimentalist work remained rare. Booksellers sold the most recent Parisian bestsellers, while book clubs promoted discussion of new ideas.[31] Since the 1760s, theatres programmed sentimental plays as well. Already in 1761, the *Annonces et avis divers des Pays-Bas* commented on 'the delicious pleasure of shedding tears' in a review of a performance of Diderot's bourgeois drama *Le Père de famille* in Brussels.[32] In the 1780s, some periodicals criticised French-loving 'sentimental lads'.[33] It should not surprise, then, that at the death of Empress Maria Theresa in 1780, Cornelis Franciscus de Nelis, who spoke a eulogy in Brussels, reported that the whole kingdom was 'in tears', which people 'shed with abundance'.[34]

In criminal courts, the emotional practices that I described in the previous section partially continued in the records of 1770s and 1780s. Men whose honour was challenged continued to be reported as angry and violent. Men and women alike continued to profess shock and sadness after committing or witnessing crime. People still shed tears after finding out that someone close had died. Remarkably, however, whereas between 1750 and 1770, I have not found a single report of male weeping, the records now revealed nine men to be weeping too – as compared to only seven women (in a total of sixty-two cases).[35] The numbers are not huge, but clearly contrast with the earlier period. Moreover, these men did not just cry out of shock for what had just happened, but they also expressed grief of a different nature.

Let me expand on two cases. The first one concerns Jacob Ceulemans, a miller in his twenties, living in Laken near Brussels, in 1781. While playing cards, Ceulemans got in a row with Jan van Heijmbeeck, who insulted him. Both were 'in gruesome anger'. After some arguing, Ceulemans walked away, with Heijmbeeck in pursuit. In a dark alley, they started fighting. Ceulemans pulled a knife, stabbed his opponent and ran off. Passers-by found Heijmbeeck and called for a surgeon, but his intervention was to no avail: Heijmbeeck soon died of his injuries. Later that night, Ceulemans went to the same surgeon, asking him to come to attend to his father, who was supposedly ill. While they walked together, Ceulemans asked him 'whether nothing had happened in the parish' and the surgeon told him that

Heijmbeeck had died. 'It's a sad time for the one who did it', Ceulemans replied. When they reached the mill where Ceulemans' father lived, the surgeon soon realised that no-one was ill. He saw Ceulemans go into the kitchen with his father and witnessed them weep together, as the father told his son to flee.[36]

A second case took place in Antwerp in 1782. A group of textile worker friends went to an inn for a drink. While heading home, they ran into a fight between Jan De Corte and another man, who objected to De Corte having looked into his daughter's eyes for too long. Things escalated and De Corte fled into his house. Some people followed him and fighting continued. Ten minutes later, the corpse of one of the textile workers was found in the house. De Corte was the prime suspect, but there were apparently no witnesses. When the victim's friends headed to the mayor to report the killing, people saw that they were weeping and moaning. When the judges interrogated them, they asked why they had done so. 'We were pitying the deceased, as well as his killer', one of them said. Another claimed to have said to his friends 'let us, instead of weeping, rather read a paternoster for his soul'.[37]

In these two cases, people explicitly commented upon men's tears. These men cried in a distinct way: they were not weeping alone, they were weeping together with other men. Moreover, certainly in the second case, they were not weeping out of shock or for their own sad fate, but because they sympathised with others. It is remarkable that in both cases, men were ostensibly eliciting compassion not only with the victim, but also with the killer – even if, in Ceulemans' case, this turned out to be self-pity. This agrees very well with the values of sentimentalism: men of feeling were not supposed to worry about themselves, but primarily about others.[38] All the same, these men were still closely involved in the situation they wept about: Ceulemans' father wept about his son's fate, and the textile workers' tears led judges to question whether the killer had not been a friend of them. While this is contrary to some sentimentalist authors who suggested that men of feeling should also feel for strangers, it agrees with David Hume's observation that sympathy was strongest when resemblance was the highest, and that therefore 'the sentiments of others have little influence when far remov'd from us'.[39]

Between 1770 and 1785, I have found roughly four scenarios in the trial records in which crying occurred. First, as in the previous period, some women cried upon discovering a dead body, out of shock. Men were never reported to be crying out of shock. Second, as in the examples above, some men and women were reported to weep out of sadness, perhaps even out of compassion. A third scenario has people weeping after they had done something, or something had happened to them, that they knew was reprehensible. It was a way of practising regret, shame or guilt. For instance, in 1777,

Catharina Tusson's daughter had had sex with a man and received money. She claimed that she had been forced to do so. To support her innocence, her mother said that she was 'still weeping every day'.[40] Similarly, while Peter Hengs was committing sodomy with an older man, he 'continually wept out of regret', despite his partner's reassurances.[41] Finally, crying could occur when people were in a very grim situation, as a practice of desperation and misery. When Jan De Corte continued to deny the murder allegations, judges saw fit to chain him in a dark and cold cellar, where during one visit, they found him weeping.[42]

The cult of sensibility is often associated with the 'middle class' or the 'bourgeoisie', as part of their attempts to distinguish themselves from the aristocracy on the one hand and from common people on the other.[43] I have not encountered any aristocratic weeping men in the court records, but that is probably due to their infrequent appearances in criminal court. The writings of the Prince de Ligne reveal that at least some of them happily participated in the new emotional culture.[44] The weeping men whom I have found, however, are certainly not all of the higher 'middle class': the textile workers in the case against Jan De Corte were not even able to write their own name, and millers Jacob Ceulemans and his father were hardly among the better sorts. Most of the people who testified about weeping would certainly not have read intellectual works on sensibility – although some of them may have seen a sentimental play or read a novel.[45] Most were skilled artisans, mainly associates and some masters: weavers, millers, cobblers. No journeymen or beggars were reported weeping, but people of the lower middling sorts did apparently take part in the new emotional culture. It seems to have had a wider reach than just the 'bourgeoisie'.

The increased – but still limited – reporting of male tears could again be interpreted in different ways. It could be that men wept more often; that witnesses reported this more often; that judges or clerks found this more noteworthy. But that does not change the conclusion that apparently between around 1770 and 1785 the official records of the criminal court, which resulted from a compromise between all the actors involved, show that it was not unthinkable that men, even those of the lower social orders, wept in particular circumstances. In contrast with the angry women, people did not evaluate this negatively. These findings suggest that, between 1770 and 1785, the culture of sensibility had an impact on emotional practices in the Southern Netherlands. However, these emotional practices were perhaps not so much influenced by an intellectual 'sensibility', as by a more visible and more tangible 'sentimentalism', which stimulated the overt display of tears. In plays, novels and eulogies, but also in society at large, people witnessed the rise of tears and learned its uses. The interactions and official recordings in criminal courts further normalised the new practices of weeping.

Suing with sympathy

In 1796, Jan Hofman's bourgeois drama *Den onbermhartigen schuld-eiss-cher* was performed in Kortrijk for the first time. In its opening lines, count Verhulst, the merciless creditor in the title, demanded immediate payment of overdue rents by the poor old Lambrecht. While Lambrecht lamented on his poverty ('That I had to be your debtor, I have deplored with bitter tears'), his daughter Lidia bemoaned the count's ruthlessness ('Your heart lacks all compassion').

Verhulst, however, would not bend, on the contrary, in all his villainy, he suddenly revealed Lidia's best-kept secret: that her so-called sister Julia was actually her illegitimate daughter. Lidia fainted. Upon recovering, she confessed to Julia that indeed, she was not her sister: 'No, my Julia! I am your own mother'. Only after many exclamation marks, suspension points, sighs and tears, it was revealed that the rightful heir of the county was not Verhulst, but Julia's father, Lidia's lover. When Verhulst was dethroned, but pardoned by the new count, he finally realised that greed had led him to abandon virtue, in particular compassion with the poor, and promised to mend his ways.[46]

In the last twenty years of the eighteenth century, the original production of sentimental works in the Southern Netherlands finally took off. Sentimental outpourings were no longer limited to eulogies. In the bourgeois dramas of middle-class rhetoricians such as Hofman in Kortrijk and Pieter-Joost de Borchgrave in Wakken, emotional display stood central.[47] Cornelis Franciscus de Nelis' collection of dialogues *L'aveugle de la montagne* opened with a recently blind father telling his moaning son not to pity him too much.[48] In 1785, the *Vlaemschen Indicateur* published a story about a man pitying his suffering dog, while in another story, a young man wept out of sympathy with a stranger who had lost his house in a flood.[49]

In neighbouring countries, however, sentimentalism was starting to receive criticism. At the end of the eighteenth century, the 'man of feeling' who recited poetry and wept in sympathy with the sad fate of his fellow human beings was increasingly considered unmanly. The cult of sensibility was found to be passive, lacking in activity. Feelings had to be put into action.[50] People raised doubts about the sincerity of public emotional expressions.[51] The political turmoil at the turn of the century and the new focus on rigid gender identities left little room for male sentimentalism: honour once again became the guiding principle for male behaviour. The uses of tears as a practice of masculinity became more restricted, as male tears once again were more commonly seen as unmanly, shameful and unnatural. Sensibility became a female and private affair.[52] This renewed gendering of sensibility was what Mary Wollstonecraft argued against in her *Vindication of the Rights of Woman* in 1792: men had successfully claimed that they were governed by reason, not sensibility. While she was ambiguous about female sensibility, she nevertheless argued that for women, too, this 'play-thing of outward circumstances' must be 'moderated by reason'.[53]

The trial records I consulted from between 1785 and 1795 seem to confirm this picture. They reveal no more weeping men. Illuminating in this respect is the case of Maria Reps in 1789. Reps was married, but had been sleeping with another man, Joannes Dingemans, for several years. For unclear reasons – adultery was almost never prosecuted at the time – the case came to court and after her interrogation, the clerk noted that Reps 'has fallen on her knees before the commissioners and shown great grief over her mistakes, and cried bitter tears, begging and requesting' a settlement. When Dingemans was questioned, he too asked for forgiveness, but it the record simply stated that he requested a settlement for having kept a relationship with Reps while she was married. The woman wept, the man did not.[54]

The sentimental plays seem like an anomaly. They were, admittedly, late examples of the sentimental style. But they already bear the mark of changing emotional practices, for, while Lambrecht claims to have wept bitterly over his debts, clearly Lidia and Julia are most overtly sentimental, constantly trembling, sighing, weeping and fainting on stage. Moreover, the central theme of the play – the virtue of compassion – was still a pressing issue. As I mentioned above, sympathy and fellow feeling lay at the heart of the sentimental project. In the philosophy of sensibility, feelings of sympathy would lead to a better, more moral world.[55] This ideal led to a more positive appreciation of emotions and especially of tears, as symbolised by the weeping men I discussed in the previous section. Slightly later, it also resulted in more people explicitly referring to sympathy in criminal courts. Thus, in the Southern Netherlands, the age of sensibility was not entirely over. While the most visible expressions of sentimentalism, male tears, were disappearing, its underlying principle started to flourish precisely in this period.

Between 1780 and 1795, sympathy and compassion were more often referred to in trial records than before. Of course, compassion had always had a place in criminal trials. When applying for grace, supplicants appealed to the compassion of the king. While this display of compassion was the prerogative of the sovereign, magistrates and prosecutors were asked for advice and also framed this in terms of compassion. When Peter Coelembier applied for grace in 1765, the prosecutor advised that his 'gruesome malice merits punishment rather than compassion'.[56] In the case of Nicolas Kreijsscher in 1772, however, both the judges and the prosecutor suggested that he was 'worthy of commiseration'.[57] Outside the sphere of grace, however, the language of compassion or sympathy was rarely spoken in criminal court. In his legal manual, J.G. Thielen warned judges that they should not let themselves be 'moved by misplaced compassion'.[58]

However, starting in the 1770s, the language of compassion began to occur in witness statements. Compassion occurs as an active sentiment, clearly rooted in ideals of Catholic *Misericordia*, in the idea that people had to assist fellow Christians in need to ensure their own salvation.[59] While these ideals were centuries old, they are not referred to in the trials of the 1750s and the 1760s. In 1774, however, a spinner told judges that she had employed and sheltered Anna Catharina Van den Rijn, suspected of infanticide, 'out of compassion'.[60] Another woman had lodged a suspected prostitute 'out of pure sympathy' in Antwerp in 1787, which yet another woman in Brussels had equally done 'out of compassion' in 1791, as the prostitute in question had been 'almost naked'.[61] These and other women, some of them literate, some of them not, used the language of compassion to protect themselves and take distance from the reprehensible individuals whom they had apparently supported. Surprisingly, perhaps, they used a language that was intended to connect people as a tool to stress difference and superiority. But the fact that they were able to use this language shows its growing importance. They practised a socially oriented self and stressed the prominence of feelings for others.

It was not only women who referred to this patronising form of *caritas*-like compassion. Men similarly used the language of compassion to create distance from other people. This could be particularly urgent for men suspected of sodomy. Such was the case for Peter Stocker, a cobbler tried in Antwerp in 1781. Two young men had told the judges that Stocker had seduced them and had intercourse with them. When the magistrates questioned Stocker, they asked him why one of them, Philip Mainard, had spent so much time at his house. Stocker said that Mainard came to his house because he did not have fire at his own place, and 'that he sometimes gave him some bread out of compassion', but denied all other allegations.[62] In the same year, when Joannes Le Febure claimed that Georges Beauclerk, Duke of Saint-Albans, had tried to buy his sexual services in Brussels, the Duke asserted that he had only given Le Febure a little money 'out of compassion'.[63]

In the 1780s, this form of compassion was joined by another, more passive and more egalitarian form. This form was often called 'sympathy' in English literature, but contemporaries in the Southern Netherlands do not seem to have made such a difference between terms like 'compassie', 'meedoogen' or 'medelijden' – they could all refer to both active, patronising and passive, egalitarian sentiments.[64] The more egalitarian sentiment can be witnessed in the cases that I discussed in the previous section: the companions of Jan de Corte wept out of sympathy with the victim and the perpetrator of the crime, while Jacob Ceulemans expressed his pity for the killer (although it was ill-disguised self-pity). People also testified of such passive forms of compassion during the revolutionary turmoil of the late 1780s and early 1790s. The case against Joannes Bulens in 1791 is emblematic in this respect.

In October 1790, Willem van Kriecken, a supporter of the more radical revolutionary faction, the Vonckists, was publicly hanged by supporters of the opposing faction, the Statists, among them Joannes Bulens. Although the Statists were in power at the time, the hanging had not been officially sanctioned. Shortly afterwards, the Austrian government was restored and in early 1791, the perpetrators of the hanging were prosecuted. Witnesses of the execution, which had taken place on the Grand Place in Brussels, were plenty. However, many of the witnesses allegedly left after they had become aware of what was happening. One twenty-eight-year-old fish seller told judges that he had encountered the crowd escorting their victim and 'seeing this, he felt great compassion, and quickly retired'. When he later saw them again on the Grand Place, he 'couldn't bear to watch' and left. Many other witnesses, all men of the middling sorts, testified that they were unable to watch such atrocities because they sympathised with the victim, or that they were perturbed afterwards.[65] The state of 'shock' that many witnesses testified of is testament to the sensibilities of the time.[66] It also shows that compassion was not only a practice of social orientation, but also of individuality and interiority.

Even prosecutors started to frame their demands in terms of sympathy and compassion. They traditionally took the harsh stance. While they could show clemency by not prosecuting someone, when they did prosecute, their most affectionate outpourings were calls for severity and, though infrequently, impatience or anger. In the case against Joannes Bulens, however, the prosecutor used the language of sympathy: the defendant had been granted a solicitor, who was stalling the case, to the annoyance of the prosecutor. He claimed that the solicitor was acting against the interests of his client and portrayed himself as concerned with the well-being of 'the poor prisoner', whom the solicitor 'made suffer in prison all this time'. Given that Bulens could be convicted to death, we should probably not take the prosecutor at his word, but it is significant that he used the language of sympathy to make his case.[67]

Sympathy, it could be said, had become an intrinsic part of criminal justice, just like anger had been before. In Kortrijk in 1788, Augustin Strobbe even went so far as to suggest that the display of sympathy destroyed his guilt. In 1787, Strobbe was drinking in an inn. The innkeeper refused to serve Strobbe any more beer, judging that he was already too drunk. Strobbe answered that he still had all his strength and to prove this he went outside to move a cart. The owner of the cart, however, tried to stop Strobbe from doing so. Strobbe then hit the owner, who fell badly, had a severe head injury and died several weeks later. In his defence, Strobbe's solicitor argued that Strobbe was acting 'uncontrollably and tempered'. Moreover, the solicitor continued, after the fall, Strobbe had helped to carry his victim to his house, 'which sympathy clearly shows that the defendant was not in wrath'.[68] As the excuse value of anger had diminished, defendants could now use sympathy to remove guilt.

A form of sensibility closer to its intellectual origins thus found its way into the criminal courts and into society through the language of sympathy and compassion, be it slightly later than the language of tears. In its totality, sensibility stimulated a socially oriented self: the origins of feeling were supposed to be social – the suffering of others – and the expression of feelings was supposed to be social – public tears. Nevertheless, the culture of sensibility also implied individuality and interiority, as in practice, most people felt about themselves and people close to them, and often in semi-private settings. Their sensibility was portrayed as an essential part of themselves. When people claimed that *they* could not bear to watch others suffer, they implied that this was a strong feeling within themselves – not simply a social orientation.

Save your tears

'Who will relieve me of the sighs and tears', baron Frédéric de Reiffenberg sighed in 1825, 'of this bland writer who complains without pain'. He was not at all impressed by the weeping and sighing youth, who 'defamed the existence without having lived' (note that Reiffenberg was only thirty years old himself). 'Renounce, my friend, renounce this vain mania, and cease this crying to prove your genius'. For Reiffenberg, a member of the Belgian intellectual elite – he was a member of the Royal Academy for Science and the Arts and would later become head of the National Library – the sentimentalist movement had gone out of fashion.[69] Public displays of feeling through tears and sighs had become a sign of superficiality rather than of sophistication.

Reiffenberg did not object to all sentimentality, however. Indeed, he told the fictional youngsters devoured by *Weltschmerz*, 'I have suffered more than you'. He had been an orphan, 'alone, thrown in the world at the end of childhood'. But God had 'taught [him] to suffer without murmuring'. Rather than praising others for their sympathies with the world's evils; rather than feeling compassion for their sorrows, he stressed that his own life (as an orphan of noble ancestry) was more pitiable. Rather than eliciting feeling for others, he elicited feeling for himself. And preferably, sorrow was not publicly expressed in sighs and tears, but borne without murmuring.[70]

Reiffenberg was hardly a full-blown romantic. Although he was familiar with French romanticist work, he generally showed little concern for exploring his deepest inner depths.[71] He is generally characterised as an eclectic; in many ways he adhered to the eclectic ideas of the French philosopher Victor Cousin.[72] At the same time, Reiffenberg portrayed many traits of a sort of 'everyday romanticism' that was in vogue in Belgium and France in the 1810s and 1820s.[73] With the romantics, Reiffenberg shared his distaste of the Enlightenment *philosophes* and the French Revolution. Their philosophy of fragmentation, he argued, had brought about 'immorality, dizziness, disorder and atheism'. It had resulted in the violence of the revolutions.[74] Reiffenberg denounced Robespierre, the *philosophes* and their sentimental style. True feeling was experienced in private.

The early nineteenth century thus saw the waning of sentimentalism as a style of public emotional expression. Speaking of an 'erasure' of sentimentalism, as William Reddy does for France, is perhaps too strong.[75] Sentimentalist outpourings continued in the early nineteenth century, and the distinction with romantic sentiments is not always clear cut. The 'progressive' authors of the late eighteenth century, like Hofman and De Borchgrave, continued to produce new work after 1800, and they continued to write sentimental scenes; if perhaps less explicitly than before. Sentiment was also heavily present in poetry (and other writings) about love and love-sickness.[76] With some exceptions, most sentimental scenes took place in private settings, alone or among intimate friends or family. After the horror of the violence of the French Revolution and the Napoleonic wars, sentimentalism remained very important in shaping love and affective family life, but lost its currency in public settings.[77]

As we have seen, male tears were already disappearing in the trial records of the Southern Netherlands after 1785, even if people still praised the virtues of sympathy. There seems to have been a short-lived revival of the sentimental style in the early days of the new regime, between 1795 and 1800. In that period, the records of the forty-one cases I studied mention eight weeping men (including two adolescents), and only five weeping women. Cobbler Gerard Cosijn, for instance, had fought his father, who later died as a result of his injuries. Cosijn's partner testified that when Cosijn got home, 'he started crying' and complained about his relationship with his father.[78] Two years later, scutcher Martin Cuvelier told a witness that 'I have wept that I have killed Martijn Van Dooslaere', adding that he had helped to bring his victim home.[79] In 1799, finally, day labourer Guillaume Durnez confessed that after he had (allegedly by accident) shot his uncle, 'he left, weeping, and went home without saying anything'.[80]

These men wept as a practice of remorse, to show their families, friends or judges that they regretted their actions. Note, however, that in the 1750s and 1760s, men in similar situations practised regret by sighing and lamenting, but stopped short of weeping (or clerks did not write this down). The influence of a more positive appreciation of male tears is therefore still visible in the narratives of the 1790s.

The case record of Dominique Vandenbroeck, a weaver and innkeeper in 1799, contained even more explicit sentimental scenes. Vandenbroeck was suspected of the murder of his wife. According to the public prosecutor, he had hit his wife to death and then fled the scene. According to Vandenbroeck himself, she had been very drunk and had had a bad fall, resulting in her death. While he went to the city to borrow money for her funeral (so he later declared), he had heard that magistrates were at his house to arrest him and fled. He had stayed away out of shame for not having properly buried his wife. At his house, he had left a note, explaining that his wife had been 'seduced by jenever', and asking the people who found the note to 'pray for the soul of the woman and especially the man', and to 'look after the children'.

His children were the reason why Vandenbroeck came back after having been in Germany for six weeks. He returned to his house, but did not dare to enter. Through a window, he saw his children play. 'And not having the strength to support this spectacle, he went to lie down on the dunghill, where he has wept severely'. Because he felt that he could not help his children, he then left the town again for some time. When he returned, again to see his children, police officers arrested him. In Vandenbroeck's story, weeping was a sign of love for his children and his regrets about his inability to provide them with sufficient care. He explicitly tried to elicit compassion with his situation. This seems to have been convincing, for he was found innocent.[81]

The case of Henry Janssens in 1800 also contained an explicit sentimental scene, but at the same time shows the waning of sentimentalism. The forty-eight-year-old day labourer was suspected of poisoning his wife. The prosecutor argued that he had had many rows with his wife, continuously drank too much, neglected his work and sold their housewares to sustain his drinking habits. He had also threatened to kill his wife. The afternoon before he had presented his wife with poisoned sausages, witnesses had seen him in a pub, where his wife came to fetch him. As he saw his wife, 'he burst out into tears' and said 'go away, for when I see you...'. The prosecutor interpreted this as a sign of remorse for his vile plans, as some sort of scruples. This public display of sentiment surprised the witnesses in the pub, to the extent that 'it was still the subject of conversation the next day'. While sentimentalism was therefore still reported, it was commented upon as a strange event in the local community.[82]

After 1800, the number of weeping men reported in the trial records declined sharply. Between 1801 and 1830, only six men were reported as weeping, as opposed to twenty-eight women (on a total of 208 cases). All of the men wept out of regret or for themselves, rather than for the fate of others. In 1805, day labourer Jean Joseph Ladon was suspected of having killed his father by hitting him with a pair of fire tongs. Among the evidence against him were witness statements of people who had seen him 'testify of much regret' and heard him saying that 'he desired to be dead'. As his father lay on his deathbed, witnesses saw Ladon asking him for a pardon, praying and weeping.[83] In 1810, labourer Jean Ronse had 'his soul touched & tears in his eyes' as he finally told his interrogators that he would confess, after they had presented him with 'overwhelming' evidence.[84] Similarly, after farmer Pieter Deplace had killed his wife in 1828, he went to the local officer of justice to confess his crime. He grabbed him by his jacket while 'weeping and crying and saying Jesus Mary up to three times while trembling, adding I have done an accident'. The shock of killing his wife and confessing his crime brought Deplace to tears.[85] The same story for craftsman Joannes Baptiste Van Kerkhoven: in 1829, a man testified that Van Kerkhoven had come to his place and 'while weeping confessed that he was the perpetrator of the assault'. He asked the witness in question to testify in his favour should a trial follow, fearing that he would have to spend the rest of his life in prison.[86] Shock, regret and fear seemed to bring men to tears (and even then only rarely), rather than compassion or sympathy.

The decline of sentimentalism is sometimes linked to the French Revolution and the violence of the Terror – in this view, the fall of Robespierre epitomises the end sentimentalism.[87] My findings in the legal archives do not seem to confirm this; indeed, the Southern Netherlands saw perhaps a short revival of sentiment in the first years of the French annexation, after the Terror and Robespierre's fall. It rather seems that the waning of sentimentalism coincided with the decline of the *Directoire*, with the ascent of Napoleon and with the coming of the Napoleonic wars. Napoleon and his regime were distinctly unsentimental.[88]

But even the Napoleonic regime did not entirely erase all traces of sentimentalism. Certainly, people tended to take their explicit distance from sentimentalism. Reiffenberg and others explicitly denounced the 'seas of tears' that had been fashionable before: many people found sentimentalism unmanly.[89] But while the weeping men became less common, they did not entirely disappear from the trial records. In line with the romantically inspired tendencies of the day, however, their tears became more individualised – they mainly wept for themselves – and more explicitly profound. When men were weeping, something was *seriously* wrong. Moreover, most tears were shed in private or semi-private settings: alone, with their close ones or when making a confession.[90] While this is not in direct contrast with the tears of the 1770s and 1780s – some of the weeping men in that period were also weeping out of regret, about their own sad fate and alone or with close ones – the less frequent appearance of weeping men and the very specific scenarios in which they wept show that something had changed. The self that was practised through feeling was less socially oriented, more individualised and more interior.

While male tears were in decline, female sentiment was blossoming. Weeping women were more than four times as frequently reported as weeping men between 1801 and 1830; which is even more significant as there were many more male suspects in my sample.[91] In many cases, women wept for the same reasons as men: after they had committed a crime – most often after committing infanticide – or when they were making a confession.[92] But their occasions for weeping were more diverse. As before, some women wept when they witnessed a dead body.[93] Unlike men, women were also sometimes reported to weep when something happened to their husbands, lovers or children.

In 1803, innkeeper and farmer Benoit Toulouse was suspected of murdering his former maid. After Toulouse had left the maid's house, witnesses heard his wife (who had had been waiting outside) weeping and cursing. While they walked home, Toulouse later confessed to his interrogators, 'his wife wept and lamented a lot' and said that 'if he had given the mortal blow, he had to flee abroad'. He implied that he had not wept.[94] In 1804, a witness reported that Marie Dirickx, who was illiterate, was crying when she heard that her husband had committed a crime.[95] Anne De Bruyn, a servant, ascribed her premature delivery, also in 1804, to the fact that her lover had been very ill, which had made her cry all the time.[96] In 1821, finally, Pieter Hendrickx, the local police constable, shot a man with whom he had a long-standing feud. When Hendrickx's wife learned this news, a neighbour heard her 'moaning and weeping bitterly'. The day after Hendrickx was arrested she went to a friend, who also testified that she 'was weeping a lot over this incident'. The friend tried to comfort her, saying that her husband must have been a vile man. Yes, she answered while weeping, adding that the incident could have occurred much earlier, but she had hidden his gun. On that note, she left, 'very dispirited and weeping'.[97]

Unlike men, people still expected women to feel for others, particularly for others they knew very well, and to practise these feelings with tears. They continued to practise a more socially oriented self. While it may not seem surprising that women whose husbands had committed a murder were weeping, nobody said that men had cried when their wives had committed crimes; nor did they frequently say this of women in the eighteenth century. It became acceptable for women and perhaps even expected of women that they felt and wept for the fate of their husbands and children; and it became acceptable to report these feelings in criminal court. As I will discuss more extensively in the next chapter, female tears even became 'naturalised': it was seen as part of a woman's constitution that she wept at particular occasions. Already in 1797, magistrates told a suspect, who said he had acted weirdly because his wife had been weeping, that 'there is nothing more natural than that a mother is sensitive when seeing her child die'.[98]

In emotional practices, gender difference was constructed and affirmed: in the early nineteenth century, women were becoming the 'weeping sex', and perhaps even more broadly, the 'feeling sex'. This explains – and is exemplified by – a phenomenon that we have encountered in chapter 1. As interrogation techniques became more sophisticated in the early nineteenth century, women accused of infanticide in particular were put under much emotional pressure. Interrogators confronted them with the corpse of their supposed infant or with its clothes. They asked them whether they did not feel 'interior movements'. While interrogators also used intricate techniques on men, they were rarely as explicitly emotional. Interrogators seemed to suspect that they would yield more success with women.

Indeed, when a woman was *not* emotional after something terrible had happened, this was sometimes interpreted as a sign of their guilt in the early nineteenth century. Emotionlessness had also been noted before, and also of men, but in different contexts. If a crime had been committed 'in cold blood', this was more serious than when it had happened in 'a moment of heat', as we have seen in chapter 3. But what was new in the early nineteenth century was the interest in emotionlessness not at the moment of the crime, but afterwards – and this interest was particularly strong when the suspects were women. In 1812, for instance, a clerk noted that Elisabeth Fisscher, a servant, did 'not appear very distressed' when she made her confession.[99] In 1823, a magistrate asked witnesses whether they had noticed anything about Joanna Mees, an illiterate woman on poor relief, when a child was found in the privy. Two witnesses declared that they had 'found no dismay' in her and that she was 'of a cold mind [*gemoed*]'. The alderman who had first interrogated her declared that she was 'not dismayed' and the local clerk confirmed that she was 'looking not dismayed at all' during the interrogation.[100] Both Fisscher and Mees had confessed to infanticide. The remarks on their emotions only served as character testimony: they were cruel women, incapable of proper feeling.

Judges were perhaps most far-going in the case of Hermina Van Welbergen in 1824. Van Welbergen was suspected of murdering her husband, a soldier, but she denied the accusations, claiming that her husband had been injured when he came home and had later died of his injuries. The police commissioner who was investigating the case was convinced of her guilt. Therefore, 'in order to see Hermina Van Welbergen, if she has caused the death of her husband, have remorse over her crime & if such is not existent, at least see her become sensitive over her loss', he decided to take her to see the corpse of her husband. But Van Welbergen did not become sensitive: 'we have observed nor despair, nor sadness in her, having showed herself entirely insensitive'. The other people present in the room testified of their surprise at this behaviour. In the end, the judge of instruction concluded that 'the cold-bloodedness and indifference that you have shown at various unhappy occasions has made you highly suspect'.[101] A woman who did not feel was seen as a monster – and very likely the perpetrator.

Magistrates rarely made such analyses for men. Only in the case of Yves Delva – whose sanity was questioned, as discussed in chapter 3 – was his lack of feeling made into an issue. Even men, this case makes clear, were not supposed to be entirely cold-blooded after they had committed murder.[102] In general, however, the courts expected men to express their emotions less publicly and in a more controlled way than women. As we have seen in chapter 2, and as has been extensively argued by scholars such as Martin Wiener and William Reddy, people commonly expected men to behave reasonably and responsibly, in accordance with rules of honour and personal interest.[103] The criminal trial records reflect this gendered approach to feeling. Interrogators reported and expected uncontrolled sentiment more often of women and were more surprised when they did not show feeling.

The case against Constant Pringiers and Barbara Dufossé exemplifies the tensions around proper gendered feelings in the early nineteenth century. In 1829, innkeeper Peter Van Craeyneste was found dead in his home in Kortrijk. Although his wife and children first claimed that he had fallen off the stairs, it soon transpired that Van Craeyneste's wife Barbara Dufossé was in fact having an affair with Constant Pringiers, and that the latter had beaten Van Craeyneste. Dufossé was, moreover, suspected of having assisted in the maltreatments of her husband by holding him, rendering him defenceless. All suspects and most witnesses in this case were illiterate. Nevertheless, several witnesses testified about Dufossé's harshness. Her maid declared that while Pringiers was beating her husband, she said 'let it be; he has to be beaten to death one time, he has brought me enough sorrow'. At Van Craeyneste's funeral, witnesses had seen that Dufossé's brother reprimanded his sister over her behaviour and 'burst into tears over the loss of his brother-in-law'. While weeping at funerals was not unheard of for men, Dufossé told her brother off: 'you'd better save your tears to cry when I will be exposed on the market square of Kortrijk, and even then, I will not cry'. She suggested that his abundant tears were inappropriate and that she herself had more control over her feelings. But this capacity did not play to her advantage: witnesses denounced her lack of feeling over the death of her husband. The indictment retained these opinions and portrayed Dufossé as a woman devoid of proper feelings for her husband. Although the evidence against her was meagre, she was found guilty of assault and battery (not of complicity to murder) and convicted to two years of imprisonment and a fine.[104]

What the tears of a killer can tell us

The history of emotions allows us to approach the history of the self from a new perspective: emotions are practices that often travel between body and mind and between the inside and the outside. They are sometimes thought to be actively evoked, and sometimes seen as involuntary movements. They can be connected to an inner core or to a moment of dispossession. Feeling was a way to practise the self. The analysis of the cultures of sensibility, sentimentalism and romanticism therefore complements the insights in previous chapters and reveals an important shift in the way people practised emotions: as in many other domains, there was a turn inwards in the early nineteenth century. Through the changing emotional practices, the self increasingly gained depth.

Between 1750 and 1830, emotions functioned in roughly three ways in criminal trials in the Southern Netherlands. First, when the accused had practised certain emotions after their supposed crime, judges were eager to consider this as a sign of their guilt. For instance, in some cases judges asked suspects why they had been weeping, with a distinct indication that this confirmed that they had done something wrong.[105] A second reason for the legal interest in emotions was, as we have seen in chapter 3, that they could explain behaviour and even be seen as a reduction of responsibility. Defendants or witnesses sometimes cited a 'state of anger' or 'desperation' in their favour as a cause for doing something they would otherwise not have done. Finally, practising and naming emotions in court was a way of provoking sympathy among judges. Defendants took responsibility for their actions, but practised guilt, shame or regret, hoping to gain a more favourable sentence.

Given this pragmatic interest in emotions in the criminal justice system, the changing emotional practices in criminal trial records can be interpreted in different ways. Very minimally, they can be seen as mere changes in the fashionable writing style of trial records, or as changes in the (legal) priorities of judges, solicitors and clerks: as they became more interested in tears and sympathy, they started to record it more often; as they increasingly feminised tears, they hesitated to record male tears. A slightly broader interpretation could suggest that the emotional practices reported in criminal courts were indeed not the result of changing emotions among witnesses and defendants, but the result of their changing ideas about what judges wanted to hear. If people started to refer more to tears or to compassion, this interpretation would suggest, this was not because they wept more often or were moved by others' misery, but because they expected that judges wanted to hear this. The final and most generous interpretation would allow that people's changing emotional practices in court actually reflected their changing emotional practices elsewhere and that criminal court records therefore provide reliable evidence of everyday emotional lives.

None of these interpretations do justice to the emotional practices found in criminal court records. What I have argued in the introduction – with respect the practices of the self – similarly affects emotional practices: criminal trial records provide more than just a glimpse into the specific emotional setting of the criminal court or even into the emotional lives of the people involved. Criminal law and criminal trials not only reflected models of society, but also provided models for society. Criminal courts are 'emotional institutions'.[106] They are formative of emotions, shape their language, suggest which emotions are acceptable or commendable and which are not. In the courts, judges, prosecutors, solicitors, witnesses, victims and defendants evaluated, stimulated and repressed emotional practices. Criminal trials involved many people, who were influenced by its negotiations and decisions and who in turn influenced others, precisely because of the status of the court. Considering the criminal court as formative of emotional practices allows us to bridge the gap between court and society, just like the concept of emotional practices itself bridges the gap between expression and experience.[107] While we should not ignore strategic statements and power dynamics, what happened in criminal court should not be dismissed as *just* strategical. Like novels and magazines, trials and their records form people's emotions, even if, like these other sources, they only show a particular context of emotions.

The criminal records have allowed me to distinguish four phases – four emotional cultures, perhaps. These cultures did not simply 'succeed' one another nor were they monolithic and inescapable – like the self, emotions could always have multiple, sometimes contradictory meanings and people could negotiate them in different ways. Distinguishing them, however, allows me to reveal certain shifts in expectations and common practices. In a first phase, between 1750 and around 1770, anger and sadness were the dominant emotions I have encountered. Only women were occasionally reported as weeping. This changed in the 1770s and early 1780s: although weeping was still not reported very often, criminal courts now accepted that men also wept, even in public. These visible practices of sentimentalism were initially not accompanied by references to the all-important emotion of sympathy.

In the 1780s and 1790s, male tears were already disappearing again, while explicit references to compassion, sympathy and pity found their way into both trial records and literary productions. Between 1795 and 1800, there was a short revival of male tears, coinciding with the first years of the French occupation. Afterwards, tears and the public display of feeling were increasingly feminised, and women 'sentimentalised'. Many people believed that women were 'naturally' more emotional, while men should behave more honourably and reasonably; at least in most public settings.

The occurrence of weeping men in the Southern Netherlands coincided with what has been called a 'trivialisation' of sentimentalism in France and Germany in the 1770s and 1780s. With respect to this visible expression of sensibility, the Southern Netherlands therefore seem to have followed a similar chronology as its neighbouring countries. However, the intellectual underpinning of sentimentalism, the expression of sympathy, only came up much later than in neighbouring countries. In French, British and American novels, essays, newspapers and pamphlets, for instance, the language of sympathy gained currency from the 1740s on.[108] In Dutch literary reviews, in contrast, sympathy only became a popular theme from 1770 on.[109] Like in the Northern Netherlands, then, it seems that the subtler form of sentimentalism arrived later in the Southern Netherlands than its visible expression through male tears.

Similarly, the waning of sentimentalism coincides with the waning of sentimentalism in other countries. As the revolutionary fervour was ending, so were the emotional practices of sensibility. In the Napoleonic and post-Napoleonic days, sentiment was primarily reserved for women – even though men occasionally continued to be involved in sentimental scenarios. A romantic culture, in which feeling was more private and more profound, replaced the cult of sentiment.

Sensibility most visibly affected male emotional practices. Contrary to what is commonly accepted, I have found that the changing weeping practices did not only affect 'bourgeois' men: at least some noblemen and perhaps more surprisingly, some illiterate men also wept in a new way. With respect to references to sympathy, social and gender differentiation is less clear. The most visible changes here are among prosecutors and solicitors, but lower middling men and women, literate and illiterate, also began to refer more often to various forms of compassion and sympathy. The culture of romanticism brought important changes to gendered emotional practices: weeping became more inherently feminine, to the extent that it came to be seen as problematic when women did not cry in certain circumstances. Male tears were increasingly relegated to private life.

In many ways, this chapter confirms the findings of William Reddy and others concerning France. But in some ways, what I have found is more radical than what Reddy has suggested. Reddy's analysis mainly uses printed sources. Largely relying upon Sarah Maza's analysis of pre-revolutionary *causes célèbres*, Reddy also integrates sentimentalism in (civil) trials in his argument. For his argument on the erasure of sentimentalism in the early nineteenth century, he refers to civil trials again, primarily as the press reported them. Reddy argues that civil cases were more concerned with everyday conflict than criminal trials and therefore less distorted.[110] As a result, however, he is mostly concerned with lawyers' pleas, rather than common people's testimonies. Even when he does attend to the individuals involved in the trial, they are mainly of the upper sorts: poor people more rarely went to civil court. By relying on criminal trials – which may have been quite disruptive but demanded an increased accentuation of emotional practices – I have been able to incorporate common people in my analysis. While their recorded words were always the result of negotiations with others, their involvement in the trial allows us to get a better look at the social differentiation of sentimentalism. My analysis shows that the changing emotional cultures of the late eighteenth and early nineteenth century were not only an affair of the rich and famous, but also affected common men and women. My findings mainly include day labourers, farmers, servants and artisans, some of them illiterate. The truly destitute were less present – I have not found many references to their emotional practices – but sentimentalism and romanticism were certainly not only 'bourgeois' affairs.

My findings also show the contrast with the emotional performances in early nineteenth-century Irish courts, as studied by Katie Barclay. In part, the differences may be due to different sources: whereas Barclay has studied press reports of public trials, I have primarily studied private, pre-trial court records. Both genres of trial reports had different aims and conventions. Whereas Barclay learns much about the reported behaviour of lawyers, magistrates and audiences, my sources mostly focus on suspects and witnesses. Yet it is striking that male emotional display remained, in the early nineteenth century, so much more visible in the Irish courts. Despite similar discourses of the necessity of emotional restraint, the practices of sentimentalism continued to dominate the courts for a much longer time in Ireland than in the Southern Netherlands and many other European countries.[111]

The transforming cultures of feeling reveal changing practices of self. The emotional culture of the 1750s and 1760s was oriented towards external events or unintended consequences of people's own actions. There was little concern for the personal experience of feelings. The arrival of sensibility, first with its focus on weeping and then with its focus on sympathy, brought about a more explicit social orientation of the self. In practice, however, it also stimulated interiority and individuality, as it seemed that most tears and most feelings of sympathy occurred in private settings, concerned close friends or family and were seen as something personal and inner. These practices radicalised in the early nineteenth century, as male feelings were increasingly oriented towards themselves and male tears increasingly implied profoundness. The male self was increasingly individualised and oriented towards the inner side. Many women continued to practise a more socially oriented self, as they occasionally wept for their partners' or children's fate. However, for them, too, feeling was increasingly deep and affected their whole being. Both men and women could use feelings to turn inwards.

Notes

1 On the intellectual origins of sensibility and sympathy, see Frank Baasner, *Der Begriff 'sensibilité' im 18. Jahrhundert: Aufstieg und Niedergang eines Ideals* (Heidelberg: Winter, 1988); William M. Reddy, 'Sentimentalism and its erasure: the role of emotions in the era of the French Revolution', *The Journal of Modern History*, 72 (2000), 119–24; Ute Frevert, *Emotions in History: Lost and Found* (Budapest: Central European University Press, 2011), pp. 153–205.

2 G. J. Barker-Benfield, *The Culture of Sensibility: Sex and Society in Eighteenth-Century Britain* (Chicago, IL: University of Chicago Press, 1992); David Denby, *Sentimental Narrative and the Social Order in France, 1760–1820* (Cambridge: Cambridge University Press, 1994); Annemieke Meijer, *The Pure Language of the Heart: Sentimentalism in the Netherlands 1775–1800* (Amsterdam: Rodopi, 1998); Dorothée Sturkenboom, *Spectators van hartstocht. Sekse en emotionele cultuur in de achttiende eeuw* (Hilversum: Verloren, 1998).

3 On the role of tears and weeping in sentimentalism, see Anne Vincent-Buffault, *Histoire des larmes: XVIIIe–XIXe siècles* (Paris: Rivages, 1986); Bernard Capp, '"Jesus wept" but did the Englishman? Masculinity and emotion in early modern England', *Past & Present*, 224:1 (2014), 75–108; Thomas Dixon, *Weeping Britannia: Portrait of a Nation in Tears* (Oxford: Oxford University Press, 2015), chaps 6–7.

4 Porter cited in Wahrman, *The Making of the Modern Self*, p. 186; Hunt, *Inventing Human Rights*, p. 48.

5 Wahrman, *The Making of the Modern Self*, pp. 37–40 and pp. 185–90; Sarah Knott, *Sensibility and the American Revolution* (Williamsburg, NC: University of North Carolina Press, 2009), p. 112.

6 Nicole Eustace, *Passion Is the Gale: Emotion, Power, and the Coming of the American Revolution* (Williamsburg, NC: University of North Carolina Press, 2008), p. 279.

7 The first three sections of this chapter are a revised version of an article published as Elwin Hofman, 'The tears of a killer: criminal trials and sentimentalism in the Austrian Netherlands', *BMGN – Low Countries Historical Review*, 132:2 (2017), 3–26. In contrast with the other chapters, I do not rely on the grace records here.

8 Barker-Benfield, *The Culture of Sensibility*; Dorothée Sturkenboom, 'Historicizing the gender of emotions: changing perceptions in Dutch Enlightenment thought', *Journal of Social History*, 34 (2000), 55–75; Knott, *Sensibility and the American Revolution*.

9 Georges Vigarello, 'L'émergence du mot "émotion"', in Georges Vigarello (ed.), *Histoire des émotions. T. 1: De l'Antiquité aux Lumières* (Paris: Seuil, 2016), pp. 219–24.

10 Dixon, *From Passions to Emotions*; Thomas Dixon, '"Emotion": the history of a keyword in crisis', *Emotion Review*, 4:4 (2012), 338–44. But see the qualifications in Kirk Essary, 'Passions, affections, or emotions? On the ambiguity of 16th-century terminology', *Emotion Review*, 9:4 (2017), 367–74.

11 Scheer, 'Are emotions a kind of practice'.

12 Voltaire cited in Bram Van Oostveldt, *The Théâtre de la Monnaie and the Theatre Life in the 18th Century Austrian Netherlands: From a Courtly-Aristocratic to a Civil-Enlightened Discourse?* (Ghent: Academia Press, 2000), p. 19.

13 Van Oostveldt, *The Théâtre de la Monnaie*, pp. 61–5. On the new theatrical fashion in Paris, see Colin Jones, *The Smile Revolution in Eighteenth Century Paris* (Oxford: Oxford University Press, 2014), pp. 59–60.

14 FA, V, 103 (Jacob Mol 1750).

15 Cf. Keetley, 'From anger to jealousy', 272.

16 FA, V, 103 (Jacob Mol 1750).

17 Sturkenboom, 'Historicizing the gender', 59; Gwynne Kennedy, *Just Anger: Representing Women's Anger in Early Modern England* (Carbondale, IL: Southern Illinois University Press, 2000).

18 Cf. Stearns, '"Lord help me walk"', pp. 51–2.

19 FA, V, 103 (Francis Verlinden 1752).

20 SAK, OCAK, 8343.

21 Capp, '"Jesus wept"', 75–104.

22 FA, V, 103 (Francis Verlinden 1752).

23 SAK, OCAK, 10790.

24 FA, V, 103 (Nijt van der Neusen 1752).

25 FA, V, 105 (Van der Goes 1759).

26 Cited in Friedrich Melchior Freiherr von Grimm and Denis Diderot, *Mémoires historique, littéraires & anecdotiques* (London: Colburn, 1813), vol. 1, pp. 57 8.

27 Charles Joseph de Ligne, *Lettres et pensées du Maréchal Prince de Ligne, publiées par Mad. la Baronne de Staël Holstein. Troisième édition, revue et augmentée* (Paris, 1810), p. 325.

28 Jones, *The Smile Revolution*, p. 61.

29 Baasner, *Der Begriff sensibilité*, pp. 333–46; Reddy, 'Sentimentalism and its erasure', 125–6.

30 Sturkenboom, 'Historicizing the gender', 60–4; Capp, '"Jesus wept"', 106.

31 Hugo De Schampeleire, 'Verplichte lectuur te Antwerpen en Parijs in de 18e eeuw. Een comparatief quantitatief leesonderzoek naar Voltaire, Rousseau en

de Encyclopedie', in Roland Mortier and Hervé Hasquin (eds), *L'influence française dans les Pays-Bas autrichiens et la Principauté de Liège au temps de Voltaire et de Jean-Jacques Rousseau* (Brussels: Université de Bruxelles, 1979), pp. 132–53; Karel Bostoen, 'Verlichte letteren in de Zuidelijke Nederlanden?', in Andreas Hanou (ed.), *Verlichte letteren in Noord en Zuid* (Leuven: Peeters, 2004), pp. 393–403, p. 396.

32 Cited in Van Oostveldt, *The Théâtre de la Monnaie*, p. 70.

33 Published in *Den Vlaemschen Indicateur* in 1787; cited in Jozef Smeyers, 'Mevrouw de mode in de Vlaemschen Indicateur (1779–1787)', in *Literair- en cultuurhistorische bijdragen: van Rousseau en Amerika tot Aalst en Brussel* (Brussels: Studiecentrum 18de-eeuwse Zuidnederlandse Letterkunde, 2004), p. 74. See also Verschaffel, *De weg naar het binnenland*, pp. 177–8.

34 Cornelius Franciscus Nelis, *Oraison funèbre de Marie-Thérèse* (Brussels: Lemaire, 1781), p. 3 and p. 23. Cf. Verschaffel, *De weg naar het binnenland*, pp. 228–35.

35 Note that as a consequence of increasing criminal litigation and better preservation, the number of cases for this period greatly exceeds that of the periods before and immediately after. This may have increased the probability of encountering weeping men. I do not think, however, that this significantly affects my analysis.

36 CAB, *HA Trials*, 6920.

37 FA, V, 116 (Jan de Corte 1782).

38 Eustace, *Passion Is the Gale*, pp. 244–7.

39 Cited in Frevert, *Emotions in History*, pp. 153–5. On the necessity of feeling for strangers, see Sturkenboom, *Spectators van hartstocht*, pp. 306–7.

40 CAB, *HA Trials*, 7673.

41 FA, *731*, 1514/2.

42 FA, V, 116 (Jan de Corte 1782).

43 Sturkenboom, 'Historicizing the gender', 62–3; Knott, *Sensibility and the American Revolution*, pp. 17–18.

44 See, for instance, his autobiography, replete with sentimental language: Ligne, *Fragments de l'histoire*.

45 On literacy in the Southern Netherlands, see Gerrit Verhoeven, '"Le pays où on ne sait pas lire": Literacy, Numeracy and Human Capital in the Commercial Hub of the Austrian Netherlands (1715–75)', *European History Quarterly*, 44:2 (2014), 223–43.

46 Jan Baptist Jozef Hofman, *Den onbermhartigen schuld-eisscher, of de deugdzaame in armoede* (Kortrijk: Gambar, 1796).

47 Verschaffel, *De weg naar het binnenland*, pp. 168–77.

48 Cornelius Franciscus Nelis, *L'aveugle de la montagne* (Amsterdam: Gabriel-Henri Nicolle, 1799), pp. 4–5.

49 'Merkwaerdig voorbeeld van getrouwheyd in eenen hond', *Den Vlaemschen indicateur*, 14:7 (13 August 1785), 106–8; 'Beloning der neerstigheyd', *Den Vlaemschen indicateur*, 14:22 (26 November 1785), 343–4.

50 Frevert, *Emotions in History*, p. 173; Halttunen, 'Humanitarianism', 308.

51 Reddy, *The Navigation of Feeling*, pp. 270–1; Jones, *The Smile Revolution*, p. 152.

52 Reddy, 'Sentimentalism and its erasure', 145; Sturkenboom, 'Historicizing the gender', 65–9; Capp, '"Jesus wept"', 107. This view has been complicated, however, in studies of successful politicians in the late eighteenth century, who continued to use tears in their self-fashioning: Edwina Hagen, 'Fashioning the emotional self: the Dutch statesman Rutger Jan Schimmelpenninck (1761–1825) and the cult of sensibility', *BMGN – Low Countries Historical Review*, 129:2 (2014), 138–62; David Andress, 'Living the revolutionary melodrama: Robespierre's sensibility and the construction of political commitment in the French Revolution', *Representations*, 114 (2011), 103–28.

53 Wollstonecraft, *A Vindication*, p. 110. See also Isabelle Bour, 'Epistemological ambiguities: reason, sensibility and association of ideas in Mary Wollstonecraft's Vindication of the Rights of Woman', *XVII–XVIII. Revue de la Société d'études anglo-américaines des XVIIe et XVIIIe siècles*, 49:1 (1999), 299–310; Boddice, *A History of Feelings*, pp. 118–24.

54 FA, V, 122 (Maria Reps 1789).

55 Sturkenboom, *Spectators van hartstocht*, pp. 299–303; Eustace, *Passion Is the Gale*, pp. 239–79; Frevert, *Emotions in History*, pp. 153–61.

56 SAK, OCAK, 10790.

57 FA, V, 108 (Nicolas Kreijsscher 1772).

58 Thielen, *Forme et manière*, pp. 53–4. The case was similar in England, where judges were expected to control their emotions in the court: Amy Milka and David Lemmings, 'Narratives of feeling and majesty: mediated emotions in the eighteenth-century criminal courtroom', *The Journal of Legal History*, 38:2 (2017), 164–5.

59 On the difference between *misericordia* and sympathy, see Frevert, *Emotions in History*, pp. 167–8.

60 FA, V, 110 (Anna Catharina Van den Rijn 1774).

61 FA, V, 120 (Catharina Van Laer 1787); CAB, *HA Trials*, 10071.

62 FA, 731, 1514/2.

63 CAB, *HA Trials*, 8209.

64 The same goes for the French terms: 'compassion', 'pitié', 'misericorde' and 'commiseration' could all be used in active and passive ways in the trial records, although 'pitié' has a more condescending connotation in intellectual culture. On the English and French terminology, see Katherine Ibbett, 'Fellow-feeling', in Susan Broomhall (ed.), *Early Modern Emotions: An Introduction* (London: Routledge, 2017), pp. 61–4.

65 CAB, *HA Trials*, 7124 and 8146.

66 More generally on the public's sensibility during executions, see Friedland, *Seeing Justice Done*, chap. 7.

67 CAB, *HA Trials*, 7124.

68 SAK, OCAK, 15131.

69 On Reiffenberg, see J. Stecher, 'Reiffenberg (Baron Frédéric-Auguste-Ferinand-Thomas de)', in *Biographie nationale de Belgique* 18 (Brussels: Bruylant, 1905), pp. 887–918.

70 Frédéric de Reiffenberg, *Poésies diverses, suivies d'épîtres et de discours en vers* (Paris: Dondey-Dupré, 1825), pp. 125–32.

71 On the characterisation of romanticism as concerned with uncovering inner depths, see Peter Gay, *The Bourgeois Experience Victoria to Freud, Vol. 4: The Naked Heart* (New York, NY: Norton, 1995); Tim Blanning, *The Romantic Revolution: A History* (New York, NY: Modern Library, 2012).

72 Kevin Donnelly, *Adolphe Quetelet, Social Physics and the Average Men of Science, 1796–1874* (London: Pickering & Chatto, 2015), pp. 37–8.

73 Cf. Jan Goldstein's characterisation of Victor Cousin as a 'generic romantic': Goldstein, *The Post-Revolutionary Self*, p. 155.

74 Cited in Donnelly, *Adolphe Quetelet*, p. 37.

75 Reddy, 'Sentimentalism and its erasure'.

76 See e.g. the poem cited in Jan Frans Willems, *Verhandeling over de Nederduytsche tael- en letterkunde, opzigtelyk de Zuydelyke provintien der Nederlanden* (Antwerp: Schoesetters, 1819), 228–30. See also Gustave Charlier, *Le mouvement romantique en Belgique 1815–1850*, 2 vols. (Brussels: Palais des Académies, 1948).

77 Cf. Reddy, *The Navigation of Feeling*, chap. 8. See also Andress, 'Living the revolutionary melodrama', 105.

78 SABE, *AC-ANT*, 70.

79 SABR, *AC-WEST*, 129–137bis.

80 SABR, *AC-WEST*, 137–222.

81 SABE, *AC-ANT*, 126.

82 NA2, *AC-BRA*, 1609.

83 SABR, *AC-WEST*, 184–640.

84 SABR, *AC-WEST*, 228–1081.

85 SABR, *AC-WEST*, 393–1414.

86 SABE, *AC-ANT*, 1583. His fears were correct: he was convicted to forced labour for life.

87 Reddy, *The Navigation of Feeling*, p. 201; Dixon, *Weeping Britannia*, pp. 108–11.

88 Jones, *The Smile Revolution*, p. 173.

89 Cf. Marleen Brock, '"Houdt ons voor geen sentimenteele knapen!" Natuur en emoties in Brieven, geschreven op eene wandeling door een gedeelte van Duitschland en Holland, in den zomer van 1809', *Tijdschrift voor Geschiedenis*, 126:4 (2013), 552–3.

90 Cf. Dixon, *Weeping Britannia*, pp. 141–5.

91 In 128 trials, one or more men were suspected, while in only 73 trials one or more women were suspected. 7 trials concerned suspects of both sexes. While witnesses could also be weeping, most of the reports concern suspects.

92 E.g. SABR, *AC-WEST*, 106–34, 200–784, 230–1097, 259–195, 394–1423; NA2, *AC-BRA*, 1685, 248–452, 2195; SABE, *AC-ANT*, 787.

93 E.g. SABR, *AC-WEST*, 235–1146; SABE, *AC-ANT*, 1100.

94 SABR, *AC-WEST*, 164–449.

95 SABE, *AC-ANT*, 371.

96 SABE, *AC-ANT*, 372.
97 SABE, *AC-ANT*, 1229.
98 SABR, *AC-WEST*, 116–81. Cf. Dixon, *Weeping Britannia*, p. 116.
99 SABE, *AC-ANT*, 787.
100 SABE, *AC-ANT*, 1288.
101 SABE, *AC-ANT*, 1340.
102 SABR, *AC-WEST*, 236–227. See the discussion of this case in chapter 6.
103 Wiener, *Reconstructing the Criminal*, chaps 1–3; Reddy, *The Invisible Code*; Reddy, *The Navigation of Feeling*, chap. 8.
104 SABR, *AC-WEST*, 398–1460.
105 E.g. in the case of Norbert Tomas: FA, V, 113 (Norbert Tomas 1778).
106 Biess *et al.*, 'History of emotions', 75.
107 Scheer, 'Are emotions a kind of practice'.
108 Rabin, *Identity, Crime, and Legal Responsibility*, p. 71; Eustace, *Passion Is the Gale*, p. 552n69.
109 Sturkenboom, *Spectators van hartstocht*, p. 296.
110 Reddy, *The Navigation of Feeling*, pp. 260–2.
111 Barclay, *Men on Trial*, pp. 113–14.

5

The ambiguities of nature: self-talk as a challenge and as an opportunity

In previous chapters, I have discussed how people practised different discourses of the self through regulations of the courts, through the use of criminal trials as technologies of the self and through interpretations of the self. I have not yet given much attention to the words people actually used to talk about the self, for 'self-talk' and for the conceptions of self this implied. That is what this chapter is about: the transformation of the self in criminal courts took place alongside a transformation of the language of the self. An important means to talk about the self were words relating to 'nature'. The tensions inherent in and between different words referring to some form of 'nature' illustrate the changes in the importance and morality of the self.

Nature had many meanings in the eighteenth and nineteenth centuries. People could talk about nature in a general sense, as 'human nature', or in a more individual sense, as an 'inner nature', as a means to talk about the self. Both conceptions of nature were increasingly important, and both could have positive and negative connotations. They could provide challenges and opportunities. Tracing the ambiguous meanings of the concept of nature in the discourses of criminal justice, I will show that there were important evolutions during the period under review: if nature was, in the second half of the eighteenth century, mainly seen as generalised and negative, and rarely discussed in criminal court, it became more positive in some instances in the early nineteenth century, and at the same time more individualised and more commonly mentioned.

Talking nature, talking self

Nature was a key concept for eighteenth- and early nineteenth-century philosophers. Whether their writings concerned law, politics, science, literature, theatre, morality or indeed, the self, nature seemed the unavoidable term to relate to, in descriptions of specific and local natures and in the search for the universal natural laws that guided the universe and humankind.[1] The ubiquity of nature was unhindered – and perhaps even facilitated – by its vagueness. The *Encyclopédie*, heavily relying on the seventeenth-century natural philosopher Robert Boyle, distinguished at least eight meanings of the term:

(1) The system of the world, the universe
(2) As in 'human nature' or 'divine nature'
(3) The essence of a thing
(4) The natural order as studied by physicists
(5) The opposite of the 'supernatural'
(6) The force of a body, as in 'his nature is strong'
(7) Divine provision
(8) God.[2]

The *Encyclopédie* thus portrayed nature as a concept with many meanings, but the overview lacked a sense of nature as a person's disposition or character – nature as (related to) the self. This meaning was discussed in a separate entry, under the headword 'le naturel (morale)', written by the 'slave of the *Encyclopédie*' (he wrote no less than a quarter of its articles), the Chevalier de Jaucourt. The natural, Jaucourt wrote, is 'the temperament, the character, the humour, the inclinations a man tends to from his birth'.[3] The dictionary of the *Académie française* gave a similar definition, both in the 1762 and the 1798 editions. Nature could mean 'complexion, temperament' and 'a certain disposition & inclination of the mind'.[4] For Jaucourt and many of his learned contemporaries, one of the meanings of nature was what we would call the self; nature was a means to talk about the individual psyche. It was the closest the *Encyclopédie* came to including a specific headword about the self – there was no headword on 'soi' and only a grammatical entry on 'moi'.

Given its cultural salience, 'nature' would therefore seem a good starting point to analyse self-talk in the criminal records. Remarkably, however, in these records, the word 'nature' (*natuur, natuer, nature, naturel*) was rarely used in any of the senses that the *Encyclopédie* described, or only tangentially. In my sample of trial records, people mainly used it:

(1) To refer to the divine order, as in the 'crime against nature'
(2) To refer to biological or physical patterns (e.g. 'death from natural causes'; or, three months ago, he had sex with her for the first time, so he could not be the father of her new-born child 'due to the course of nature')
(3) To describe a logical, self-evident course of action, as in 'naturally'
(4) To describe to what kind something belonged, as in 'the nature of the crime'

(5) As in 'natural child' to refer to illegitimate offspring
(6) To refer to semen (a meaning curiously absent from the dictionaries of the time).

A list quite different from the one in the *Encyclopédie*: the concepts of inner nature, human nature and nature as essence were missing. Luckily, Jaucourt's definition of the natural and the explanation in the dictionary of the *Académie* provide us with a set of related words to talk about nature as a part of the self – words that did occur in the trial records: *caractère, tempérament, disposition, inclination, penchant, humeur, passion, instinct*. Jan Des Roches' French-Dutch dictionary (1769) allows us to add related Dutch terms: *aerd, drift, genegentheyd, hertstogt, inborst, natuer* and *neyging*.[5] By tracing this set of words, we can uncover the meanings of nature and self not only in the learned communities of the *philosophes* or the *Académie française*, but also in everyday practice. At the risk of being rather enumerative, I will try to ascertain how people used these terms and how they related to the self. I will thus seek to uncover to what extent talking about nature implied talking about the self; and what this meant for the self.

Instinct and urge

Let us start with the least individualised of the terms I just discussed: 'instinct' and 'urge' (*instinct, impulsion, drift*). Instinct, the dictionary of the *Académie française* noted, was 'a certain movement that nature has given to animals'.[6] As the dictionary continued, and the trial records confirm, it was also said about humans when they acted without reflection. So in 1791, when Jacques Honton requested grace, he admitted that he had hit an assailer multiple times while one blow would have sufficed, but said that he had done so 'in a first moment of agitation and trouble where, when one is in danger, one obeys only his instinct'.[7] So, as in the many stories discussed in chapter 3, Honton claimed to have lost his reasonable self and reverted to a sort of natural, animal state which led him to commit atrocities. Similarly, in 1824, inhabitants of the Jodestraat in Antwerp complained against a brothel in their neighbourhood, arguing that the public women 'inflame in the children certain urges which are not proper'.[8] In both cases, people referred to instincts that were natural, universal and morally reprehensible. In a somewhat altered form, ideas of such natural urges that people need to repress continue to exist up to this day. People did not consider the instincts as inherent to the self, but more as part of a general human nature that the self had to control. The instincts were quasi-animal movements that were active when the self was displaced. Talking about instincts did not particularly contribute to a greater valuation of the self.

Humour and temperament

The term 'humour' (*humeur* both in French and in Dutch; but the word was infrequently used in Dutch, Des Roches suggested translating it as the catch-all *aerd*) was slightly more individualised and related to an individual physical constitution which affected the mind. Its use goes back to the humoral theories of antiquity, which continued to shape popular understandings of nature.[9] The term had a double meaning. As today, people could be in a 'good humour' or a 'bad humour'.[10] In these cases, humour referred to a temporary mood. But in some cases, people referred to a more permanent kind of humour. Jacob Mol, for instance, could not 'accommodate [his wife's] humour' in 1750.[11] In 1770, a certain Gentil was renowned for 'his turbulent humour'.[12] Some people were also classified in the humoral system, being 'choleric' or 'melancholic'. They had a particular 'temperament', a 'natural constitution of the human body' with a particular balance of the four humours, which influenced their behaviour.[13] Unlike the instincts, humours could be good as well: neighbours of Joseph Bellens declared in 1813 that they had always found him to be of 'a peaceful humour'.[14] By talking about humour and temperament in this way, people affirmed their individuality and practised a self that was relatively stable and oriented towards the body: the bodily fluids explained and determined the self.

Passions

People discussed the passions (*passions, hertstogten*) in a similar way: on the one hand, as discussed in chapter 3, passions figured as temporary displacements of the self, causing people to act in a moment of heat. But people could use them, too, to refer to a more permanent state that was inherent to the self. Pierre van de Wiele, in 1757, had 'an unruly passion for hunting'. Henry Janssens, in 1800, and Maria Theresia Cauwe, in 1822, both had a 'passion for drink'. Julie Thalie, in 1826, was 'like so many loose young people since long infected with the passion of chasing lovers'.[15] People also qualified passions as negative: they were excessive, uncontrolled, they were vices. In his *Premières idées*, Fierlant noted that to prevent all crime, 'one would have to reform the human race, deprive them of their passions, or of the power to abuse them'.[16] Passions, this passage again reveals, were thought to be inherent to humankind and people should control them. It is not always clear whether people believed that everyone was susceptible to the same passions – with some people just better at controlling them – or that they were more individual affairs, connected to the individual body or self. But it is clear that the language of passion could be used to talk about the self, to talk about and explain individual predilections. Compared to humours, talking of passions practised a self more oriented towards the mind or the will than to the body.

Penchants and inclinations

The passions, the *Encyclopédie* noted, were extreme forms of penchants and inclinations (*penchants, inclinations, neygingen, genygtheden*).[17] Inclination was defined as a 'disposition of the mind for something, by taste & by preference'. An inclination was a 'tendency of the will' and came forth from 'the particular mechanism of our organs', but inclinations were less violent than passions and did not trouble the regular operations of the will. Inclinations determined people's preference for music or study, or what they saw as a source of happiness. The *Encyclopédie* offered 'penchant' as a synonym with a slightly different meaning: 'Inclination is acquired, penchant is innate; penchant is violent, inclination soft'. Both could be good or bad: there were honest penchants and just inclinations; and perverse inclinations and shameful penchants.[18] There does not appear to be a similar distinction in Dutch – both terms translate as 'neyging'; and in the trial records, the distinction between inclinations and penchants was generally not made either.

Like talk of the passions, talk of inclinations and penchants served to practise the self by explaining behaviour with references to the individual mind. Indeed, frequently, people discussed penchants and inclinations in precisely the same way as the passions. In 1819, for instance, Jean Verbrugge's employer said that Verbrugge was a good employee, but that he had a 'decided penchant for drink'. Similarly, Cecile Louise Broucke was said in 1820 to work properly as a maid, but to have 'a penchant for libertinage'.[19] As was the case with passions, when people discussed inclinations or penchants in the trial records, they were always bad. In 1762, Antoine Deleporte was tried in Kortrijk for hitting a woman who had died as a result. In his defence, several witnesses testified of the woman's inappropriate behaviour. Two neighbours said that she was 'quick-tempered [*colericq*] and inclined to insult everyone'. In his justification, Deleporte's solicitor repeated that the woman was of a 'vile humour' and had repeatedly provoked the defendant. Even the victim's mother was found willing to declare before a notary that her daughter was 'naturally inclined to insult and defame anyone'.[20] Both inclination and humour served to show the woman's despicable nature.

The most positive context in which people discussed inclinations was when they said that someone did *not* have a particular inclination. Of Ambroise Vrancx and his father, aldermen in Grez advised in 1771 on an application for grace that 'neither of them is inclined to trouble society with excesses'. In her defence, Marie Anne Peccau alleged in 1772 that she had never stolen anything and that 'if she had been inclined to stealing', she would have had the occasion often enough, but she was not. Josse Van Cutsem, applying for grace in 1781, wrote that his homicide had been a traffic accident. This was not a crime of a premeditated nature, 'even less that of a man with a decided penchant to crime'. He hoped that his regular conduct and soft mores would convince His Majesty to grant him a pardon.[21] It seemed better not to have penchants and inclinations – no one was ever said to have a good inclination in my sample of trial records, even though the *Encyclopédie* explicitly mentioned this as an option.

Nature

The word 'nature' itself could also be used to refer to an individualised nature. As noted above, I have not found any uses of the term in this sense, but the Dutch word 'aerd', which Jan Des Roches used as a catch-all translation for many of the words for nature (*caractère, humeur, nature, naturel* and *tempérament*), was referred to in one instance. In 1779, Guilliam Roms was tried for the murder of his wife. He claimed that he had only defended himself against her and that she had often threatened to kill him. The Brussels magistrates then asked him whether she had given any signs that she was indeed capable of killing him. Yes, Roms claimed, for she was always fighting with him. As testimony of her 'villainous nature' [*boosaerdighen aert*], he put forward that he suspected her of having killed her infant. With 'such a woman of such nature' [*soo eene vrouwe van soo eenen aert*] he could not live safely.[22] Her nature was clearly not good. Roms used nature as an entirely individualised mental concept, to designate a stable self. By talking about this nature, the self gained importance. But as the case of Roms was the only one in my sample in which this happened, its influence remained limited.

Character

A final word used to describe people's natures was 'character' (*caractère*). Katie Barclay has found that 'character' was one of the most commonly used words to discuss the self in early nineteenth-century Irish courts, serving as a means to evaluate the credibility of witnesses.[23] While the word was not as dominant in the records of the Belgian trials I have studied, it was also occasionally used, mainly with respect to suspects. The *Encyclopédie* defined character as 'the habitual disposition of the mind, by which one is more inclined to portray, & in effect one does more often portray actions of a particular sort, rather than actions of the opposite sort'. More than the other words, character was rooted in actions and habits, rather than abstract preferences. Character was generally seen as habitual rather than inborn.[24] In practice, the difference between character and other terms for nature and self was sometimes clear – remarks on people's characters were sometimes closely tied to their actions – and sometimes not, when character, humour and inclination seemed interchangeable. In the latter case, magistrates concluded in 1780 that Guilliam Roms had 'like most mutes a suspicious character, and moreover he seems to have a violent character'. In 1798, neighbours said that Joseph De Keyser had a 'bad character'. In 1818, Augustine Henaux said that her mother-in-law was 'of a rather vile character', as she was 'always of a melancholic humour'. And so examples abound: about Augustinus Heiremans, judges asked in 1822 whether he was 'a man of a choleric and violent character'; the public prosecutor argued in 1828 that Pieter d'Halluin had 'severe character'.[25] Character was thus a word to talk about the individual self similar to the other terms, but less explicitly rooted in the body or the mind, and more in habit (but this distinction is, as the expression 'choleric character' shows, not absolute). Like the other terms, it promoted a sense of stability and uniqueness.

In some cases, however, descriptions of character were not so easily interchangeable with descriptions of temperament, 'aerd' or inclination. In these cases, character was more directly connected to specific actions. In 1753, for instance, Jean Giot applied for grace after committing a homicide. He asserted that he had always behaved impeccably and that he had the 'character of an honest man'. Local judges confirmed this: 'he has always lived irreproachably, being of a very peaceful character'. While talk about character was eschewed in further investigations, his honourable *behaviour* was mentioned several times. In 1812, magistrates interrogated Gisbert van der Linden on suspicion of murder, committed together with his wife. They asked him – a rare event – 'what his wife's character was'. Van der Linden replied that 'she had a good character, & in no way vile', adding that 'she would not harm anyone'.[26] In both these cases, character was not simply one's given nature, but closely connected to one's actions; it was, as Katie Barclay suggests, performative, something that people had to acquire through their everyday behaviour.[27]

The different words used to talk about nature imply different ways of talking about and appreciating the self. Many of these terms served to promote the idea that the self mattered: people had individual mental dispositions, linked to their body, their will or their habits. Their behaviour – their crimes or their lack of crimes – could be understood by referring to their self. But at the same time, many of the terms remained ambiguous as to what extent people's natures were truly individualised: instincts, passions and perhaps inclinations as well could refer to basic dispositions that were present in every human being, but that could and should be controlled.

Nature as a challenge (I)

Especially up to 1800, it seems that in the trial records, people predominantly referred to nature – both human nature in general and individual nature – in order to stress that something was *bad*. While the *encyclopédistes* and other scholars accepted that individual nature, humours, character, inclinations and penchants could both be good and bad, witnesses, prosecutors and defendants only rarely referred to these concepts to put someone in a favourable light (instincts and passions were always bad – there was no disagreement there).

This negative use of nature as a general concept agrees with the dismissive view of nature as something that people should control. Classical Christian doctrine promoted a dim view of human nature (without, however, frequently using the term 'human nature'). Humans were tainted by original sin – since the fall of man – and inclined to continue sinning. In their natural state, they were selfish and sensual. In sermons, the word 'nature' was often accompanied by the adjective 'corrupted'.[28] Only by exercising self-restraint could people avoid sinning. They should overcome nature; they should control it.[29] This conception of nature was general, it concerned all humans, but could be extended to individual natures.

This Christian doctrine has been found to have had an important impact on ideas about crime. Popular newssheets in early modern France frequently explained crimes by referring to human passions and the corruption of humankind. The criminal was a sinner and people had to conquer their sinful nature to avoid descending into crime.[30] Published confessions and execution sermons in seventeenth- and eighteenth-century England and Northern America, similarly, portrayed the criminal as an 'everyman', not particularly different from other people. The doctrine of universal sin provided an explanation for everyone's proclivity to commit sins and crimes. Published execution sermons and confessions served to warn communities of the dangers that were lurking in their own lives, of their own risk to hit the wrong path.[31]

In this universalist conception of crime, the psychology of the slippery slope played an important part. Crime – be it theft, murder, prostitution or sodomy – was the inevitable consequence of a progressive worsening of sins. Small sins became heavier and heavier and ended in murder. Only by interfering swiftly and actively, this descent into crime could be halted. Sinners were to repent for their sins and to control their impulses. While criminals could be born with 'vicious inclinations', it was everyone's task to try and control these inclinations.[32]

The eighteenth-century crime literature of the Southern Netherlands was less abundant than in France, England and America; at any rate, it has not been extensively studied. There were no printed execution sermons, confessions or criminal biographies. But the psychology of the slippery slope was familiar. A cursory analysis of the genre of 'murder songs', songs sold and performed at the execution of a criminal, reveals a similar conception of criminal behaviour. In 1779, for instance, Ambrosius Carton was executed in Kortrijk for thefts and murder. At this occasion, a song was distributed, detailing how Carton got on the wrong path from his early youth, soon got in the habit of stealing small things, then larger things and finally to committing murder. In its final stanza, the author recommended that parents buy a copy of the text as an example to show their children that if they were living loosely, great dangers were lurking.[33]

In learned culture, Goswin de Fierlant subscribed to the psychology of the slippery slope as well. 'A slight deviation is followed by several other slight deviations; soon it weighs on more important tasks, one commits excesses: the excesses bring delicts in sight, and from delicts one gets to crime'. Consequently, 'everything that spoils the heart opens the way to crime, bad morals, vice, laziness and idleness'. Several barriers could halt these evolutions: Fierlant made numerous specific suggestions, from a new, moral catechism to rewarding merits. The most crucial means of prevention was a proper education in religion, true honour and virtue. As we will see in the next section, Fierlant did not view nature as entirely bad, but he helped to promote a negative view of nature by agreeing with a psychology in which humans naturally tended towards crime.[34]

This psychology and the negative view of human nature complemented each other. Humans had an inherently sinful nature and were to control this nature to avoid a life of crime. The predominantly negative view of individualised human nature – individual passions, penchants, inclinations, humour and even character – seems to stem from this general view of human nature. While talk about individual nature reinforced the importance of the self, this self was mainly negative: people should renounce and control it.

Now it could be put forward that the negative view of nature was inherent to genre of crime records and publications about crime; that as a consequence, it does not necessarily reflect more general perceptions of nature. After all, the people involved had committed crimes, so they were necessarily of a bad nature. However, not only the bad was noted when people were talked about in crime records. Indeed, to their own defence and to others' defence, people often stressed their positive traits. To do so, they did generally not refer to nature: they never referred to passions or humours, rarely to penchants and inclinations and only occasionally to character. They mainly referred to specific behaviour, to people's actions.

In the grace application of Ambroise Vrancx in 1771, cited above, the statement that father and son were 'not inclined' to cause trouble was accompanied by the conclusion that they had always been of good behaviour and that they had always laboured properly. Similarly, sixteen notable citizens of Heiremans' village declared in 1822 that, contrary to reports of his violent and choleric character, he had 'always been of good and irreproachable behaviour'.[35] These statements – good behaviour and hard work – were the bread and butter of many applications for grace and cases for the defence, sometimes complemented with a recommendation of the 'Christian life' and 'honourable behaviour' of the defendants.[36] If people mainly referred to passive nature for stressing the bad, active behaviour could be referred to for stressing the good.[37] From this background, it is not surprising that when people referred to 'character' as positive, it generally appeared as active and closely related to behaviour.

Nature as an opportunity

Especially before 1800, people in the trial records mainly referred to human nature as something negative. This is a somewhat curious observation, for while early modern views of human nature are indeed known to be quite dismissive, the times were changing. Intellectual and literary historians have shown – and I have followed them when introducing this chapter – that 'nature' was a key concept in eighteenth-century thought. Nature – in its plurality of meanings – was present in all domains: in science, in morals, in religion, in education, in the arts, in theatre and in politics. And in all these domains, nature was overwhelmingly something that people desired: they wanted to study, know and follow nature.[38]

In line with this general appreciation for nature, attention for general human nature and individual nature also grew. As the eighteenth century progressed, this use of nature became increasingly positive. In 1762, the *Dictionnaire de l'académie française* noted that nature 'is also taken to mean a certain disposition & inclination of the mind. *Perverse nature. He is by nature inclined to such vice*'. In its next edition in 1798, the dictionary repeated the same definition, but added a new example: '*A happy nature*'.[39] The same thing happened in other dictionaries. Between 1750 and 1830, only two dictionaries of the Dutch language were published. In the first one, Des Roches' 1769 French–Dutch dictionary, the example with the translation of 'Naturel' was 'Mauvais naturel. Een quaden aerd'.[40] In Pieter Weiland's dictionary of the Dutch language (1799–1811), however, the example for 'aard' was: 'Een mensch van eenen goeden, zachten aard'; 'A man of a good, gentle nature'.[41] Human natures were no longer all bad.

One of the most prolific propagators of the positive approach to nature – at least in the domain of human nature and personal nature – was Jean-Jacques Rousseau. For Rousseau, '[t]he fundamental principle of all morals […] is that man is a being that is naturally good'.[42] Rousseau was not only concerned with human nature in general, but also with individual nature, which took the form of a 'voice from within'. Rousseau argued that – I am digesting – people's goals should be to liberate themselves from the constraints of society and the pressure of their peers and live according to their true nature. People's ambitions in society and their longings for honour were but 'amour propre', vain self-regard. Rousseau denounced the social orientation of the self. People should rather cultivate their true self – their biologically provided, inner nature – and make that nature actual; a practice which Rousseau termed 'amour de soi', love of the self. He stressed the importance of the self and particularly of an inner-oriented self.[43]

The positive view of human nature was also present in the *Encyclopédie*. Jaucourt's article on 'le naturel', after defining the natural as the characteristics we are born with, good or bad, tells us that 'Education, example or habit may indeed rectify the natural of which the penchant is to the bad, or spoil he who tends more happily towards the good; but however great their power is, a constrained nature betrays itself in unforeseen occasions'. True nature always shows, regardless of education. But then, departing from his earlier position that nature could be good or bad, Jaucourt put forward that 'the good nature seems to be born with us; it is one of the fruits of a happy temperament that education may cultivate with glory, but that she does not give'. Without this good nature, Jaucourt noted, no durable society would be possible in the world. The good nature is generalised; for without good nature there could be no society. So, Jaucourt concluded, as our fate depends on the natural, 'happy is he who takes a way of life conform with the character of his heart & of his spirit, he will always find pleasure & resources in his choice'. In this final movement, Jaucourt praised the authentic life: people should live in accordance with their individual true nature.[44]

Of course, not everyone was as jubilant about human nature. Many more conservative writers continued to view nature negatively, in the Christian sense. And even more progressive thinkers were not always convinced. Mary Wollstonecraft, for instance, rejected Rousseau's arguments in favour of the 'state of nature' as unsound, unphilosophical and impious: if nature was so good, God would not have given people the abilities to evolve to civilisation.[45] Others decried the 'naturalistic fallacy' of deriving moral values from nature.[46] Yet while such voices continued to disturb the positive appreciations of nature, they could not prevent the increasing attention for the inherent goodness of nature in its different forms.

This positive sense of nature did not go unnoticed in the Southern Netherlands. In theatre, for instance, 'naturalness' became a central concern in the second half of the eighteenth century.[47] The new appreciation of nature was also visible in legal thought. Goswin de Fierlant may have subscribed to the psychology of the slippery slope, as we have seen in the previous section, but he was also quite positive about nature. He argued, for instance, that the 'barriers of nature' and the 'desire of self-conservation nature has given to all animated beings' were sufficient to prevent people from committing suicide, as long as they were in their right mind.[48] In the 1790s, Rousseau's concept of the good human nature became central to the ideology of the French Revolution and indirectly influenced the revolutionary criminal justice system.[49]

After 1800, more positive uses of nature also appeared in the trial records. Some people, particularly interrogators, called upon 'feelings of nature' and 'the voice of nature'. In 1812, Elisabeth Fisscher was suspected of infanticide. She initially denied the allegations, but during her second interrogation, after a medical examination, she confessed that she had given birth and had accidentally lost her child while on the privy. The interrogators then asked her why she had not told anyone about her pregnancy and why she had not called for help during labour, 'help which the voice of nature and of motherhood imperiously command her to seek'. Fisscher admitted that she should have taken this course of action, and regretted that she had not.[50] Similarly, in 1828, the judge of instruction concluded that Pieter D'Halluin and his wife Maria Doone had killed the latter's father. This, he argued, was the result of 'greed combined with the fierce character' of the suspects. It 'made the feelings of nature almost disappear' and caused them to kill their family member.[51] The voice of nature and feelings of nature were linked to good and moral ways of living. In these instances, nature appeared as a general condition, not particularly linked to the self.

This new, positive view of general human nature was especially well articulated for women. As I have discussed in chapter 2, the eighteenth century saw an important development in intellectual attitudes towards women. If people often saw early modern women as lascivious and unable to control themselves, they could portray later eighteenth-century women more easily as chaste and virtuous. Now, while this evolution was gradual and non-linear, another important change took place in the late eighteenth century: chasteness, motherly love and care were increasingly cast as 'natural' virtues women possessed. Maternity became intertwined with the essence of femininity; deviating from this essence was 'unnatural'. As Dror Wahrman has argued, in the late eighteenth century 'prevailing gender norms were redefined as essential and natural'.[52]

This view was of course clearly articulated in the case of Fisscher, whom interrogators asked about 'the voice of nature and of motherhood'. It was also present in the case of Adrien Braem and Levine Hellebuyck in 1797. They were accused of killing their child. Braem claimed that he had had a row with his wife, their child had started crying and his wife had hit the child. Then his wife started crying too. This had led him to think that she was going mad and he had run away. Judges found this a peculiar story. It should not have surprised him that his wife was crying, they said, 'for there is nothing more natural than that a mother is sensitive when seeing her child die'. Braem acknowledged this, but claimed that he did not know that the child was dead at the time.[53] I have never encountered such references to female nature as closely connected to caring motherhood earlier in the eighteenth century. The naturalisation of the loving mother was becoming common not only in print culture, but also in the courts of law, even if, for the time being, it was mainly used by the interrogators, and rarely volunteered by witnesses or suspects. With it, the idea that nature was inherently good gained currency.

This talk of nature in criminal records was talk about a generalised human nature. People did not explicitly connect it to the self, but to femininity in general or to humanity in general. But the more positive appreciation of general human nature spilled over to talk about individual nature – about the self. More than before, in the early nineteenth century people talked about this individual nature and saw it as positive. To discuss a good individual nature, people used a new metaphor: 'the heart'. Of course, this metaphor was not really new; the heart had been used for centuries to denote 'the interior, the foundation [le fond], the disposition of the mind'.[54] Laura Kounine has found much talk about the 'heart' as a locus of sincerity and truth in sixteenth- and seventeenth-century German witch trials.[55] But it was rarely used in this way in the trial records which I consulted from between 1750 and 1800, and received a stronger moral meaning in the early nineteenth century: the heart was naturally good.

In his analysis of crime prevention, Goswin de Fierlant had already attended to the importance of the good heart in criminal justice. Recommending religion, for instance, Fierlant wrote that 'it prevented the heart from contracting that degree of corruption without which the passions would not be able germinate crime'. He railed against everything 'which extinguishes in the heart of citizens the love of order and subordination, the desire to contribute to the general good'. The heart was naturally good, he assumed, but could be corrupted.[56] More than some of the other terms for nature, such as 'passion' or the word 'nature' itself, the heart was always individualised. The language of the heart signified the individual application of the positive view of human nature.

It was only in the early nineteenth century, however, that the heart started to appear in trial records in the same way as in Fierlant's treatise: a nature that was inherently good, but that could be corrupted. In 1812, we have already seen, Gisbert van der Linden and his wife Marie Ludwig were suspected of murder. Van der Linden had declared that his wife 'had a good character, & in no way evil'. Judges disagreed, however, and put it to Ludwig that her crime was proven and that 'by denying she only demonstrates more and more the wickedness of her character, and that despite her youth her heart is already so familiar with crime that it is inaccessible to all remorse & repentance'. This is, of course one of the techniques of interrogation discussed in chapter 1. But here, it stands as testimony of the idea that an individual's nature was supposed to be good, especially during 'youth', when still uncontaminated by civilisation. Nevertheless, good nature and the good heart were easily corrupted. While human nature was expected to be good, in this case, this nature was lost, leading to a different, negative nature, represented as the character.[57] The case was similar for Francisca Van Ryckeghem, who stood trial for infanticide in 1829. After the corpse of a child had been found, Van Ryckeghem was among a party of onlookers. One of them testified that she had said 'that she couldn't understand that there were people who had such an evil heart to do such things'.[58] She commented upon the heart – an inner self – and performed surprise at the fact that it could be evil.

Talk about the heart was not only a practice of a relatively stable self, it was also a practice of inner orientation and depth. This is illustrated in the case of Josse Sersant in 1806. Sersant was suspected of the murder of Charles de Pascal in Ghent. Witnesses related that an unknown person had threatened Pascal before the murder. One witness had seen Pascal at a party and noted that he seemed to be amused. Speaking to the witness, however, Pascal declared that 'it was not wholeheartedly, for I am in fear'. The witness then 'started reflecting' and concluded that 'his gayness that day had not penetrated to his heart'. This same approach was offered in the case of Pierre De Mahieu in 1803: when a friend noticed that De Mahieu was 'occupied by sinister plans and dark projects, he pressed him to open his heart and tell him the cause of his chagrin'. In both cases, people referred to the heart to denote something deep, something hidden inside, which could or could not be reflected in outward appearance. By using the language of the heart, people practised a deeper self and attached importance to this self.[59]

Nature as a challenge (II)

The increasingly positive view of human nature posed a problem for the criminal courts. If people were supposed to be inherently good, how could it be that they committed horrible crimes? The psychology of the slippery slope was not entirely abandoned; indeed, up to this day people continue to refer to the idea that small transgressions lead to bigger ones. But by around 1800, it was no longer as self-evident as it had been before. If human nature was good, the criminal could no longer be an everyman, a common sinner. The early nineteenth-century criminal had to be explained, made sense of as an individual, in a much more elaborate way than before.

The movement to make sense of crime is quite visible, in Belgium and elsewhere in Europe.[60] In 1828, in an essay against a proposed new penal code, jurist Victor Savart reflected on criminals and punishments in general. He proposed that criminal justice was to pay more attention to human nature. All crimes had their origins in desires, he observed. When these desires became too strong, they became 'a moral malady and often even a physical malady', such as 'imbecility, fury, consumption, rupture of the arteries, a stroke, inevitable death'. The legislator should therefore not view the criminal 'as a bad person who needs to be punished, but rather as a madman who needs to be healed'.[61] While casting criminals as madmen, requiring individualised treatment and a cure, Savart also cast them as 'everymen', driven by desires. He balanced between a universalising and an individualising conception of criminality. Likewise, Belgium's most famous penal reformer, Edouard Ducpétiaux, constantly referred to human nature and asserted that criminals were driven by insanity, anger, despair, ignorance or fanaticism, but 'at heart', they were still human beings. The legislator should take their circumstances into account.[62]

The aim to understand criminals led some to adopt novel methods. From the late 1820s, some penal reformers started to refer to statistics to support their claims, among them Ducpétiaux. None became more famous for doing so than Adolphe Quetelet, the so-called 'father' of social statistics. Influenced by natural science – Quetelet was an astronomer and mathematician by education – he sought to explain crime through statistical 'laws'. He proposed that there was an 'average man' in each time and society, whose behaviour was typical for the whole nation. Using crime statistics, Quetelet investigated the probability that a person would commit a crime under similar circumstances, particularly attending to seasons, climate, education, sex and age. He found that there was a greater 'penchant' to commit crime among men and people around twenty-five. Although the poor and the uneducated had a higher penchant to commit crime, the influence of these variables was less pronounced; and he argued that it was moral education rather than knowledge; and sudden decline in wealth rather than poverty itself which stimulated crime. Although Quetelet stressed that he was not analysing at the level of the individual – everyone could choose their own destiny – he definitely did away with the idea of the criminal as an everyman. Not everyone had the same risk of committing crime. It depended on their place in society.[63]

In trial records, too, looking for and offering explanations – more particularly, looking for and offering 'motives' – became a much more common affair in the early nineteenth century. People rarely used the term 'motive' (*motif/motief*) in eighteenth-century criminal trial records or applications for grace.[64] In my sample, the word was only used in the grace case of Denis Dierens in 1780. Dierens had gotten in a fight and had the 'accident' of lethally injuring another man, upon which 'he has immediately fallen in excessive sadness and has shown his mournful heart to the victim, his father and his other friends'. In their advice, local judges noted that it seemed that a blow he had received had been 'the only motive for his crime'; as a consequence, he was granted grace. While judges sometimes asked people *why* they had committed their crime, particularly in sodomy cases, this remained relatively sporadic and was rarely a prime concern.

This was changing in the 1790s. As we have seen in chapter 1, interrogations started to become more extensive with the installation of the new criminal justice system. The abolition of the system of legal proof and the rise of 'inner conviction' as the sole guideline for determining guilt or innocence required above all that judges or juries were convinced that an individual had committed the crime. A clear explanation of *why* they should have committed this crime helped a great deal to this end. This evolution contributed to the problematisation of the self: precisely at the time that understanding crime became a legal necessity, ideas about a good generalised human nature made these understandings more difficult.

As a result, in many cases, interrogators started to ask suspects explicitly 'why' or 'for what motive' they had committed their crime; and defendants frequently used the word 'motive' in their own answers. Similarly, magistrates often asked witnesses about the perpetrator's possible motives, or the witnesses volunteered such information. So in 1798, interrogators asked Marie Therese Boyen why her assailer had attacked her; and they asked Marie Joseph Davaine why her master had supposedly killed her infant. In 1800, they asked Cuny Renaud 'what motive he has had for killing' a man. In 1812, they asked Marie Ludwig why she had lied in a previous interrogation.[65] In the 1820s, indictments started to refer to motives as well. In 1821, for instance, the indictment of Pascal Bastiaens noted that 'the motive [of the fight] were the pleasantries that Bastiaens held towards a girl'.[66] Examples like this abound: judges no longer simply wanted to establish what had happened, but also why; they needed specific motives to understand the crime.

Not everyone was able to declare such motives. In 1806, for instance, Maria Alsteens was asked about a fight between her sons, one of whom had killed the other. Asked why her son had hit his brother, she said that 'she cannot say, she can't know that, for sometimes a person has something in his head'. Rather than offering an acceptable motive, she inclined towards the explanation of displacement or mental illness.[67] And courts did not accept every motive offered. In 1795, Joseph André confessed that he had murdered his uncle and his maid. He told this in a very matter of fact way: they all ate together, he had words with the maid, took a stick and hit her on the head, after which she died. The uncle shouted from his room, asking what was happening, so André went to him and stabbed him with a knife. Then he set the building on fire.

'Why has he committed such cruel actions?' judges asked. 'Because of the words they had had, especially the servant'. The interrogation was closed with this explanation, but the president of the criminal tribunal later returned to the matter, again asking why he had committed the crimes. He said that his victims had 'received him grumpily', and that the maid 'behaved as if she was the mistress of the house' and had mistreated him. The case had to be started over because of a procedural error, and again the magistrates returned to his motives. This time, they inquired further: was his uncle rich? Would he inherit? André claimed that he did not know. Once again, in his final hearing, the substitute president of the criminal court asked if no other motive than bad words had led to his actions. André answered affirmatively but returned to the claim that they had mistreated him – not going along with the magistrates' suggestion that he was after the inheritance.[68] Clearly, however, a simple confession of the material facts of the crime did not satisfy nineteenth-century magistrates. They wanted a confession that made the crime understandable.

The increasing interest in motive is also apparent in the way the courts and the police dealt with suicide. Suicide was not punished after 1782, but courts continued to conduct *pro forma* trials until the end of the old regime. An interest in the suicide's motives was occasional and generally stemmed more from a desire to excuse suicides (because they had been insane), rather than to properly understand them. Since the French occupation, suicides were no longer part of the criminal law, but the police still reported deaths by suicide. These reports were generally very matter-of-fact and did not contain many witness statements or investigations. But more commonly than before, they recorded why the suicide had taken place. For instance, in 1803, the police wrote that it seemed that the cause of Jacques Chatenier's suicide was 'his embarrassment'; while a report noted about Albert Leonard in 1819 that 'one believes that jealousy and chagrin have taken him to this act of despair'. When the police found no clear causes, they even wrote that 'the motives for this act of desperation are unknown'.[69]

The belief in a generally good human nature thus stimulated an interest in people's individual motives. But most motives did not solve the problem.

In murder cases, the most commonly offered motives were personal gain (an inheritance or theft) and envy (personal feuds or jealousy). That suspects were after monetary gain and believed that they would be able to escape punishment squared well with the common idea of rational calculation, as discussed in chapter 2. Popular newssheets also commonly suggested such financial motives.[70] Neither this motive, nor the motive of envy was testimony of a good human nature, however. Things were even worse when no understandable motive whatsoever could even be found.

To save the idea that human nature in general was good, it was necessary to cast criminals as radically different. Instead of 'everymen', they became 'aliens', 'monsters' or 'unhuman'.[71] They could hardly be identified with; their deeds were so 'unnatural' that they evoked horror, fear and wonder.[72] As we have seen in chapter 3, for the most 'horrific' and 'unexplainable' crimes, people sometimes referred to mental illness as a way to make sense of this radical deviation from human nature. But there was a less incisive option. While human nature in general might be virtuous, these individuals had a bad individual nature.[73]

In the previous section I discussed the use of the 'heart' to discuss positive individual nature in the early nineteenth century. But this does not mean that there were no longer any negative sentiments about individual natures. Let me return to two cases discussed above. The first is the case of Marie Ludwig in 1812. Recall that her interrogator told her that 'by denying she only demonstrates more and more the wickedness of her character, and that despite her youth her heart is already so familiar with crime that it is inaccessible to all remorse & repentance'. While this quote shows that human nature (the heart) was supposed to be good, her individual 'character' was bad. The second case is that of Pieter D'Halluin and Maria Doone in 1828. Here, the judge of instruction concluded that 'Greed combined with the fierce character of [...] D'Halluin made the feelings of nature almost disappear'. Again, the judge portrayed feelings of nature as positive, while he argued that the suspect's character was bad. This way of formulating things was opposite to the pattern of the second half of the eighteenth century, when people generally called nature bad and character more often good. Of course, there were exceptions, but overall, a general bad human nature with occasional good individual characters had changed into a general good human nature with occasional bad individual characters. The general virtuous human nature could be reconciled with criminal behaviour by accepting the existence of individuals with a corrupted, monstrous and criminal nature.[74]

With the proliferation of the idea that human nature was inherently good, criminal courts needed to look more at individual nature and motivation to understand criminals. As a result, self-talk in the criminal courts increased.

More than before, courts in the early nineteenth century sought to assess suspects' individual minds – their motivations, their 'character', their self.[75] As self-talk and interpretations of self became more common in the criminal courts, people reflected on their self, deepened their self and expanded it.

The change is, of course, not neatly delineated. Talking about nature and about character occurred throughout the period and was ambiguous throughout. Character was sometimes closely connected to behaviour, while at other times it seemed to connect to innate dispositions. People mentioned good and bad characters throughout the period. But as the positive view of human nature became more popular, it became necessary to discuss character and motive as a way of highlighting an individual deviation from the good human nature.

Postscript: the strange career of the crime against nature

The concern for nature – individual or universal – provided an opportunity for increased self-talk. From the late eighteenth century on, people more than before talked about and interpreted the self (the individual psyche) in explicit terms. They questioned people's motivations and often connected these to their selves, to their character and their feelings. Interrogators sought for particular answers while suspects and witnesses offered their own versions of their motivations and motives. They related their stories to the new conceptions of good nature, individuality, interiority and stability. If nature never became the principal concern of the criminal court – throughout the period, people were expected to remain in control of their nature – its ambiguities are clearly present in the trial records. Nature appeared both as a challenge that people should overcome and as a chance for an authentic and good life.

In the second half of the eighteenth century, talk about nature in the records of criminal justice was rare. When people spoke of aspects of human or individual nature, these were mostly negative. The more positive appreciation of nature was hardly visible at all. If it occurred, it was referred to as 'character' and firmly rooted in actions. This changed after the French annexation. Talk about nature was still mostly eschewed by witnesses and suspects, but interrogators and judges sometimes formulated their questions and conclusions using the language of nature, inclination, penchant and character. Their words show us that a more positive appreciation of nature had found its way into society; at least among the elites that populated the criminal courts. This is significant, not because it is surprising that these elites were familiar with these ideas, but because they used them in the criminal justice system, thus confronting juries, witnesses, suspects and audiences from all layers of society with them. Many of the people who had to answer to questions about nature were low-skilled workers and servants, some of them were even illiterate. In response to the demands of the criminal courts, they had to reflect on themselves in terms of nature; they had to think about an inherently good nature and bemuse the horror of deviating from this nature.

At the same time, this more positive appreciation of nature posed a problem for criminal justice. If people were naturally good, how could they still commit crimes? The courts henceforth became more interested in individual motives and characters as a way to explain crime. They had to confront that at least people's individual natures were not necessarily inclined towards the good. A culture stressing self-control, honour and reason over inner nature therefore continued to be dominant in the early nineteenth century. Nature and the self thus gained a greater visibility in the discourses of criminal justice, but always remained ambiguous.

My analysis has mostly been based on the discourses of nature in the more serious cases in my sample: cases of murder during the whole period, of sodomy and suicide in the eighteenth century and of infanticide in the nineteenth century. People rarely referenced nature and only occasionally explicitly mentioned the self in cases of prostitution, or in the pederasty cases of the nineteenth century. Discourses of nature and self were most clearly articulated in cases that were grave enough to merit extensive attention; the rise of self-talk and nature-talk in the courts was contingent on social norms, laws and legal procedures. Perhaps, then, the evolutions I have sketched reveal more about the increasing problematisation of murder and infanticide than about general views of nature and self. For the remainder of this chapter, I will explore this question with an excursion on the history of homosexuality – a domain where nature has done much conceptual work.[76] I will show that while discourses on same-sex sexuality underwent a somewhat different evolution, they do not invalidate the larger evolution that I have been able to analyse mostly by reference to homicide cases.

The case of Peter Stocker, a forty-year-old cobbler who was arrested on suspicion of sodomy in Antwerp on 8 February 1781, reveals the importance of the concept of nature to the legal dealings with sodomy. One of Stocker's supposed partners, only nineteen years of age, had confessed to the officer of justice that Stocker had sodomised him on multiple occasions during the last two months. Although Stocker denied the allegations, magistrates continued their investigations and heard many more men who admitted to having had sex with Stocker.

The Antwerp mayor saw the gravity of the case and wrote to the Privy Council in Brussels for advice. Our court is considering a case, he wrote, against Peter Stocker, who is accused of the 'horrible crime against nature'.

The magistrates had taken precautions to avoid that this sensitive matter would become known among the public. How should they now proceed? The Privy Council agreed that discretion was of the highest essence. The magistrates should continue the trial, but in secret, with only the essential legal staff and with as few witnesses as possible, preferably those 'whose innocence could not be damaged too much anymore'.

In his first interrogation, the delegated magistrate did not directly ask Stocker whether he had committed sodomy. He only asked questions like 'does he know Posenaer and has he done something particular with him?' Stocker generally assented to knowing these people, but noted that he had done 'nothing in particular' with them. Judges then heard more witnesses – more partners and neighbours – and interrogated Stocker for a second time. This time, they were more explicit. They asked Stocker 'why he had taught and made different boys to spill their nature [*doen hunne natuer storten*], and how he had lost himself so far as to forcing his nature [*sijne natuer te forceren*; ejaculating] in their presence or together with them?' Stocker claimed never to have done such things, and continued to deny further allegations that he had had sexual intercourse with several young men.

Then, after a long interrogation, judges resorted to one of the interrogation techniques discussed in chapter 1, playing to Stocker's religious fears. They asked him 'whether he knows that he has a soul that he must try to save'. Stocker confirmed that he knew this. 'How does he dare, then', judges continued, 'to keep denying the truthful truth, does he not fear to be abandoned by God, and that his soul will be torn out of his disastrous body to be thrown into the abysses of hell?' Stocker said 'not to fear this, as he is falsely accused'. But the judges had planted a seed. A month later, Stocker requested to be interrogated anew. He told his judges that he would tell 'the true confession of all facts and crimes for which he thinks he is imprisoned'. And indeed, Stocker confessed to having had sex with numerous men and detailed his frequent encounters and sexual habits. His story was not a proud one, however: Stocker often professed shame and claimed to have performed sexual acts 'only because of his urges [*drift*] and beastliness'.

To some of his partners, Stocker had elaborated on his sexual preferences. When one of his partners had said 'you'd better go with women, than with boys', Stocker allegedly said 'blech, blech, that's filth!' To another partner he said 'that he wouldn't leave this trade, even if he saw the gallows erected before him'. Stocker thus professed some kind of stable sexual preference, which he linked to his urges and beastliness.[77]

The ambiguities of nature are immediately present in this case: sodomy was portrayed as a 'crime against nature', but also a result of nature. In the first sense, nature represented the divine order, to which a heinous crime such as sodomy was opposed. The label 'against nature' served to stress the severity of the crime. With the destruction of Sodom and Gomorrah, God had made His opinion of men who had sex with other men amply clear. A crime against nature was a crime contrary to the laws of God. Since it was given by God, this nature was of course good; but remained very abstract. It hardly related to human nature or individual nature.[78]

Many eighteenth-century *philosophes* agreed that sodomy was a crime against nature, but they did not necessarily refer to the divine order. They argued that as same-sex sexual relations did not produce offspring, they were contrary to the demands of nature that required the human species to preserve its own existence. But they also recognised the ambiguities of this nature and hinted at a different meaning. Voltaire, for instance, wondered how it had happened 'that a vice that would destroy the human race if it were widespread, that an infamous vice against nature, is nevertheless so natural?' Initially, Voltaire used nature in the sense just discussed, as a fundamental necessity of the human race. The second time, he referred to nature as a sort of instinct, as a sexual drive.[79]

Indeed, the trial records of Peter Stocker include similar discourses about nature, in Stocker's explanation for his behaviour with references to instinct, urge and beastliness. Nature was now portrayed as morally bad: these were natural, bodily impulses that people should conquer and control. Sometimes, this nature was individualised and related to the self: these were Stocker's individual preferences and urges, inherent to his self. At other times, however, these urges were referred to as general, universal instincts that could be present in every man.

In light of the absence of much talk about human or individualised nature in the homicide trials of the eighteenth century, all this talk about nature in this 1781 sodomy case is remarkable. Indeed, in other sodomy cases as well, discourses about nature and self were relatively well-articulated. In the same year, Joannes Baptiste Jacobs was also tried for sodomy with several young men. His victims testified that he had said that 'this is no evil', for 'what do we have this for but to use it'.[80] In this instance, Jacobs also used nature – here as the sheer existence of sexual organs and sexual pleasure – to justify his actions.

In the Dutch Republic, where sodomites were far more frequently tried in the eighteenth century, some sodomites started to offer even more sophisticated arguments in the second half of the eighteenth century. Witness reported in 1757 that preacher Andreas Klink had claimed that 'it was in his nature [*hem van natuuren eygen*], for his mother was pregnant with him while his father was away and his mother was always full of appetite and desire, which he has inherited from his mother'.[81] For Klink, his desires were inborn and (therefore) natural. Natural was used as a synonym for innate. Klink was not the only one to volunteer such ideas. Several others did the same in the later eighteenth-century Northern Netherlands.[82]

After the decriminalisation of sodomy in the Southern Netherlands in 1795, the discourses about nature also disappeared from legal and police records. The police still arrested men who had sex with other men, henceforth often called 'pederasts', and sometimes even brought them to court. They could be prosecuted under charges of public indecency, which judges interpreted very broadly – it sufficed if anyone had seen them, or even if someone *could* have seen them. However, police reports of these cases rarely contained more than a dry description of the material facts that had taken place.

Take, for instance, the case of Peter Dehaes and a certain Deraadt in Antwerp in 1825. The police report only indicated that the military watch had arrested both men on the Castle Square while they 'committed vices against nature'. 'Having taken more information on this disgrace, it results from the mutual statements of the accused that they were urinating on the said Castle Square and have touched each other with their male members'. The police officer put them at the disposal of the prosecutor but wrote nothing else on the case.[83] These were police reports, but even when a trial took place, our information remains limited. Public indecency cases were not very important, so trials and interrogations were short and focused on material facts. Magistrates did not ask about the background, motivations or explanations in any of the cases I have found. Words like inclination did not turn up in the records.

The discourses of nature and self in cases concerning 'crime against nature' therefore went through a different trajectory than the discourses in the homicide and infanticide cases. But why, then, have I taken the latter as more representative of a general movement towards more attention to nature and self in the early nineteenth century, when I could have argued the opposite by looking at sodomy cases? First, because the evolution I have sketched on the basis of homicide cases was much more outspoken. Not only were there more cases to reveal an evolution, but judges, witnesses and suspects spoke much more explicitly about an individualised nature, moral motivation, and sometimes an inner-oriented self, with words such as 'character' and the 'heart', in early nineteenth-century homicide cases than in eighteenth-century sodomy cases. If nature and self were *relatively* often spoken about in these latter cases, this is only when compared to other eighteenth-century cases, not when compared to nineteenth-century criminal cases.

The second reason why I argue that discourses in cases of same-sex sexual behaviour were the exception to a more general pattern is the changing legal status of the crime. Homicide, and especially murder, was consistently seen as a serious crime meriting extensive legal attention. Prostitution was more or less consistently seen as a minor nuisance, to be dealt with without much ado. As a result, much more discourse was recorded in homicide cases, allowing for the analyses I have made above. But sex between men changed from one of the most serious crimes up to 1795 to not a crime at all afterwards. While sodomy continued to be seen as improper and criminal, it could only be prosecuted as an offence against public decency, tried by the lower correctional courts. These cases were of minor importance and there was little time and limited means to deal with them. Legal discourses about nature and self were smothered in the everyday practice of policing and justice. The homicide cases therefore provide a more reliable guide to the general positions of the criminal court: if some crimes perhaps became seen as crueller in the early nineteenth century, and if legal records became more extensive, this was not because homicide had not been seen as meriting much attention, but because legal procedures more generally were changing. While I cannot exclude, of course, that an analysis of, for instance, property crimes would yield different results, it seems clear that the evolutions I have sketched point to an important evolution in the discourses of the law – an evolution people involved in its proceedings had to relate to.

While nature and self all but disappeared in the pederasty cases of the early nineteenth century, talk about nature could still be used in relation to same-sex sexual behaviour. The important innovation of the eighteenth and nineteenth centuries was that people increasingly saw nature as individualised and as a source of moral guidance. By the 1820s and 1830s, Swiss authors Heinrich Zschokke and Heinrich Hössli started to use the idea of a 'sexual drive' and an immutable sexual preference. Hössli even suggested that 'male love is true nature, a law of nature' – and therefore good.[84] None of the people accused of sodomy went so far in the Belgian trial records from the period before 1830; indeed, they rarely did later in the nineteenth century either.[85] But this approach to sodomy and nature – same-sex sexual desire as natural; nature as good – laid the basis of later emancipation movements. The understanding of homosexuality as an orientation and an identity was interspersed with thought about nature, while views of homosexual practices as 'unnatural' continued to abound. Up to today, homosexuality remains one of the topics where the ambiguities of nature are most clearly articulated.

Notes

1 Lorraine Daston, *Against Nature* (Cambridge, MA: MIT Press, 2019), pp. 29–31.
2 Jean le Rond d'Alembert, 'Nature (Philos.)', in Diderot and d'Alembert, *Encyclopédie*, vol. 11, p. 40.

3 Louis Jaucourt, 'Naturel, le (Morale)', in Diderot and d'Alembert, *Encyclopédie*, vol. 11, p. 45.

4 'Nature', *Dictionnaire de l'Académie française*, 4th ed. (1762), ARTFL; 'Nature', *Dictionnaire de l'Académie française*, 5th ed. (1798), ARTFL.

5 Jan Des Roches, *Nouveau dictionnaire françois-flamand* (Antwerp: Grange, 1769).

6 'Instinct', *Dictionnaire de l'Académie française*, 4th ed. (1762), ARTFL.

7 NA, *PCAP-C*, 606/A (Jacques Honton 1791).

8 FA, *MA*, 525/1 (Request of 10/6/1824).

9 Noga Arikha, *Passions and Tempers: A History of the Humours* (New York, NY: Harper Perennial, 2008), pp. 231–68. See also Rublack, 'Fluxes'.

10 E.g. in SABR, *AC-WEST*, 116–81 and 286–409.

11 FA, *V*, 103 (Jacob Mol 1750).

12 CAB, *HA Trials*, 10449.

13 'Tempérament', in Diderot and d'Alembert, *Encyclopédie*, vol. 16, p. 56.

14 SABE, *AC-ANT*, 808.

15 SAK, *OCAK*, 8343; NA2, *AC-BRA*, 1609; SABR, *AC-WEST*, 349–1014; SAK, *Court of the First Instance of Kortrijk (FIK)*, 130/1.

16 Fierlant, 'Premières idées', fo. 18v.

17 'Passions', in Diderot and d'Alembert, *Encyclopédie*, vol. 12, p. 142.

18 Louis Jaucourt, 'Inclination', in Diderot and d'Alembert, *Encyclopédie*, vol. 8, p. 651.

19 SABR, *AC-WEST*, 310–620 and 320–723.

20 SAK, *OCAK*, 8293.

21 NA, *PCAP-C*, 631/B (Ambroise Vrancx 1769); CAB, *HA Trials*, 9631; NA, *PCAP-C*, 597/A (Josse Van Cutsem 1781). See also SABR, *AC-WEST*, 232–1109.

22 CAB, *HA Trials*, 6367.

23 Barclay, *Men on Trial*, chap. 7.

24 Cf. Thomas Ahnert and Susan Manning, 'Introduction: character, self, and sociability in the Scottish Enlightenment', in Thomas Ahnert and Susan Manning (eds), *Character, Self, and Sociability in the Scottish Enlightenment* (New York, NY: Palgrave Macmillan, 2013), pp. 1–30. On the interest in character in the eighteenth- and nineteenth-century English and Irish courts, see Nicola Lacey, *Women, Crime and Character: From Moll Flanders to Tess of the D'Urbervilles* (Oxford: Oxford University Press, 2008), pp. 14–23; Katie Barclay, 'Performing emotion and reading the male body in the Irish court, c. 1800–1845', *Journal of Social History*, 51 (2017), 296.

25 CAB, *HA Trials*, 6367; SABE, *AC-ANT*, 73; NA2, *AC-BRA*, 2195; SABE, *AC-ANT*, 1236; SABR, *AC-WEST*, 393–1416.

26 NA, *PCAP-C*, 620/A (Jean Giot 1753); SABR, *AC-WEST*, 246–83.

27 Barclay, *Men on Trial*, p. 9.

28 E.g. in Joannes Verslype, *Historie en overeenkominge der vier evangelien* (Ghent: Mauritius vander Ween, 1712–1729); Petrus Franciscus Valcke, *Sermoenen op de sondagen en feest-dagen* (Ghent: A. B. Steven, 1802).

29 Dixon, *From Passions to Emotions*, p. 70; Karen Halttunen, *Murder Most Foul: The Killer and the American Gothic Imagination* (Cambridge, MA: Harvard University Press, 1998), chap. 1.

30 Maurice Lever, *Canards sanglants: naissance du fait divers* (Paris: Fayard, 1993), pp. 23–4.

31 Halttunen, *Murder Most Foul*, chap. 1.

32 Andrea McKenzie, *Tyburn's Martyrs: Execution in England, 1675–1775* (London: Hambledon Continuum, 2007), chap. 3.

33 W. L. Braekman, 'Marktlied bij een publieke executie in Kortrijk 1779', *De Leiegouw*, 49 (2007), 237–42. See also Julien De Vuyst, *Het moordlied in de Zuidelijke Nederlanden tot de XIXe eeuw* (Brussels: Aurelia, 1976).

34 Fierlant, 'Premières idées', fos. 18r-93v.

35 NA, *PCAP-C*, 631/B (Ambroise Vrancx 1769); SABE, *AC-ANT*, 1236.

36 Examples are numerous; among others see CAB, *HA Trials*, 5401; SAK, *OCAK*, 8823, 8343, 6676; NA, *PCAP-C*, 596/A (François Vanden Bossche 1780), 606/A (Charles & Henri Van Sant 1791), 620/A (François Soudan 1755), 620/B (Barthelemi Neutjes 1753); NA2, *AC-BRA*, 471–1662, 593–1232; SABE, *AC-ANT*, 407, 1288; SABR, *AC-WEST*, 360–1114, 211–883; SAK, *FIK*, 133–90.

37 Behaviour was of course not necessarily good: bad behaviour was also frequently noted, but behaviour was not as exclusively bad as nature.

38 Jean Ehrard, *L'idée de nature en France dans la première moitié du XVIIIe siècle* (Paris: Sevpen, 1963); Henry Vyverberg, *Human Nature, Cultural Diversity and the French Enlightenment* (New York, NY: Oxford University Press, 1989); Ludmilla Jordanova, *Nature Displayed: Gender, Science and Medicine, 1760–1820* (London: Longman, 1999); Christophe Madelein, *Juigchen in den adel der menschelijke natuur. Het verhevene in de Nederlanden (1770–1830)* (Ghent: Academia Press, 2011); Van Oostveldt, *Tranen om het alledaagse*.

39 'Nature', *Dictionnaire de l'Académie française*, 4th ed. (1762), ARTFL; 'Nature', *Dictionnaire de l'Académie française*, 5th ed. (1798), ARTFL. See also Taylor, *Sources of the Self*, pt. IV.

40 'An evil nature'. Des Roches, *Nouveau dictionnaire*.

41 Petrus Weiland, *Nederduitsch taalkundig woordenboek* (Amsterdam: Johannes Allart, 1799).

42 Cited in Arthur M. Melzer, *The Natural Goodness of Man: On the System of Rousseau's Thought* (Chicago, IL: University of Chicago Press, 1990), p. 15.

43 Peter Abbs, 'The full revelation of the self: Jean-Jacques Rousseau and the birth of deep autobiography', *Philosophy Now*, 68 (July 2008), 17–20; Carnevali, 'Rousseau et l'authenticité'; Udo Thiel, 'Self and sensibility: From Locke to Condillac and Rousseau', *Intellectual History Review*, 25:3 (2014), 265–70.

44 Jaucourt, 'Naturel', vol. 11, pp. 45–6.

45 Wollstonecraft, *A Vindication*, p. 39.

46 Daston, *Against Nature*, pp. 3–4.

47 Van Oostveldt, *Tranen om het alledaagse*; Verschaffel, *De weg naar het binnenland*, pp. 165–80.

48 Fierlant, 'Premières idées', fo. 1027v.
49 Carol Blum, *Rousseau and the Republic of Virtue: The Language of Politics in the French Revolution* (Ithaca, NY: Cornell University Press, 1986).
50 SABE, *AC-ANT*, 787.
51 SABR, *AC-WEST*, 393–1416.
52 Wahrman, *The Making of the Modern Self*, p. 18. Cf. Thomas Walter Laqueur, *Making Sex: Body and Gender from the Greeks to Freud* (Cambridge, MA: Harvard University Press, 1990); Tim Hitchcock, *English Sexualities, 1700–1800* (Basingstoke: Palgrave, 1997), p. 48; Sturkenboom, *Spectators van hartstocht*, pp. 327–34; Soile Ylivuori, 'Rethinking female chastity and gentlewomen's honour in eighteenth-century England', *The Historical Journal*, 59:1 (2016), 71–97.
53 SABE, *AC-WEST*, 116–81.
54 'Coeur', *Dictionnaire de l'Académie française*, 4th ed. (1762), ARTFL.
55 Kounine, *Imagining the Witch*, pp. 75–7.
56 Fierlant, 'Premières idées', fos. 19v–20r, 1027v.
57 SABR, *AC-WEST*, 246–83.
58 SABR, *AC-WEST*, 396–1444.
59 SABR, *AC-WEST*, 196–748; SABE, *AC-ANT*, 329.
60 Robert Shoemaker and Richard Ward, 'Understanding the criminal: record-keeping, statistics and the early history of criminology in England', *British Journal of Criminology*, 57 (2017), 1456.
61 Victor A. Savart, *Observations critiques sur le code pénal* (Brussels: H. Tarlier, 1828), pp. 22–4.
62 Ducpétiaux, *De la peine de mort*, pp. 152–3; Ducpétiaux, *De la justice de répression*, pp. 20–5.
63 Adolphe Quetelet, *Recherches sur le penchant au crime aux différens âges* (Brussels: Hayez, 1833). See also Beirne, *Inventing Criminology*, pp. 65–110; Kaat Wils, *De omweg van de wetenschap: het positivisme en de Belgische en Nederlandse intellectuele cultuur, 1845–1914* (Amsterdam: Amsterdam University Press, 2005), pp. 117–24.
64 Similarly, the term motive only started to be popularly used in American crime reports in the first decades of the nineteenth century: Halttunen, *Murder Most Foul*, p. 43. The word was occasionally used in eighteenth-century legal manuals and commentaries, however: e.g. Jousse, *Traité de la justice*, vol. 2, pp. 292–3; Fierlant, 'Premières idées', fo. 807r.
65 NA2, *AC-BRA*, 255–500 and 248–452; SABE, *AC-ANT*, 179.
66 NA2, *AC-BRA*, 481–1733. See also SABE, *AC-ANT*, 1473.
67 NA2, *AC-BRA*, 1873.
68 SABR, *AC-WEST*, 101–7.
69 CAB, *ADM-POL*, 438 (reports of 30 Pluviose XIII, 13/12/1819 and 6 Ventose XIII). Similar reports can be found in CAB, *ADM-POL*, 439, 440 and 441.
70 Thomas Cragin, *Murder in Parisian Streets: Manufacturing Crime and Justice in the Popular Press, 1830–1900* (Lewisburg, PA: Bucknell University Press, 2006), p. 148.
71 Cf. Halttunen, *Murder Most Foul*, pp. 35–44; McKenzie, *Tyburn's Martyrs*, pp. 87–90; Cragin, *Murder in Parisian Streets*, p. 148.

72 Daston, *Against Nature*, chap. 5.
73 Cf. Halttunen, *Murder Most Foul*, pp. 45–59.
74 SABR, *AC-WEST*, 246–83; SABR, *AC-WEST*, 393–1416.
75 Cf. Barclay, 'Performing emotion', 296.
76 For a more expansive treatment, see Elwin Hofman, 'The end of sodomy: law, prosecution patterns and the evanescent will to knowledge in Belgium, France and the Netherlands, 1770–1830', *Journal of Social History*, 54:2 (2020), 480–502.
77 FA, *731*, 1514/2; NA, *PCAP-C*, 576/B (Advice Peter Stocker 1781).
78 Harry Cocks, *Visions of Sodom: Religion, Homoerotic Desire, and the End of the World in England, c. 1550–1850* (Chicago, IL: University of Chicago Press, 2017), pp. 106–7.
79 Both quotes are taken from Merrick, 'Sodomy, suicide', 188–9.
80 City Archives, Bruges, *TBO 119*, 716, cahier 6 II. Thanks to Jonas Roelens for providing me with a transcription of this case.
81 Cited in Theo van der Meer, *Sodoms zaad in Nederland: het ontstaan van homoseksualiteit in de vroegmoderne tijd* (Nijmegen: Socialistische Uitgeverij Nijmegen, 1995), p. 316.
82 Meer, *Sodoms zaad*; Theo van der Meer, 'Sodomy and Its Discontents: Discourse, Desire, and the Rise of a Same-Sex Proto-Something in the Early Modern Dutch Republic', *Historical Reflections / Réflexions Historiques*, 33:1 (2007), 41–67.
83 FA, *Police Archives (450)*, 151 (Police report, 24 May 1825).
84 Robert Deam Tobin, *Peripheral Desires: The German Discovery of Sex* (Philadelphia, PA: University of Pennsylvania Press, 2015), pp. 27–40.
85 Wannes Dupont, 'Free-Floating Evils: A Genealogy of Homosexuality in Belgium' (PhD dissertation, University of Antwerp, 2015).

Conclusion: fragments of a history of the self

Let us leave the criminal courts for a moment and consider a more traditional source for the history of the self: the autobiographical writings of Prince Charles-Joseph de Ligne. Born in 1735 in his family home in Beloeil in the province of Hainaut, Ligne was a cosmopolitan who ostentatiously mingled with European high society. He continuously travelled, corresponded with the leading philosophers, writers and rulers of his time and was an eminent authority on gardening. He often took the role of the jester and had a distinct taste for 'adventures', inspiring Goethe to call him 'the most cheerful man of his time'.[1] For all of this, he has been characterised as 'the incarnation of the eighteenth century'.[2] And as this incarnation, he could not fail to practise that typical eighteenth-century activity of autobiographical writing.

From the 1790s onwards, Ligne started working on his *Fragments de l'histoire de ma vie*. As the perils of revolutionary times seemed to prevent a further glorious career at court and, more importantly, strained his finances, Ligne shifted his ambitions towards literary glory. He had been a fervent reader of his contemporaries' memoirs: Ligne adored Rousseau's confessions and had been one of the first readers of his friend Casanova's recollections. The *Fragments* were his own attempt at autobiographical writing.[3] While clearly inspired by Rousseau and Casanova, Ligne's tone and structure were quite different and, especially, inconsistent. Ligne alternated recollections of his youth, quasi-profound observations and assessments of his own character with amusing anecdotes and (often humorous) character sketches of both the famous and less famous people he met. As a result, his writings were, as the title suggests, quite fragmented.

In the first place, Ligne bragged about his accomplishments and acquaintances. He was self-conscious about what he was doing: he was writing for an audience, not to lay bare his soul or to 'show a man in the truth of his nature', but to impress them and entertain them.[4] In many respects, Ligne displayed a social man rather than his inner life.[5] He intended the *Fragments* for posthumous publication (he even wrote a preface 'speaking from the dead'). He was well aware that 'unpublished and posthumous work is popular these days'.[6]

Nevertheless, Ligne explicitly situated his own work in the same genre as Rousseau's. 'J.J. Rousseau', he wrote, 'your *Confessions* are better written, but not as piquant as these ones; except for your two or three crimes that you have [...] made up to appear interesting, they really are too innocent'.[7] Even though he mostly played the entertainer, Ligne was more contemplative, truer to Rousseau's model at times. In later life, when he heard people speaking in the Walloon dialect while he was far away from Beloeil and would probably never return, it had an effect on him:

> I ask myself, is this love of one's country? And these thoughts, half happy, half sombre, these memories and regrets, would they degenerate in what they call homesickness? No, I say quickly, it is the time of your youth, and the pleasures you had in your birthplace that are the source of this condition [...]. You only want to return to yourself.[8]

Towards the end of his memoir, written shortly before his death in 1814, he reflected on his life and writings:

> What contrast, they will say, between what I am, what I say and what I write. But turn to yourself, my readers, and you will also find an encyclopaedia of good and bad things in endless contradictions.[9]

The *Fragments* are certainly less pivotal to the history of the self than the *Confessions*. They did not inspire many others to take up self-writing. But like the *Confessions* for Rousseau, the *Fragments* were a technology of the self. They were a means for self-presentation and self-reflection. Ligne presented himself as a man who pretended to be jolly and somewhat shallow; but was in fact also profound and reflective. This was self-conscious self-fashioning, of course, but it was also a way for Ligne to get to know himself. His writings were a way of practising a particular self, of valuing his life history and of adding depth to his self.

Ligne's memoirs have not occupied a central place in this study, nor have any similar sources. While I have occasionally cited them, for Ligne's views on sensibility and on duelling, elite self-writing and the fashion of autobiography have only played a marginal role in this story. Elite men have already received more than their share of historiographical attention. The surge of autobiographical writing among such men (and to a lesser extent, women) in the late eighteenth and early nineteenth centuries may be indicative of changing practices and discourses of self. But they do not tell all there is to say. Memoirs, diaries, autobiographies and letters do not show how models of self spread nor how people from broad layers of society put them into practice. They do not show how people were often asked to give an account of themselves. By placing common people front and centre and studying discourses and practices of the self in institutions of criminal justice, this study has attempted to enrich the inherently fragmented history of the self.

Doing the self during the age of revolutions

The period between 1750 and 1830 was a time of tremendous legal, political, literary and intellectual changes in Europe, epitomised by the movements of the late enlightenment, the revolutions and early romanticism. These changes brought along – and were to some extent brought about by – new practices and changing discourses of the self, many of them visible in criminal court records. The most prominent change in this study has been the increased importance of interiority, which also influenced discourses of individuality and collectivity, holism and fragmentation, stability and malleability and self-control and dispossession. During the second half of the eighteenth century, the psychology of sensationalism, which stressed the importance of external impressions, dominated intellectual culture. In criminal courts, people often combined this philosophy with the older idea of 'the slippery slope', which saw crime as a consequence of a universal human tendency towards sin. In line with these psychological assumptions, criminal interrogations focused mainly (though not exclusively) on external material facts, rather than inner morality or motivations. The culture of sensibility, in vigour from the 1770s to the 1790s, moreover, stressed the importance of fellow feeling and the public display of tears. All these practices tended towards an outward orientation of the self; a self that was relatively fragmented and malleable.

By the turn of the century, however, penal theory and practice started to move away from its focus on impressions and universality, towards a more holist and individualised approach. The universal 'slippery slope' made way for an interest in individual motives for crimes and individual criminal selves. Along with this development, criminal interrogations started to give more attention to inner experiences and played more to feelings of remorse and relief to obtain answers. The culture of sensibility developed into an early romantic culture, in which people primarily felt for themselves and cultivated great torments, but did not often express these publicly. In the courts and elsewhere, talk about an individual nature was on the rise. There was a decreasing focus on the social, the body and the universal, and increasing attention on the individualised inner, relatively stable and holist self. In the early nineteenth century, I have found a greater stress on 'inner depth' in several domains.

Yet these developments were not quite so straightforward. I do not con-sider the increasing stress on inner depth as an element in the making of a 'modern self', but as an evolution that is interesting in its own right and that was accompanied by complementary and conflicting tendencies. Talk about motivations and inclinations and practices of a bad conscience were rarer, but not entirely absent from eighteenth-century records. Throughout the period, honour and reputation remained important for many people appearing in the courts. Regardless of the greater insistence on inner lives, many continued to attach more value to outward presentation; to the keep-ing up of appearances. In some respects, the idea of universality even saw a revival in the early nineteenth century. The criminal justice system often supposed an anthropology in which all humans (but especially men) were principally rational beings, who made decisions by calculating benefits and losses – at least as long as they were in control of themselves. When they did not act rationally, people were thought 'not to be themselves', because they were drunk or insane. These boundaries had often been less articulate in the earlier period, when people had been understood to lose self-control in more diverse ways. By the late eighteenth century, however, the interest in the individual psyche became especially great in cases where reason was not found.

In spite of grand narratives about the coming of the modern self, its his-tory was therefore not linear, not sudden and not inevitable. We can ana-lyse change over time yet still appreciate the diversity and contradictions in the history of self. The challenge is to interpret these contradictions and to seek out developments in their constellations, however unstable, piecemeal and incomplete they may be. Conflicting discourses of the self often became more prominent at the same time: people referred with more frequency to both reason and dispossession, both interiority and outer orientation, and both stability and malleability during the same period, despite apparent contradictions. The self remained pluralistic and could be practised in dif-ferent ways depending on local circumstances.

The criminal courts brought – to some extent – discursive unity to the self across different social groups. The movements towards both greater interi-ority and greater rationality have often been observed by scholars of the self across the eighteenth and nineteenth centuries. They have generally limited their conclusions to the upper and upper-middling sorts: to people who were educated, who read books and wrote letters. But social distinctions, I have shown, are not so clear. In the courts, people of all social strata encountered the new models of the self. They had to answer questions about their inner lives, they had to respond to imputations of particular motives and they were expected to make sense of their behaviour in ways that satisfied the court. While not everyone participated in the new senses of self, and there were plenty of opportunities for resistance, excluding lower social groups from the changing models of self is not helpful in understanding the history of the self. Just as Matt Houlbrook has found for England in the twentieth century, changing conceptions of self around 1800 'traversed hierarchical social structures and cultural forms'.[10] One of the main aims of this book has been to show that we must include common people in our analysis of the history of the self, not because their sense of self was necessarily different, but because it cannot be taken for granted.

That does not mean, of course, that there were no social and gendered differences. Criminal courts mainly accepted claims to a reasonable self when they came from elite men. As such, they could more easily evade discussion of their interiority. People generally expected men of a lower social status and women to behave reasonably to some extent, but the courts more rarely accepted this as an explanation when they committed a crime. It seemed far more likely that people of a lower social status would lose control over themselves (especially by drinking), than that educated people would. Particularly in the early nineteenth century, the courts could link this to their inner dispositions. People from the very lowest social groups – the destitute, beggars, vagrants and some prostitutes – were perhaps taking the least part in the changing cultures of the self; as was most visible in their limited participation in the culture of sensibility. But even they had to answer to the changing demands of judges, who reserved some of their most inner-oriented questions on feelings and nature for poor servants accused of infanticide.

The same holds true for gender relations. The criminal justice system was tailored towards men: they made up the entire staff of lawmakers, judges, policemen, clerks and lawyers. A majority of homicide and suicide suspects, and all sodomy suspects, were men. Conversely, all suspected prostitutes and most suspected of infanticide were women. Criminal laws did not tend to prescribe a different treatment for men and women, but criminal courts did enact and reinforce discourses of masculinity and femininity in their everyday practice. As such, the coming of a more interior self went along with stricter gender norms. Masculine and feminine behaviour was increasingly 'naturalised' in the early nineteenth-century courts: magistrates supposed that men were reasonable, at least in public, and in control of themselves; while women were 'naturally' more feeling and more emotional. Their inner life was more important, but their self was less stable. Suspects and witnesses had to relate to such ideas. Nevertheless, for both men and women, honour and shame remained vital principles. Women themselves continued to claim reasonability for their actions, for instance in some cases of infanticide and in cases of prostitution, even if judges only rarely accepted this. There continued to be multiple ways to bring masculinity and femininity into practice.

Despite the growing attention for the inner side of the individual, there was still little concern for the 'authentic life' as propagated by Rousseau. Courts expected that people would behave in accordance with the social rules of honour and that they would say anything to avoid a conviction rather than spontaneously come clean. Interrogators, for instance, needed to use all their effort to convince people that confessing was good for themselves. The self – as practised in the courts – was thus more similar to Ligne than to Rousseau: full of endless contradictions, occasionally profound and looking inwards, but mainly performing for an audience.

Beyond borders

The Prince de Ligne's travels took him all over the European continent. While he enjoyed pointing out cultural differences, conceptions of self were not among them. The history of the self has often been seen as a broad European affair. Both Charles Taylor's and Michel Foucault's landmark histories of selfhood and subjectivity tell stories that surpass nations and localities. Even some more historically specific accounts, such as Dror Wahrman's, argue that 'the history of identity and self, in its broadest outlines, was not confined by Western national borders', even though 'the unfolding of the developments [...] was likely to have taken a specific and different form in each national context'.[11] In contrast with historians who stress the local or national over these major developments, or contrast Catholic with Protestant regions, I provisionally tend to agree. While local specificities certainly deserve attention, they should not conceal that similar developments were occurring in a greater geographical area.

Although most of the sources I have referred to in this study pertain to Belgium, I have aimed to tell a story that reaches beyond its borders, as the region did not exist in isolation. Intellectual, religious, political and legal influences from neighbouring countries were strong. The influence of French culture was especially high. The cultural elite of the country spoke French and many (like Ligne) idolised French culture – provoking, of course, criticism from others. For fifteen years, the Southern Netherlands were even a part of France, and during this time the French legal system was adopted. Thus, although there has been little research on the relationships between criminal courts and the self in eighteenth- and nineteenth-century France, it seems that there would be many similarities with Belgium. There were differences in timing and impact of ideas, practices and institutions, but France knew similar legal evolutions and shared (or instigated) many of the changing philosophical preferences with its smaller neighbour: the abolition of torture and the inward turn of interrogations; the coming and waning of sensibility and romanticism; the decline of sensationalism and the rise of Cousinianism; the increasing valuation of nature and the rise of psychiatry. It seems, therefore, that the ambiguous developments of the self followed a similar course in France as in the Southern Netherlands.

Yet for all their similarities, we might also suspect some differences between conceptions of self in Belgium and in France, or at least in some French regions. One notable difference, for instance, was the much more advanced state of policing in Paris, which may have contributed, among other things, to a greater – or at least more visible – self-consciousness among sodomites in the late eighteenth century.[12] In this respect, Belgium followed a trajectory that was perhaps more similar to France's provincial departments than to its capital. Another important difference with France was the greater influence of Catholicism in Belgium. Anticlericalism was (in this period) much more limited than in France. It is not immediately clear how this affected the self: penance, for instance, was an important practice for the doing of the self, and people took the sacrament with much greater frequency in Belgium than in France.[13] This would suggest a greater emphasis on self-reflection. Yet the great religiosity of the Belgian people could also be (and has been) interpreted in another way: it was a sign of their backwardness and conservatism.[14] This interpretation merits serious doubts. Not only did the latest French productions find their way into Belgium, how people practised religion also changed in accordance with the sensibilities of the times. For instance, the ritual of penance increasingly focused on providing peace of mind from the early nineteenth century onwards.[15]

If France is, due to the many shared characteristics, the most obvious country for showing the relevance of my analysis, comparison between England and Belgium allows for attention to more differences. Many of the institutions and practices that stood central in my analysis of the self in Belgium were different in England. The legal system was accusatory rather than inquisitorial and as a result, the interrogation of suspects played a minor role. The visible impact of criminal trials was much higher, as they took place in public and the press often reported on them.[16] The dominant Protestant tradition implied the absence of penance and a greater prominence of autobiography, also among less elite people.[17] The genre of criminal confessions and last dying speeches, which could be bought at executions and beyond, was much more popular than on the continent.[18]

Despite all these differences, the history of the self in England shared many characteristics with its overseas counterparts. During the eighteenth century, up to around 1780, Dror Wahrman has suggested, selves were more malleable and more socially oriented. In the criminal courts, they could easily be 'displaced', Dana Rabin has argued. There was little regard for a stable, inner core, in the criminal court or elsewhere. The culture of sensibility reigned. Around 1780, this started to change: according to Wahrman, there came a greater stress on an inner essence, on uniqueness and on rigid identity categories. By the early nineteenth century, Martin Wiener has suggested, the English criminal courts also began to assume reason and responsibility as their guiding principles, and insanity as the main explanation for losing self-control.[19] While I have not observed a shift as sudden and all-encompassing as Wahrman has, and while it seems that many of the major changes took place slightly later – around 1800 – in the Southern Netherlands, these developments are in many respects similar in both countries.

The changing discourses and practices of self were therefore not local or national affairs. As scholars ranging from Charles Taylor to Michel Foucault have suggested, it was a broader, Northwest-European, European or perhaps even 'Western' trend. While there were certainly local differences, in timing and in the way specific institutions, discourses and practices formed the self, the double movement towards a more interior and more reasonable self in the late eighteenth and early nineteenth centuries was shared by several regions. The rough lines of the history of the self in Belgium run parallel with other European countries.

The remaking of the mind

As this history of the self in Belgium runs parallel with histories in other countries, it also fits within a longer history of the self. While I must remain speculative, by tracing this wider frame, I hope to illuminate the relevance of the period under study. The discourses of the self in the 1750s were already the result of a long and complex history: of the responsibility-based criminal justice system that had been in place since the late medieval period; of the courtly cultures of renaissance self-fashioning; and since the seventeenth century, of the declining belief in possession and other supernatural influences on the self and the increasing importance of religious confession (mainly in Catholic regions) and autobiography (mainly in Protestant regions). The sixteenth- and seventeenth-century conceptions of self were certainly not devoid of individuality, interiority or self-control, but except in certain intellectual and religious movements, the inner self was given relatively little attention. People had a sense of interiority, but this inner side was not particularly 'deep', nor particularly important. Honour, work, family and religion were the main sources of identities, rather than an individualised inner nature.[20] The eighteenth century added another layer to the self. Sensationalism – in its many varieties – became an influential system to understand the workings of the human mind, facilitating a fragmented and malleable sense of self. Moreover, external influences could easily displace this self.[21]

The later eighteenth and early nineteenth century saw, as I have argued, an increased concern for the self and especially for its inner depths. In the early nineteenth century, this was combined with a renewed concern for honourable and reasonable conduct. More than before, people examined the inner self and brought it to the outside, in the criminal justice system and elsewhere. The inner side became more difficult to access and was at the same time more commonly seen as a source of truth, morality and identity.

By the late nineteenth century, it seems that this ambiguity by which both inner- and the outer-oriented discourses of the self were given great importance was (at least in some circles) increasingly problematised. The inner self was not just a source of truth and identity, but a moral imperative. Doctors in hermaphrodite cases, for instance as Geertje Mak has shown, began to look for an individual's 'inner sex' instead of their social position in society when they tried to determine someone's 'real' sex. Earlier concerns with the inner were taken to new domains: with psychoanalysis and other techniques, people 'discovered' previously unknown depths of the mind and brought them to the spotlight. It was a period that witnessed the medicalisation of sexuality, which physicians explicitly linked to an inner and stable 'orientation'.[22]

The role of criminal courts as sites for negotiating discourses and practices of the self in early modern and late nineteenth-century society still requires more detailed study. Yet I have shown that, certainly between 1750 and 1830 in Belgium, and elsewhere in Europe as well, questions about the self abounded in criminal courts. Criminal trials were often trials of the self: they engaged with discourses of inner and outer orientation, of stability and malleability, of a unified and fragmented self, and of self-control and dispossession. In criminal trials, magistrates, defendants and witnesses solicited, arbitrated, interpreted and regulated particular discourses. In this process, no 'modern self' was found: the discourses of the self in the criminal courts remained pluralistic and unstable; contradicting practices occurred at the same time. Nevertheless, I have noted that discourses also changed between 1750 and 1830, in ways I have discussed above. Through the practices solicited by the courts in response to murder and mayhem, the ways people thought and felt changed. In the criminal courts, people remade the mind.

Notes

1 For a more extensive biographical portrait of Ligne, see Philip Mansel, *Prince of Europe: The Life of Charles-Joseph de Ligne 1735–1814* (London: Phoenix, 2005).

2 Paul Morand, *Le prince de Ligne* (Paris: Mercure de France, 1964), p. xii.

3 On the *Fragments* as an autobiography (and its relationship to other con-temporary autobiographical work), see Basil Guy, 'Rousseau improv'd: The Prince de Ligne's "Fragments de l'histoire de ma vie"', *Romanic Review*, 71:3 (1980), 281–94; Raymond Trousson, 'Le Prince de Ligne et l'autobiographie', *Nouvelles annales Prince de Ligne*, 12 (1998), 93–115.

4 The quote is from Jean-Jacques Rousseau, *Les Confessions* (Paris: Launette, 1889), p. 1.

5 Cf. Trousson, 'Le Prince de Ligne et l'autobiographie'.

6 Quoted in Guy, 'Rousseau improv'd', 291.

7 Ligne, *Fragments de l'histoire*, vol. 1, p. 244.

8 Ligne, *Fragments de l'histoire*, vol. 1, p. 209. On nostalgia, selfhood and auto-biography, see Thomas Dodman, *What Nostalgia Was: War, Empire, and the Time of a Deadly Emotion* (Chicago, IL: University of Chicago Press, 2018); Joanne Begiato, 'Selfhood and "nostalgia": sensory and material memories of the childhood home in late Georgian Britain', *Journal for Eighteenth-Century Studies*, 42:2 (2019), 229–46.

9 Ligne, *Fragments de l'histoire*, vol. 1, p. 407.

10 Matt Houlbrook, *Prince of Tricksters: The Incredible True Story of Netley Lucas, Gentleman Crook* (Chicago, IL: University of Chicago Press, 2016), p. 8.

11 Wahrman, *The Making of the Modern Self*, p. 312.

12 Hofman, 'The end of sodomy', 8.

13 Rombauts, *Het Paasverzuim*, p. 123.

14 Cf. Luc Dhondt, *Verlichte monarchie, Ancien Régime en revolutie: een insti-tutionele en historische procesanalyse van politiek, instellingen en ideologie in de Habsburgse, de Nederlandse en de Vlaamse politieke ruimte (1700/1755–1790)* (Brussels: Algemeen Rijksarchief, 2002), vol. 3, p. 501.

15 Hofman, 'A wholesome cure'.

16 David Lemmings, 'Introduction: criminal courts, lawyers and the public sphere', in David Lemmings (ed.), *Crime, Courtrooms, and the Public Sphere in Britain, 1700–1850* (Farnham: Ashgate, 2012), pp. 4–5.

17 Michael Mascuch, *The Origins of the Individualist Self: Autobiography and Self-Identity in England, 1591–1791* (Cambridge: Polity Press, 1997).

18 Andrea McKenzie, 'From true confessions to true reporting? The decline and fall of the ordinary's account', *The London Journal*, 30:1 (2005), 55–70.

19 Wahrman, *The Making of the Modern Self*; Rabin, *Identity, Crime, and Legal Responsibility*; Wiener, *Reconstructing the Criminal*.

20 The argument on the early modern self is not yet settled, of course: debates are ongoing between those who argue that individuality and interiority were crucial for the early modern self and those who suggest that this was a later development; and between those who argue that interiority was new in the renaissance and those who stress continuities with the middle ages. My own synthesis is therefore necessarily speculative and based on my assessment of the arguments as well as my own findings on legal and penance manuals from

the sixteenth and seventeenth centuries, as discussed in the earlier chapters. See also Hofman, 'Sources of the self'.

21 Wahrman, *The Making of the Modern Self*; Rabin, *Identity, Crime, and Legal Responsibility*.

22 The late nineteenth-century self has, in recent times, received surprisingly less scholarly attention than the early modern and eighteenth-century self (especially concerning common practices rather than intellectual discourses), but see Geertje Mak, *Doubting Sex: Inscriptions, Bodies and Selves in Nineteenth-Century Hermaphrodite Case Histories* (Manchester: Manchester University Press, 2012); Gay, *The Naked Heart*; Carolyn Steedman, *Strange Dislocations: Childhood and the Idea of Human Interiority, 1780–1930* (Cambridge, MA: Harvard University Press, 1995).

Bibliography

Primary sources

Main archives

Felix Archives, Antwerp (FA)
    High Tribunal (V): interrogations and examinations, requests and regulations, record books
    Modern City Archives (731 and MA): police reports, prostitution administration
    Police Archives (450): police reports

State Archives, Beveren (SABE)
    Assize Court of Antwerp (R79): trial records
    Court of the First Instance of Antwerp (R19): court sessions report books

State Archives, Bruges (SABR)
    Assize Court of West-Flanders (R82): trial records

National Archives, Brussels (NA)
    Privy Council Austrian Period – Cartons (T460): advice and decisions of the council, criminal legislation reforms, grace records

National Archives 2 – Joseph Cuvelier Repository, Brussels (NA2)
    Assize Court of Brabant (I113): trial records

City Archives, Brussels (CAB)
    Administrative Archives: police reports, prostitution administration
    Historical Archives: crime books, trial records

State Archives, Kortrijk (SAK)
    Court of the First Instance of Kortrijk (200/11): correctional case records
    Old City Archives (101/3): judicial investigations, trial records

Manuscripts, print and published sources

Beccaria, Cesare, *An Essay on Crimes and Punishments* (London: Newbery, 1767).
Bioche, Charles-Jules-Armand, *Dictionnaire des juges de paix et de police ou manuel théorique et pratique en matière civile, criminelle et administrative*, 2 vols (Paris: Videcoq Fils ainé, 1852).

Code pénal du 25 septembre – 6 octobre 1791. https://ledroitcriminel.fr/la_legislatio n_criminelle/anciens_textes/code_penal_25_09_1791.htm

Code des délits et des peines du 3 brumaire, an 4 [25 October 1795], contenant les Lois relatives à l'instruction des affaires criminelles. https://ledroitcriminel.fr/la_ legislation_criminelle/anciens_textes/code_delits_et_peines_1795.htm

Code pénal de 1810. https://ledroitcriminel.fr/la_legislation_criminelle/anciens_text es/code_penal_de_1810.htm

Commission permanente du congrès médicale de Belgique, *Exposé des causes les plus fréquentes de la propagation de la maladie vénérienne et des moyens à y opposer* (Brussels: Etablissement Encyclographique, 1836).

Cupis de Camargo, Sébastien Joseph Antoine, *Lettres de Cang-ti, grand mandarin de la Chine, recueillies par Mylord Shaftesbury*, ed. Jeroom Vercruysse (Paris: Champion, 2009).

Den Vlaemschen indicateur (1779–1787).

Des Roches, Jan, *Nouveau dictionnaire françois-flamand* (Antwerp: Grange, 1769).

De Wolf, Jozef, *Den geest der reden* (Amsterdam [Ghent]: Wed. Boklar, 1777).

Dictionnaire de l'Académie française, 4th ed. (1762) and 5th ed. (1798). https://artfl -project.uchicago.edu

Diderot, Denis and Jean le Rond d'Alembert, eds, *Encyclopédie, ou Dictionnaire raisonné des sciences, des arts et des métiers* (Paris: Briasson, 1751–1772). https:// encyclopedie.uchicago.edu

Ducpétiaux, Edouard, *De la justice de répression et particulièrement de l'inutilité et des effets pernicieux de la peine de mort* (Brussels: Cautaerts, 1827).

Ducpétiaux, Edouard, *De la peine de mort* (Brussels: H. Tarlier, 1827).

Duverger, François, *Manuel des juges d'instruction*, 2 vols (Niort: Robin, 1844).

Fierlant, Goswin de, 'Premières idées sur la réformation des loix criminelles' (ca. 1773–1782). NA, *Diverse Manuscripts (I 115)*, 2119–2120.

Grimm, Friedrich Melchior Freiherr von and Denis Diderot, *Mémoires historique, littéraires & anecdotiques*, 4 vols (London: Colburn, 1813).

Hélie, Faustin, J. S. G. Nypels and Léopold Hanssens, *Traité de l'instruction criminelle: ou Théorie du Code d'instruction criminelle*, 3 vols (Brussels: Bruylant-Christophe et compagnie, 1865).

Hennequin, Antonius, *Nieuw-jaers-giften ofte Sermoonen op nieuw-jaers-dag. Sermoonen voor d'eerste communicanten*, 2 vols (Antwerp: Hubert Bincken, 1772).

Hofman, Jan Baptist Jozef, *Den onbermhartigen schuld-eisscher, of de deugdzaame in armoede* (Kortrijk: Gambar, 1796).

Hume, David, *Essays on Suicide and the Immortality of the Soul* (London: Thoemmes Press, 1783).

Jousse, Daniel, *Traité de la justice criminelle de France*, 4 vols (Paris: Debure, 1771).

Kant, Immanuel, 'Beantwortung der Frage: Was ist Aufklärung?', *Berlinische Monatsschrift*, 4:12 (1784), 481–94.

Kant, Immanuel, *Critique of Practical Reason*, trans. Thomas Kingsmill Abbott (London: Longmans, 1873).

Kant, Immanuel, *The Metaphysics of Morals*, ed. and trans. Mary Gregor (Cambridge: Cambridge University Press, 1991).

Ligne, Charles Joseph de, *Lettres et pensées du Maréchal Prince de Ligne, publiées par Mad. la Baronne de Staël Holstein. Troisième édition, revue et augmentée* (Paris, 1810).

Ligne, Charles Joseph de, *Fragments de l'histoire de ma vie*, 2 vols (Paris: Champion, 2000).

Locke, John, *An Essay Concerning Human Understanding*, ed. Peter Harold Nidditch (Oxford: Clarendon, 1975).

Loys, Ferdinandus, *Den nieuwen spiegel der jongheyd, of gulden A.B.C.* (Ghent: Judocus Begyn, 1772).

Merlin, Philippe-Antoine, ed., *Répertoire universel et raisonné de jurisprudence*, 17 vols, 4th ed. (Paris: Garnery, 1812–1825).

Nelis, Cornelius Franciscus, *Oraison funèbre de Marie-Thérèse* (Brussels: Lemaire, 1781).

Nelis, Cornelius Franciscus, *L'aveugle de la montagne* (Amsterdam: Gabriel-Henri Nicolle, 1799).

Ogier, Willem, *De gulsigheydt, speel-ghewys vertoont op de kamer vanden Olyftack den 18. october anno 1639. binnen Antwerpen*, ed. Willem Van Eeghem (Antwerp: De Sikkel, 1921). http://www.dbnl.org/tekst/ogie002toon01_01/

Paine, Thomas, *The Age of Reason: Being an Investigation of True and Fabulous Theology* (Paris: Barrois, 1794).

Pauwels, Jan Antoon Frans, *Rechtveerdig klagt-dicht, ofte Generaele redenvoeringe van verschyde staeten, conditien en persoonen, gedaen aen den uytvinder van den drank en bevelhebber over den-zelven Bacchus, rakende het misbruyk en ongevallen hier door veroorzaekt* (Antwerp: J. P. de Cort, 1778).

Quetelet, Adolphe, *Recherches sur le penchant au crime aux différens âges* (Brussels: Hayez, 1833).

Reiffenberg, Frédéric de, *Poésies diverses, suivies d'épîtres et de discours en vers* (Paris: Dondey-Dupré, 1825).

Rossi, Pellegrino, *Traité de droit pénal*, 2 vols (Brussels: Société typographique belge, 1850).

Rousseau, Jean-Jacques, *Les Confessions* (Paris: Launette, 1889).

Savart, Victor A., *Observations critiques sur le code pénal* (Brussels: H. Tarlier, 1828).

Terribles et désolantes reflexions d'un ex-conseiller en premiere instance dans le Brabant: sur quelques abus de justice (Imprimerie Patriotique, 1787).

Thielen, J. G., *Forme et manière de procéder en criminel, calquées sur les ordonnances & quantité d'arrêts, & jugemens notables* (Herve: Imprimerie du Journal général de l'Europe, 1789).

Valcke, Petrus Franciscus, *Sermoenen op de sondagen en feest-dagen*, 7 vols (Ghent: A.B. Steven, 1802).

Vanden Bossche, Petrus, *Den katholyken pedagoge, ofte Christelyken onderwyzer in den catechismus* (Ghent: Jan Meyer, 1767).

Vander Sloten, Ferdinandus Josephus, *Sermoonen op de zondagen des jaers*, 5 vols (Antwerp: Bincken, 1805).

Verheyen, Petrus, *Ziele-spys ofte christelyke leeringe*, 5 vols (Antwerp: Hubertus Bincken, 1764).

Verslype, Joannes, *Historie en overeenkominge der vier evangelien* 17 vols (Ghent: Mauritius vander Ween, 1712–1729).

Vervisch, P. F. D., *Wonderbaer en rugtbaer leven van den ex-pater Auxilius van Moorslede, alias Pieter-Francis-Dominiq Vervisch*, 2 vols (Maastricht: Wauter Dronkers, 1791).

Weiland, Petrus, *Nederduitsch taalkundig woordenboek* (Amsterdam: Johannes Allart, 1799).

Wielant, Filips, *Corte instructie in materie criminele*, ed. Jos Monballyu (Brussels: Koninklijke academie voor wetenschappen, letteren en schone kunsten van België, 1995).

Willems, Jan Frans, *Verhandeling over de Nederduytsche tael- en letterkunde, opzigtelyk de Zuydelyke provintien der Nederlanden* (Antwerp: Schoesetters, 1819).

Wollstonecraft, Mary, *A Vindication of the Rights of Woman*, ed. Eileen Hunt Botting (New Haven: Yale University Press, 2014).

Secondary sources

Abad, Reynald, *La grâce du roi: les lettres de clémence de Grande Chancellerie au XVIIIe siècle* (Paris: Presses de l'université Paris-Sorbonne, 2011).

Abbs, Peter, 'The full revelation of the self: Jean-Jacques Rousseau and the birth of deep autobiography', *Philosophy Now*, 68 (July 2008), 17–20.

Ahnert, Thomas and Susan Manning, 'Introduction: character, self, and sociability in the Scottish Enlightenment', in Thomas Ahnert and Susan Manning (eds), *Character, Self, and Sociability in the Scottish Enlightenment* (New York, NY: Palgrave Macmillan, 2013), pp. 1–30.

Allen, Robert, *Les tribunaux criminels sous la Révolution et l'Empire 1792–1811* (Rennes: Presses Universitaires de Rennes, 2005).

Andress, David, 'Living the revolutionary melodrama: Robespierre's sensibility and the construction of political commitment in the French Revolution', *Representations*, 114 (2011), 103–28.

Andrew, Donna T., *Aristocratic Vice: The Attack on Duelling, Suicide, Adultery, and Gambling in Eighteenth-Century England* (New Haven, CT: Yale University Press, 2013).

Arikha, Noga, *Passions and Tempers: A History of the Humours* (New York, NY: Harper Perennial, 2008).

Arnold, John H., 'The historian as inquisitor: the ethics of interrogating subaltern voices', *Rethinking History*, 2:3 (1998), 379–86.

Auspert, Sarah, 'La prostitution à Namur sous le régime français (1795–1813)', in Sarah Auspert, Philippe Bagard and Vincent Bruch (eds), *Namur de la conquête française à Waterloo (1792–1815). Armées, société, ordre public et urbanisme* (Namur: Société royale Sambre et Meuse, 2015), pp. 133–44.

Baasner, Frank, *Der Begriff 'sensibilité' im 18. Jahrhundert: Aufstieg und Niedergang eines Ideals* (Heidelberg: Winter, 1988).

Baggerman, Arianne, 'Autobiography and family memory in the nineteenth century', in Rudolf Dekker (ed.), *Egodocuments and History: Autobiographical Writing in Its Social Context since the Middle Ages* (Hilversum: Verloren, 2002), pp. 161–73.

Baggerman, Arianne, Rudolf Dekker and Michael Mascuch, 'Introduction', in Arianne Baggerman, Rudolf Dekker and Michael Mascuch (eds), *Controlling Time and Shaping the Self: Developments in Autobiographical Writing since the Sixteenth Century* (Leiden: Brill, 2011), pp. 13–32.

Bähr, Andreas, 'Between "self-murder" and "suicide": the modern etymology of self-killing', *Journal of Social History*, 46:3 (2013), 620–32.

Bähr, Andreas, 'Condemning oneself to death: The semantics of suicide in self-narratives of the German enlightenment', in Claudia Ulbrich, Kaspar von Greyerz and Lorenz Heiligensetzer (eds), *Mapping the 'I': Research on Self-Narratives in Germany and Switzerland* (Leiden: Brill, 2015), pp. 166–89.

Bandes, Susan A., 'Remorse and criminal justice', *Emotion Review*, 8:1 (2016), 14–19.

Banks, Stephen, *A Polite Exchange of Bullets: The Duel and the English Gentleman, 1750–1850* (Woodbridge: Boydell Press, 2010).

Barclay, Katie, 'Performing emotion and reading the male body in the Irish court, c. 1800–1845', *Journal of Social History*, 51 (2017), 293–312.

Barclay, Katie, *Men on Trial: Performing Emotion, Embodiment and Identity in Ireland, 1800–45* (Manchester: Manchester University Press, 2019).

Barker-Benfield, G. J., *The Culture of Sensibility: Sex and Society in Eighteenth-Century Britain* (Chicago, IL: University of Chicago Press, 1992).

Bassiri, Nima, 'What kind of history is the history of the self? New perspectives from the history of mind and brain medicine', *Modern Intellectual History*, 16:2 (2019), 653–65.

Beam, Sara, 'Rites of torture in Reformation Geneva', *Past & Present*, 214:suppl 7 (2012), 197–219.

Becker, Peter, '"Recht schreiben" – Disziplin, Sprachbeherrschung und Vernunft. Zur Kunst des Protokollierens im 18. und 19. Jahrhundert', in Michael Niehaus and Hans-Walter Schmidt-Hannisa (eds), *Das Protokoll: Kulturelle Funktionen einer Textsorte* (Frankfurt am Main: Peter Lang, 2005), pp. 49–76.

Begiato, Joanne, 'Selfhood and "nostalgia": sensory and material memories of the childhood home in late Georgian Britain', *Journal for Eighteenth-Century Studies*, 42:2 (2019), 229–46.

Beirne, Piers, *Inventing Criminology: Essays on the Rise of Homo Criminals* (New York, NY: University of New York Press, 1993).

Berger, Emmanuel, *La justice pénale sous la Révolution: les enjeux d'un modèle judiciaire libéral* (Rennes: Presses Universitaires de Rennes, 2008).

Berger, Emmanuel, 'La poursuite pénale sous le Directoire (1795–1799) et l'Empire (1811–1814) dans les départements belges. Evolutions et ruptures des modèles judiciaires français', in Emmanuel Berger (ed.), *L'acculturation des modèles policiers et judiciaires français en Belgique et au Pays-Bas (1795–1815)* (Brussels: Archives générales du royaume, 2010), pp. 85–98.

Berger, Emmanuel *et al.*, 'La justice avant la Belgique: tentatives autrichiennes, influences françaises et expériences néerlandaises (1780–1830)', in Margo De Koster, Dirk Heirbaut and Xavier Rousseaux (eds), *Tweehonderd jaar justitie. Historische encyclopedie van de Belgische justitie / Deux siècles de justice. Encyclopédie historique de la justice belge* (Bruges: Die Keure, 2015), pp. 26–50.

Bernos, Marcel, '"Yvrognerie": où commence le péché ?', *Rives méditerranéennes*, 22 (2005), 49–63.

Bever, Edward, 'Witchcraft prosecutions and the decline of magic', *Journal of Interdisciplinary History*, 40:2 (2009), 263–93.

Blanning, Tim, *The Romantic Revolution: A History* (New York, NY: Modern Library, 2012).

Blom, Philipp, *A Wicked Company: The Forgotten Radicalism of the European Enlightenment* (New York, NY: Basic Books, 2010).

Blum, Carol, *Rousseau and the Republic of Virtue: The Language of Politics in the French Revolution* (Ithaca, NY: Cornell University Press, 1986).

Boddice, Rob, *The History of Emotions* (Manchester: Manchester University Press, 2018).

Boddice, Rob, *A History of Feelings* (London: Reaktion Books, 2019).

Boer, Edwige de, 'Les registres de la grâce', *Sociétés & Représentations*, 36 (2013), 251–65.

Bossy, John, 'The social history of confession in the age of the Reformation', *Transactions of the Royal Historical Society*, 25 (1975), 21–38.

Bostoen, Karel, 'Verlichte letteren in de Zuidelijke Nederlanden?', in Andreas Hanou (ed.), *Verlichte letteren in Noord en Zuid* (Leuven: Peeters, 2004), pp. 393–403.

Boswell, John, *Christianity, Social Tolerance, and Homosexuality: Gay People in Western Europe from the Beginning of the Christian Era to the Fourteenth Century* (Chicago, IL: University of Chicago Press, 1980).

Bour, Isabelle, 'Epistemological ambiguities: reason, sensibility and association of ideas in Mary Wollstonecraft's Vindication of the Rights of Woman', *XVII–XVIII. Revue de la Société d'études anglo-américaines des XVIIe et XVIIIe siècles*, 49:1 (1999), 299–310.

Bourke, Joanna, *The Story of Pain: From Prayer to Painkillers* (Oxford: Oxford University Press, 2014).

Braekman, W. L., 'Marktlied bij een publieke executie in Kortrijk 1779', *De Leiegouw*, 49 (2007), 237–42.

Brennan, Thomas Edward, *Public Drinking and Popular Culture in Eighteenth-Century Paris* (Princeton, NJ: Princeton University Press, 1988).

Brock, Marleen, '"Houdt ons voor geen sentimenteele knapen!" Natuur en emoties in Brieven, geschreven op eene wandeling door een gedeelte van Duitschland en Holland, in den zomer van 1809', *Tijdschrift voor Geschiedenis*, 126:4 (2013), 548–63.

Brooks, Peter, *Troubling Confessions: Speaking Guilt in Law & Literature* (Chicago, IL: University of Chicago Press, 2000).

Broomhall, Susan, 'Feeling the wynds. Media representation of affective practices in urban Scotland in the first half of the nineteenth century', in Susan Broomhall (ed.), *Spaces for Feeling: Emotions and Sociabilities in Britain, 1650–1850* (Abingdon: Routledge, 2015), pp. 202–22.

Burckhardt, Jacob, *Die Kultur der Renaissance in Italien* (Basel: Schwabe, 1978 [1860]).

Butler, Judith, *Giving an Account of Oneself* (New York, NY: Fordham University Press, 2005).

Cahn, Zilla Gabrielle, *Suicide in French Thought from Montesquieu to Cioran* (New York, NY: Peter Lang, 1998).

Campagna, Norbert, Luigi Delia and Benoît Garnot (eds), *La torture, de quels droits? Une pratique de pouvoir, XVIe–XXIe siècle* (Paris: Imago, 2014).

Capp, Bernard, '"Jesus wept" but did the Englishman? Masculinity and emotion in early modern England', *Past & Present*, 224:1 (2014), 75–108.

Carnevali, Barbara, 'Rousseau et l'authenticité. Le concept d'authenticité chez Rousseau', in Yves Citton and Jean-François Perrin (eds), *Jean-Jacques Rousseau et l'exigence d'authenticité. Une question pour notre temps* (Paris: Classiques Garnier, 2014), pp. 23–34.

Charlier, Gustave, *Le mouvement romantique en Belgique 1815–1850*, 2 vols (Brussels: Palais des Académies, 1948).

Chauvaud, Frédéric, 'La parole captive: l'interrogatoire judiciaire au XIXe siècle', *Histoire et archives*, 1 (1997), 33–60.

Chauvaud, Frédéric, 'Le prétoire, la monomanie et l'expertise judiciaire: la difficile naissance des "experts de l'âme" (1791–1832)', in Philippe Artières and Emmanuel Da Silva (eds), *Michel Foucault et la médecine: lectures et usages* (Paris: Kimé, 2001), pp. 213–30.

Clark, Anna, *Alternative Histories of the Self: A Cultural History of Sexuality and Secrets, 1762–1917* (London: Bloomsbury Academic, 2017).

Cocks, Harry, *Visions of Sodom: Religion, Homoerotic Desire, and the End of the World in England, c. 1550–1850* (Chicago, IL: University of Chicago Press, 2017).

Cohen, Elizabeth S., 'She said, he said: situated oralities in judicial records from early modern Rome', *Journal of Early Modern History*, 16:4–5 (2012), 403–30.

Cohen, Paul, 'Torture and translation in the multilingual courtrooms of early modern France', *Renaissance Quarterly*, 69 (2016), 899–939.

Coleman, Charly, *The Virtues of Abandon: An Anti-Individualist History of the French Enlightenment* (Stanford, CA: Stanford University Press, 2014).

Colson, O., 'La sorcellerie au pays wallon. Etat actuel de la croyance', *Wallonia*, 6 (1898), 55–64.

Cosemans, Arthur, 'Alcoholisme en drankbestrijding in vroeger eeuwen', *Handelingen van de Zuid-Nederlandse Maatschappij voor Taal- en Letterkunde en Geschiedenis*, 10 (1956), 81–127.

Cragin, Thomas, *Murder in Parisian Streets: Manufacturing Crime and Justice in the Popular Press, 1830–1900* (Lewisburg, PA: Bucknell University Press, 2006).

Creasman, Allyson F., 'Fighting words: anger, insult, and "self-help" in early modern German law', *Journal of Social History*, 51:2 (2017), 272–92.

Crocker, Lester G., 'The discussion of suicide in the eighteenth century', *Journal of the History of Ideas*, 13:1 (1952), 47–72.

Dabhoiwala, Faramerz, *The Origins of Sex: A History of the First Sexual Revolution* (Oxford: Oxford University Press, 2012).

Daston, Lorraine, 'Enlightenment calculations', *Critical Inquiry*, 21:1 (1994), 182–202.

Daston, Lorraine, *Against Nature* (Cambridge, MA: MIT Press, 2019).

Davies, Bronwyn and Jane Speedy, 'Who was Pierre Rivière? Introduction to the special issue', *Emotion, Space and Society*, 5:4 (2012), 207–15.

Davis, Nathalie Zemon, 'Boundaries and the sense of self in sixteenth-century France', in Thomas C. Heller and Morton Sosna (eds), *Reconstructing Individualism: Autonomy, Individuality and the Self in Western Thought* (Stanford, CA: Stanford University Press, 1986), pp. 53–75.

Davis, Nathalie Zemon, *Fiction in the Archives. Pardon Tales and Their Tellers in Sixteenth-Century France* (Stanford, CA: Stanford University Press, 1987).

Deceulaer, Harald, 'Introduction', in Harald Deceulaer, Sébastien Dubois and Laetizia Puccio (eds), *Het pleit is in den zak! Procesdossiers uit het ancien régime en hun perspectieven voor historisch onderzoek. Acta van de studiedag gehouden op het Algemeen Rijksarchief (11–03–2013)* (Brussels: Algemeen Rijksarchief, 2014), pp. 9–38.

Dekker, Rudolf, 'Introduction', in Rudolf Dekker (ed.), *Egodocuments and History: Autobiographical Writing in Its Social Context since the Middle Ages* (Hilversum: Verloren, 2002), pp. 7–20.

Delumeau, Jean, *Le péché et la peur: la culpabilisation en Occident (XIIIe–XVIIIe siècles)* (Paris: Fayard, 1983).

Denby, David, *Sentimental Narrative and the Social Order in France, 1760–1820* (Cambridge: Cambridge University Press, 1994).

Denys, Catherine, *La police de Bruxelles entre réformes et révolutions (1748–1814): police urbaine et modernité* (Turnhout: Brepols, 2013).

De Schampeleire, Hugo, 'Verplichte lectuur te Antwerpen en Parijs in de 18e eeuw. Een comparatief quantitatief leesonderzoek naar Voltaire, Rousseau en de Encyclopedie', in Roland Mortier and Hervé Hasquin (eds), *L'influence française dans les Pays-Bas autrichiens et la Principauté de Liège au temps de Voltaire et de Jean-Jacques Rousseau* (Brussels: Université de Bruxelles, 1979), pp. 132–53.

Deschrijver, Sonja, 'From sin to insanity? Suicide trials in the Spanish Netherlands, sixteenth and seventeenth Centuries', *Sixteenth Century Journal*, 42:4 (2011), 981–1002.

De Vuyst, Julien, *Het moordlied in de Zuidelijke Nederlanden tot de XIXe eeuw* (Brussels: Aurelia, 1976).

Dhondt, Luc, *Verlichte monarchie, Ancien Régime en revolutie: een institutionele en historische procesanalyse van politiek, instellingen en ideologie in de Habsburgse, de Nederlandse en de Vlaamse politieke ruimte (1700/1755–1790)*, 6 vols (Brussels: Algemeen Rijksarchief, 2002).

Dinges, Martin, *Der Maurermeister und der Finanzrichter: Ehre, Geld und soziale Kontrolle im Paris des 18. Jahrhunderts* (Göttingen: Vandenhoeck & Ruprecht, 1994).

Dixon, Thomas, *From Passions to Emotions: The Creation of a Secular Psychological Category* (Cambridge: Cambridge University Press, 2003).

Dixon, Thomas, '"Emotion": the history of a keyword in crisis', *Emotion Review*, 4:4 (2012), 338–44.

Dixon, Thomas, *Weeping Britannia: Portrait of a Nation in Tears* (Oxford: Oxford University Press, 2015).

Dodman, Thomas, *What Nostalgia Was: War, Empire, and the Time of a Deadly Emotion* (Chicago, IL: University of Chicago Press, 2018).

Dolan, Frances E., *True Relations: Reading, Literature, and Evidence in Seventeenth-Century England* (Philadelphia, PA: University of Pennsylvania Press, 2013).

Donnelly, Kevin, *Adolphe Quetelet, Social Physics and the Average Men of Science, 1796–1874* (London: Pickering & Chatto, 2015).

Douxchamps-Lefevre, C., 'A propos de la sorcellerie dans le Namurois au 18e siècle – le procès à charge de Joseph Saucin, manant de Spy (1762–1763)', in Marie-Sylvie Dupont-Bouchat (ed.), *La sorcellerie dans les Pays-Bas sous l'Ancien Regime: aspects juridiques, institutionnels et sociaux. De hekserij in de Nederlanden onder het Ancien Regime: juridische, institutionele en sociale aspecten* (Heule: UGA, 1987), pp. 71–7.

Doyon, Julie, 'Les enjeux médico-judiciaires de la folie parricide au XVIIIe siècle', *Crime, Histoire & Sociétés / Crime, History & Societies*, 15:1 (2011), 5–27.

Duerloo, Luc *et al.*, 'Bestuur en politiek op een Schoon Verdiep', in Marnix Beyen *et al.* (eds), *Het stadhuis van Antwerpen: 450 jaar geschiedenis* (Antwerp: Pandora, 2015), pp. 171–216.

Dumont, Louis, *Essais sur l'individualisme: une perspective anthropologique sur l'idéologie moderne* (Paris: Seuil, 1983).

Dupont, Wannes, 'Free-Floating Evils. A Genealogy of Homosexuality in Belgium' (PhD dissertation, University of Antwerp, 2015).

Dupont-Bouchat, Marie-Sylvie, 'Sorcellerie et superstition: l'attitude de l'Eglise dans les Pays-Bas, XVIe–XVIIIe siècle', in Hervé Hasquin (ed.), *Magie, sorcellerie, parapsychologie* (Brussels: Editions de l'Université de Bruxelles, 1984), pp. 61–83.

Dupont-Bouchat, Marie-Sylvie, 'La reforme du droit penal dans les Pays-Bas autrichiens à la fin de l'Ancien Régime (1765–1787)', in Georges Macours (ed.), *Cornua legum: actes des journées internationales d'histoire du droit et des institutions* (Antwerp: Kluwer, 1987), pp. 71–88.

Dupont-Bouchat, Marie-Sylvie, 'Le diable apprivoisée. La sorcellerie revisitée: magie et sorcellerie au XIXe siècle', in Robert Muchembled (ed.), *Magie et sorcellerie en Europe du Moyen Age à nos jours* (Paris: Colin, 1994), pp. 235–66.

Dupont-Bouchat, Marie-Sylvie, 'Culpabilisation et conscience individuelle. L'individu, l'Église et l'État à l'époque moderne (XVIe–XVIIIe s.)', in *La Belgique criminelle. Droit, justice, société (XIVe–XXe siècles)* (Louvain-la-Neuve: Academia-Bruylant, 2006), pp. 75–105.

Dupont-Bouchat, Marie-Sylvie, 'La prison pénale. Modèles et pratiques: "Révolution" ou "évolution"? (1775–1815)', in *La Belgique criminelle. Droit, justice, société (XIVe–XXe siècles)* (Louvain-la-Neuve: Academia-Bruylant, 2006), pp. 357–84.

Ehrard, Jean, *L'idée de nature en France dans la première moitié du XVIIIe siècle* (Paris: Sevpen, 1963).

Eibach, Joachim, 'Violence and masculinity', in Paul Knepper and Anja Johansen (eds), *The Oxford Handbook of the History of Crime and Criminal Justice* (Oxford: Oxford University Press, 2016), pp. 229–49.

Eigen, Joel Peter, *Witnessing Insanity: Madness and Mad-Doctors in the English Court* (New Haven, CT: Yale University Press, 1995).

Eigen, Joel Peter, *Mad-Doctors in the Dock: Defending the Diagnosis, 1760–1913* (Baltimore, MD: Johns Hopkins University Press, 2016).

Enenkel, Karl A. E. and Anita Traninger, 'Introduction: discourses of anger in the early modern period', in Karl A. E. Enenkel and Anita Traninger (eds), *Discourses of Anger in the Early Modern Period* (Leiden: Brill, 2015), pp. 16–45.

Essary, Kirk, 'Passions, affections, or emotions? On the ambiguity of 16th-century terminology', *Emotion Review*, 9:4 (2017), 367–74.

Eustace, Nicole, *Passion Is the Gale: Emotion, Power, and the Coming of the American Revolution* (Williamsburg, NC: University of North Carolina Press, 2008).

Faber, Sjoerd, 'De verzachting van de Code Pénal in Nederland (1813) en België (1814–1815)', *Pro Memorie*, 15 (2013), 243–60.

Foucault, Michel (ed.), *Moi, Pierre Rivière, ayant égorgé ma mère, ma soeur et mon frère... Un cas de parricide au XIXe siècle* (Paris: Julliard, 1973).

Foucault, Michel, *The History of Sexuality. Volume I: An Introduction* (New York, NY: Pantheon Books, 1978).

Foucault, Michel, *Discipline and Punish: The Birth of the Prison* (New York, NY: Vintage Books, 1995).

Foucault, Michel, *History of Madness* (New York, NY: Routledge, 2006).

Foucault, Michel, *Mal faire, dire vrai: fonction de l'aveu en justice* (Louvain-la-Neuve: Presses Universitaires de Louvain, 2012).

Frevert, Ute, *Men of Honour: A Social and Cultural History of the Duel* (Cambridge: Polity Press, 1995).

Frevert, Ute, *Emotions in History: Lost and Found* (Budapest: Central European University Press, 2011).

Frevert, Ute, 'Honour and/or/as passion: Historical trajectories of legal defenses', *Rechtsgeschichte – Legal History*, 22 (2014), 245–55.

Friedland, Paul, *Seeing Justice Done: The Age of Spectacular Capital Punishment in France* (Oxford: Oxford University Press, 2012).

Garnot, Benoît, 'La justice pénale et les témoins en France au 18e siècle: de la théorie à la pratique', *Dix-huitième siècle*, 39:1 (2007), 99–108.

Gay, Peter, *The Bourgeois Experience Victoria to Freud, Vol. 4: The Naked Heart* (New York, NY: Norton, 1995).

Geertz, Clifford, '"From the native's point of view": on the nature of anthropological understanding', *Bulletin of the American Academy of Arts and Sciences*, 28 (1974), 26–45.

Gent, Jacqueline van, *Magic, Body and the Self in Eighteenth-Century Sweden* (Leiden: Brill, 2009).

Gijswijt-Hofstra, Marijke, 'Witchcraft after the witch-trials', in *Witchcraft and Magic in Europe: The Eighteenth and Nineteenth Centuries* (London: Athlone, 1999), pp. 95–188.

Godineau, Dominique, *S'abréger les jours: le suicide en France au XVIIIe siècle* (Paris: Colin, 2012).

Goldstein, Jan, *Console and Classify: The French Psychiatric Profession in the Nineteenth Century* (Cambridge: Cambridge University Press, 1987).

Goldstein, Jan, 'Foucault's technologies of the self and the cultural history of identity', in John Neubauer (ed.), *Cultural History after Foucault* (New York, NY: de Gruyter, 1999), pp. 37–54.

Goldstein, Jan, *The Post-Revolutionary Self: Politics and Psyche in France, 1750–1850* (Cambridge, MA: Harvard University Press, 2005).

Gouverneur, Romy, 'La perception et la prise en charge des insensés dans le Namurois au XVIIIe siècle', in Sarah Auspert, Isabelle Parmentier and Xavier Rousseaux (eds), *Buveurs, voleuses, insensés et prisonniers à Namur au XVIIIe: déviance, justice et régulation sociale au temps des Lumières* (Namur: Presses Universitaires de Namur, 2012), pp. 83–113.

Gowing, Laura, *Common Bodies: Women, Touch and Power in Seventeenth-Century England* (New Haven, CT: Yale University Press, 2003).

Green, Thomas A., 'Societal concepts of criminal liability for homicide in mediaeval England', *Speculum*, 47:4 (1972), 669–94.

Green, Thomas A., 'The jury and criminal responsibility in Anglo-American history', *Criminal Law and Philosophy*, 9:3 (2015), 423–42.

Greenberg, David F., *The Construction of Homosexuality* (Chicago, IL: University of Chicago Press, 1988).

Guignard, Laurence, *Juger la folie: la folie criminelle devant les Assises au XIXe siècle* (Paris: Presses universitaires de France, 2010).

Guignard, Laurence, 'La genèse de l'article 64 du code pénal', *Criminocorpus. Revue d'Histoire de la justice, des crimes et des peines*, 22 April 2016. http://journals.openedition.org/criminocorpus/3215

Guillet, François, *La mort en face: histoire du duel de la Révolution à nos jours* (Paris: Aubier, 2008).

Guy, Basil, 'Rousseau improv'd: The Prince de Ligne's "Fragments de l'histoire de ma vie"', *Romanic Review*, 71:3 (1980), 281–94.

Habermas, Rebekka, *Thieves in Court: The Making of the German Legal System in the Nineteenth Century* (New York, NY: Cambridge University Press, 2016).

Hagen, Edwina, 'Fashioning the emotional self: the Dutch statesman Rutger Jan Schimmelpenninck (1761–1825) and the cult of sensibility', *BMGN – Low Countries Historical Review*, 129:2 (2014), 138–62.

Hailwood, Mark, '"It puts good reason into brains": Popular understandings of the effects of alcohol in seventeenth-century England', *Brewery History*, 150 (2013), 39–53.

Halperin, David M., *How to Do the History of Homosexuality* (Chicago, IL: University of Chicago Press, 2002).

Halttunen, Karen, 'Humanitarianism and the pornography of pain in Anglo-American culture', *The American Historical Review*, 100 (1995), 303–34.

Halttunen, Karen, *Murder Most Foul: The Killer and the American Gothic Imagination* (Cambridge, MA: Harvard University Press, 1998).

Hardwick, Julie, *Family Business: Litigation and the Political Economies of Daily Life in Early Modern France* (Oxford: Oxford University Press, 2009).

Hasquin, Hervé, 'A propos d'exorcisme au siècle des Lumières. Les réactions d'un fonctionnaire "éclairé"', in Hervé Hasquin (ed.), *Magie, sorcellerie, parapsychologie* (Brussels: Editions de l'Université de Bruxelles, 1984), pp. 99–105.

Heijden, Manon van der, *Misdadige vrouwen. Criminaliteit en rechtspraak in Holland 1600–1800* (Amsterdam: Prometheus – Bert Bakker, 2014).

Hitchcock, Tim, *English Sexualities, 1700–1800* (Basingstoke: Palgrave, 1997).

Hitchcock, Tim and Robert Shoemaker, *London Lives: Poverty, Crime and the Making of a Modern City, 1690–1800* (Cambridge: Cambridge University Press, 2015).

Hoegaerts, Josephine, '"L'homme du monde est obligé de se battre". Duel-vertogen en praktijken in en rond het Belgische parlement, 1830–1900', *Tijdschrift voor Geschiedenis*, 124:2 (2011), 190–205.

Hoegaerts, Josephine, *Masculinity and Nationhood, 1830–1910: Constructions of Identity and Citizenship in Belgium* (Basingstoke: Palgrave Macmillan, 2014).

Hoegaerts, Josephine and Tine Van Osselaer, 'De lichamelijkheid van emoties. Een introductie', *Tijdschrift voor geschiedenis*, 126:4 (2013), 452–65.

Hofman, Elwin, 'An obligation of conscience. Gossip as social control in an eighteenth-century Flemish town', *European Review of History*, 21:5 (2014), 653–70.

Hofman, Elwin, 'How to do the history of the self', *History of the Human Sciences*, 29:3 (2016), 8–24.

Hofman, Elwin, 'Heksenwaan. De nadagen van magie in de Zuidelijke Nederlanden', *Historica*, 40:2 (2017), 19–24.

Hofman, Elwin, 'The tears of a killer: criminal trials and sentimentalism in the Austrian Netherlands', *BMGN – Low Countries Historical Review*, 132:2 (2017), 3–26.

Hofman, Elwin, 'A wholesome cure for the wounded soul: confession, emotions, and self in eighteenth- and nineteenth-century Catholicism', *Journal of Religious History*, 42 (2018), 222–41.

Hofman, Elwin, 'Corporeal truth: conscience, fear and the body in French criminal interrogations, 1750–1850', *Cultural and Social History*, advance online access (2020). doi:10.1080/14780038.2020.1752107

Hofman, Elwin, 'Sources of the self from the renaissance to the 20th century', in Wade E. Pickren (ed.), *The Oxford Encyclopedia of the History of Psychology* (Oxford: Oxford University Press, 2020). doi: 10.1093/acrefore/9780190236557.013.685

Hofman, Elwin, 'Spatial interrogations: space and power in French criminal justice, 1750–1850', *law&history*, 7 (2020) in press.

Hofman, Elwin, 'The end of sodomy: law, prosecution patterns and the evanescent will to knowledge in Belgium, France and the Netherlands, 1770–1830', *Journal of Social History*, 54:2 (2020), 480–502.

Holland, Dorothy and Andrew Kipnis, 'Metaphors for embarrassment and stories of exposure: the not-so-egocentric self in American culture', *Ethos*, 22 (1994), 316–42.

Houlbrook, Matt, *Prince of Tricksters: The Incredible True Story of Netley Lucas, Gentleman Crook* (Chicago, IL: University of Chicago Press, 2016).

Hubert, Eugène, *Un chapitre de l'histoire du droit criminel dans les Pays-Bas autrichiens au XVIIIe siècle: les mémoires de Goswin de Fierlant* (Brussels: Hayez, 1895).

Hubert, Eugène, *La torture aux Pays-Bas autrichiens pendant le XVIIIe siècle: son application, ses partisans et ses adversaires, son abolition* (Brussels: Hayez, 1896).

Hunt, Lynn, *Inventing Human Rights: A History* (New York, NY: W. W. Norton, 2007).

Ibbett, Katherine, 'Fellow-feeling', in Susan Broomhall (ed.), *Early Modern Emotions: An Introduction* (London: Routledge, 2017), pp. 61–4.

Johnstone, Gerry, 'From vice to disease? The concepts of dipsomania and inebriety, 1860–1908', *Social & Legal Studies*, 5:1 (1996), 37–56.

Jones, Colin, *The Smile Revolution in Eighteenth Century Paris* (Oxford: Oxford University Press, 2014).

Jordanova, Ludmilla, *Nature Displayed: Gender, Science and Medicine, 1760–1820* (London: Longman, 1999).

Judge, Jane C., *United States of Belgium: The Story of the First Belgian Revolution* (Leuven: Leuven University Press, 2018).

Kamali, Elizabeth Papp, *Felony and the Guilty Mind in Medieval England* (Cambridge: Cambridge University Press, 2019).

Kästner, Alexander, *Tödliche Geschichte(n): Selbsttötungen in Kursachsen im Spannungsfeld von Normen und Praktiken (1547–1815)* (Konstanz: Universitätsverlag Konstanz, 2012).

Keetley, Dawn, 'From anger to jealousy: explaining domestic homicide in antebellum America', *Journal of Social History*, 42:2 (2008), 269–97.

Kennedy, Gwynne, *Just Anger: Representing Women's Anger in Early Modern England* (Carbondale, IL: Southern Illinois University Press, 2000).

Knott, Sarah, *Sensibility and the American Revolution* (Williamsburg, NC: University of North Carolina Press, 2009).

Koolhaas-Grosfeld, Eveline, 'Behind the mask of civility: physiognomy and unmasking in the early eighteenth-century Dutch Republic', in Arianne Baggerman, Rudolf Dekker and Michael Mascuch (eds), *Controlling Time and Shaping the Self: Developments in Autobiographical Writing since the Sixteenth Century* (Leiden: Brill, 2011), pp. 247–66.

Kounine, Laura, *Imagining the Witch: Emotions, Gender, and Selfhood in Early Modern Germany* (Oxford: Oxford University Press, 2018).

Krause, Virginia, *Witchcraft, Demonology, and Confession in Early Modern France* (Cambridge: Cambridge University Press, 2015).

Lacey, Nicola, *Women, Crime and Character: From Moll Flanders to Tess of the D'Urbervilles* (Oxford: Oxford University Press, 2008).

Laingui, André, *La responsabilité pénale dans l'ancien droit (XVIe–XVIIIe siècle)* (Paris: Pichon et Durand-Auzias, 1970).

Laingui, André and Arlette Lebigre, *Histoire du droit pénal. T. 2: La procédure criminelle* (Paris: Cujas, 1979).

Lambert, Karine, *Itinéraires féminins de la déviance: Provence 1750–1850* (Aix-en-Provence: Université de Provence, 2012).

Langbein, John H., *Torture and the Law of Proof: Europe and England in the Ancien Régime* (Chicago, IL: University of Chicago Press, 1977).

Laqueur, Thomas Walter, *Making Sex: Body and Gender from the Greeks to Freud* (Cambridge, MA: Harvard University Press, 1990).

Leboutte, René, 'Offense against family order: infanticide in Belgium from the fifteenth through the early twentieth centuries', *Journal of the History of Sexuality*, 2 (1991), 159–85.

Lejeune, Philippe, 'Crime et testament. Les autobiographies de criminels au XIXe siècle', in Philippe Lejeune (ed.), *Récits de vie et institutions* (Paris: Centre de Sémiotique Textuelle, 1986), pp. 73–98.

Lemmings, David, 'Introduction: criminal courts, lawyers and the public sphere', in David Lemmings (ed.), *Crime, Courtrooms, and the Public Sphere in Britain, 1700–1850* (Farnham: Ashgate, 2012), pp. 1–22.

Lenders, Piet, 'De eerste poging van J.J.P. Vilain XIIII tot het bouwen van een correctiehuis (1749–1751)', *Handelingen van de Zuid-Nederlandse Maatschappij voor Taal- en Letterkunde en Geschiedenis*, 12 (1958), 167–87.

Levack, Brian P., 'The decline and end of witchcraft prosecutions', in *Witchcraft and Magic in Europe: The Eighteenth and Nineteenth Centuries* (London: Athlone, 1999), pp. 1–93.

Levack, Brian P., *The Devil within: Possession & Exorcism in the Christian West* (New Haven, CT: Yale University Press, 2013).

Lever, Maurice, *Canards sanglants: naissance du fait divers* (Paris: Fayard, 1993).

Liliequist, Jonas, 'From honour to virtue: The shifting social logics of masculinity and honour in early modern Sweden', in Carolyn Strange, R. B. Cribb and Christopher E. Forth (eds), *Honour, Violence and Emotions in History* (London: Bloomsbury, 2014), pp. 45–67.

Lis, Catharina and Hugo Soly, *Te gek om los te lopen? Collocatie in de 18de eeuw* (Turnhout: Brepols, 1990).

Lorcy, Maryvonne, 'Stratégie et tactique dans la procédure criminelle du XVIIIe siècle d'après les archives judiciaires bretonnes' (PhD dissertation, Lille 3, 1987).

Macpherson, C. B., *The Political Theory of Possessive Individualism: Hobbes to Locke* (Oxford: Clarendon, 1962).

Maddens, Niklaas, 'De nieuwe tijd', in Niklaas Maddens (ed.), *De geschiedenis van Kortrijk* (Tielt: Lannoo, 1990), pp. 147–363.

Madelein, Christophe, *Juigchen in den adel der menschelijke natuur. Het verhevene in de Nederlanden (1770–1830)* (Ghent: Academia Press, 2011).

Mak, Geertje, *Doubting Sex: Inscriptions, Bodies and Selves in Nineteenth-Century Hermaphrodite Case Histories* (Manchester: Manchester University Press, 2012).

Mansel, Philip, *Prince of Europe: The Life of Charles-Joseph de Ligne 1735–1814* (London: Phoenix, 2005).

Marland, Hilary, 'Getting away with murder? Puerperal insantiy, infanticide and the defence plea', in Mark Jackson (ed.), *Infanticide: Historical Perspectives on Child Murder and Concealment, 1550–2000* (Aldershot: Ashgate, 2002), pp. 168–92.

Martin, A. Lynn, *Alcohol, Sex, and Gender in Late Medieval and Early Modern Europe* (Basingstoke: Palgrave, 2001).

Martin, John Jeffries, *Myths of Renaissance Individualism* (Basingstoke: Palgrave Macmillan, 2004).

Martin, Luther H., Huck Gutman and Patrick H. Hutton (eds), *Technologies of the Self: A Seminar with Michel Foucault* (Amherst, MA: University of Massachusetts, 1988).

Mascuch, Michael, *The Origins of the Individualist Self: Autobiography and Self-Identity in England, 1591–1791* (Cambridge: Polity Press, 1997).

Mat, Michèle, 'Boeken, ideeën, genootschappen in het Oostenrijkse "België"', in Hervé Hasquin (ed.), *Oostenrijks België, 1713–1794: de Zuidelijke Nederlanden onder de Oostenrijkse Habsburgers* (Brussels: Gemeentekrediet, 1987), pp. 239–62.

Matt, Susan J. and Peter N. Stearns (eds), *Doing Emotions History* (Urbana, IL: University of Illinois Press, 2014).

Maynard, Steven, 'Police/archives', *Archivaria*, 68 (2009), 159–82.

McIntosh, Mary, 'The homosexual role', *Social Problems*, 16 (1968), 182–92.

McKenzie, Andrea, 'From true confessions to true reporting? The decline and fall of the ordinary's account', *The London Journal*, 30:1 (2005), 55–70.

McKenzie, Andrea, *Tyburn's Martyrs: Execution in England, 1675–1775* (London: Hambledon Continuum, 2007).

McManners, John, *Death and the Enlightenment: Changing Attitudes to Death among Christians and Unbelievers in Eighteenth-Century France* (Oxford: Clarendon, 1981).

McSheffrey, Shannon, 'Detective fiction in the archives: court records and the uses of law in late Medieval England', *History Workshop Journal*, 65:1 (2008), 65–78.

Mechant, Maja, 'Hoeren, pauwen ende ondeughende doghters. De levenslopen van vrouwen in de Brugse prostitutie (1750–1790)' (PhD dissertation, University of Ghent, 2018).

Meer, Theo van der, *Sodoms zaad in Nederland: het ontstaan van homoseksualiteit in de vroegmoderne tijd* (Nijmegen: Socialistische Uitgeverij Nijmegen, 1995).

Meer, Theo van der, 'Sodomy and its discontents: discourse, desire, and the rise of a same-sex proto-something in the early modern Dutch Republic', *Historical Reflections / Réflexions Historiques*, 33:1 (2007), 41–67.

Meewis, Wim, *De vierschaar: de criminele rechtspraak in het Oude Antwerpen van de veertiende tot het einde van de achttiende eeuw* (Kapellen: Pelckmans, 1992).

Meijer, Annemieke, *The Pure Language of the Heart: Sentimentalism in the Netherlands 1775–1800* (Amsterdam: Rodopi, 1998).

Melzer, Arthur M., *The Natural Goodness of Man: On the System of Rousseau's Thought* (Chicago, IL: University of Chicago Press, 1990).

Merrick, Jeffrey, 'Sodomy, suicide, and the limits of legal reform in eighteenth-century France', *Studies in Eighteenth-Century Culture*, 46 (2017), 183–203.

Michalik, Kerstin, 'The development of the discourse on infanticide in the late eighteenth century and the new legal standardization of the offense in the nineteenth century', in Ulrike Gleixner and Marion W. Gray (eds), *Gender in Transition: Discourse and Practice in German-Speaking Europe, 1750–1830* (Ann Arbor, MI: University of Michigan Press, 2006), pp. 51–71.

Milka, Amy and David Lemmings, 'Narratives of feeling and majesty: mediated emotions in the eighteenth-century criminal courtroom', *The Journal of Legal History*, 38:2 (2017), 155–78.

Minois, Georges, *Histoire du suicide. La société occidentale face à la mort volontaire* (Paris: Fayard, 1995).

Monballyu, Jos, 'De Raad van Vlaanderen en de hervorming van het strafrecht (1756–1787)', *Tijdschrift voor Rechtsgeschiedenis*, 64 (1996), 47–75.

Monballyu, Jos, 'De decriminalisering van de zelfdoding in de Oostenrijkse Nederlanden', *Revue belge de philologie et d'histoire*, 78:2 (2000), 445–69.

Monballyu, Jos, *Six Centuries of Criminal Law: History of Criminal Law in the Southern Netherlands and Belgium (1400–2000)* (Leiden: Brill, 2014).

Monballyu, Jos and Nanouche Heeren, 'Prostitutie en vrouwenhandel in de Nieuwe Tijd', in Lieve De Mecheleer (ed.), *Van badhuis tot eroscentrum. Prostitutie en vrouwenhandel van de middeleeuwen tot heden* (Brussels: Algemeen rijksarchief, 1995), pp. 23–49.

Morand, Paul, *Le prince de Ligne* (Paris: Mercure de France, 1964).

Moscoso, Javier, *Pain: A Cultural History* (Basingstoke: Palgrave Macmillan, 2012).

Muller, Caroline, 'Ce que confessent les journaux intimes: un nouveau regard sur la confession (France, XIXe siècle)', *Circé. Histoires, Cultures et Sociétés*, 4 (2014). http://www.revue-circe.uvsq.fr/ce-que-confessent-les-journaux-intimes-un-no uveau-regard-sur-la-confession-france-xixe-siecle

Murray, D. W., 'What is the western concept of the self? On forgetting David Hume', *Ethos*, 21 (1993), 3–23.

Musin, Aude and Michel Nassiet, 'Les récits de rémission dans la longue durée. Le cas de l'Anjou du XVe au XVIIIe siècle', *Revue d'histoire moderne et contemporaine*, 57:4 (2010), 51–71.

Myers, W. David, *'Poor, Sinning Folk': Confession and Conscience in Counter-Reformation Germany* (Ithaca, NY: Cornell University Press, 1996).

Nahoum-Grappe, Véronique, 'Le boire et l'ivresse dans la pensée sociale sous l'ancien régime en France (XVIe–XVIIIe siècles)', in *Histoire et alcool* (Paris: L'Harmattan, 1999), pp. 15–99.

Nicholls, James, *The Politics of Alcohol: A History of the Drink Question in England* (Manchester: Manchester University Press, 2009).

Niehaus, Michael, '"Wirkung einer Naturkraft". Das Geständnis und sein Motiv in Diskursen um 1800', in Jo Reichertz and Manfred Schneider (eds), *Sozialgeschichte des Geständnisses: zum Wandel der Geständniskultur* (Wiesbaden: VS Verlag für Sozialwissenschaften, 2007), pp. 43–73.

Niehaus, Michael and Christian Lück, 'Konfrontationen und Lügenstrafen. Akten zur Geständnisarbeit um 1800', in Jo Reichertz and Manfred Schneider (eds), *Sozialgeschichte des Geständnisses: zum Wandel der Geständniskultur* (Wiesbaden: VS Verlag für Sozialwissenschaften, 2007), pp. 115–41.

Nietzsche, Friedrich, *On the Genealogy of Morals*, trans. Walter Kaufmann and R. J. Hollingdale (New York, NY: Random House, 1967).

Nutz, Thomas, *Strafanstalt als Besserungsmaschine: Reformdiskurs und Gefängniswissenschaft, 1775–1848* (München: Oldenbourg, 2001).

Nye, Robert A., *Masculinity and Male Codes of Honor in Modern France* (New York, NY: Oxford University Press, 1993).

Nye, Robert A., 'How the duel of honour promoted civility and attenuated violence in western europe', in Carolyn Strange, R. B. Cribb and Christopher E. Forth (eds), *Honour, Violence and Emotions in History* (London: Bloomsbury, 2014), pp. 183–202.

Oosterhuis, Harry, *Stepchildren of Nature: Krafft-Ebing, Psychiatry, and the Making of Sexual Identity* (London: University of Chicago Press, 2000).

Parmentier, Romain, 'Dans l'ombre d'un pendu: justice et mentalités autour du suicide à la fin du XVIIe siècle', *Dix-septième siècle*, 271 (2016), 303–26.

Pirenne, Henri, *Histoire de Belgique: des origines au commencement du XIVe siècle* (Brussels: Henri Lamertin, 1900).

Pirotte, Kevin, 'Les grâces du Vendredi saint et le gouvernement autrichien dans les Pays-Bas sous Marie-Thérèse (1740–1780): procédure, pouvoir central et normes judiciaires face à l'homicide' (master's dissertation, UCLouvain, 2013).

Plamper, Jan, *The History of Emotions: An Introduction* (Oxford: Oxford University Press, 2015).

Pohl-Zucker, Susanne, *Making Manslaughter: Process, Punishment and Restitution in Württemberg and Zurich, 1376–1700* (Leiden: Brill, 2017).

Pol, Lotte van de, *Het Amsterdams hoerdom. Prostitutie in de zeventiende en achttiende eeuw* (Amsterdam: Wereldbibliotheek, 1996).

Porret, Michel, *Beccaria: le droit de punir* (Paris: Michalon, 2003).

Porret, Michel, *Sur la scène du crime: pratique pénale, enquête et expertises judiciaires à Genève (XVIIIe–XIXe siècle)* (Montréal: Presses de l'Université de Montréal, 2008).

Porter, Roy, 'Introduction', in Roy Porter (ed.), *Rewriting the Self: Histories from the Renaissance to the Present* (London: Routledge, 1997), pp. 1–14.

Porter, Roy, 'Witchcraft and magic in enlightenment, romantic and liberal thought', in *Witchcraft and Magic in Europe: The Eighteenth and Nineteenth Centuries* (London: Athlone, 1999), pp. 191–282.

Poullet, Edmond, *Histoire du droit pénal dans le duché de Brabant, depuis l'avénement de Charles-Quint jusqu'à la réunion de la Belgique à la France, à la fin du XVIIIe siècle* (Brussels: Hayez, 1870).

Rabin, Dana, 'Bodies of evidence, states of mind: infanticide, emotion and sensibility in eighteenth-century England', in Mark Jackson (ed.), *Infanticide: Historical Perspectives on Child Murder and Concealment, 1550–2000* (Aldershot: Ashgate, 2002), pp. 73–92.

Rabin, Dana, 'Searching for the self in eighteenth-century English criminal trials, 1730–1800', *Eighteenth-Century Life*, 27:1 (2003), 85–106.

Rabin, Dana, *Identity, Crime, and Legal Responsibility in Eighteenth-Century England* (Basingstoke: Palgrave Macmillan, 2004).

Rabin, Dana, 'Drunkenness and responsibility for crime in the eighteenth century', *Journal of British Studies*, 44:3 (2005), 457–77.

Rabin, Dana, '"For the shame of the world, and fear of her mother's anger": Emotion and child murder in England and Scotland in the long eighteenth century', in Carolyn Strange, Robert Cribb and Christopher E. Forth (eds), *Honour, Violence and Emotions in History* (London: Bloomsbury, 2014), pp. 69–87.

Raeymaekers, Dries, '"Pour fuyr le nom de vilayn et meschant." Het duel in de Zuidelijke Nederlanden: aspecten van eer en oneer in de Nieuwe Tijd' (licentiate's dissertation, KU Leuven, 2004).

Raeymaekers, Dries, '"Grosses querelles & haines mortelles". De centrale overheid versus het duel om eer in de Zuidelijke Nederlanden (1550–1650)', *Tijdschrift voor Geschiedenis*, 120:3 (2007), 316–31.

Reddy, William M., 'Against constructionism: the historical ethnography of emotions', *Current Anthropology*, 38:3 (1997), 327–51.

Reddy, William M., *The Invisible Code: Honor and Sentiment in Postrevolutionary France, 1814–1848* (Berkeley, CA: University of California Press, 1997).

Reddy, William M., 'Sentimentalism and its erasure: the role of emotions in the era of the French Revolution', *The Journal of Modern History*, 72 (2000), 109–52.

Reddy, William M., *The Navigation of Feeling: A Framework for the History of Emotions* (Cambridge: Cambridge University Press, 2001).

Reddy, William M., 'Historical research on the self and emotions', *Emotion Review*, 1:4 (2009), 302–15.

Riskin, Jessica, *Science in the Age of Sensibility: The Sentimental Empiricists of the French Enlightenment* (Chicago, IL: University of Chicago Press, 2002).

Robert, Yann, *Dramatic Justice: Trial by Theater in the Age of the French Revolution* (Philadelphia, PA: University of Pennsylvania Press, 2019).

Roberts, Benjamin, 'Drinking like a man: the paradox of excessive drinking for seventeenth-century Dutch youths', *Journal of Family History*, 29:3 (2004), 237–52.

Robertson, Stephen, 'What's law got to do with it? Legal records and sexual histories', *Journal of the History of Sexuality*, 14:1/2 (2005), 161–85.

Robisheaux, Thomas, 'Penance, confession, and the self in early modern Lutheranism', in Marjorie Elizabeth Plummer and Robin Barnes (eds), *Ideas and Cultural Margins in Early Modern Germany: Essays in Honor of H.C. Erik Midelfort* (Farnham: Ashgate, 2009), pp. 117–30.

Roegiers, Jan and N. C. F. van Sas, 'Revolution in the North and South, 1780–1830', in J. C. H. Blom and Emiel Lamberts (eds), *History of the Low Countries* (New York, NY: Berghahn, 2006), pp. 275–316.

Roets, Anne-Marie, '"Rudessen, dieften ende andere crimen". Misdadigheid te Gent in de zeventiende en achttiende eeuw: een kwantitatieve en kwalitatieve analyse' (PhD dissertation, University of Ghent, 1987).

Rombauts, W., *Het Paasverzuim in het bisdom Brugge (1840–1911)* (Leuven: Nauwelaerts, 1971).

Rose, Nikolas, *Inventing Our Selves: Psychology, Power and Personhood* (Cambridge: Cambridge University Press, 1996).

Rose, Nikolas, *Governing the Soul: The Shaping of the Private Self* (London: Free Association Books, 1999).

Rosenthal, Laura J., *Infamous Commerce: Prostitution in Eighteenth-Century British Literature and Culture* (Ithaca, NY: Cornell University Press, 2006).

Rosenwein, Barbara H. and Riccardo Cristiani, *What Is the History of Emotions?* (Cambridge: Polity Press, 2018).

Rousseaux, Xavier, 'Les tribunaux criminels en Brabant sous le Directoire (1795–1800). Acculturation et résistance à la justice républicaine', in J. Craeybeckx and F. Scheelings (eds), *De Franse Revolutie en Vlaanderen: de Oostenrijkse Nederlanden tussen oud en nieuw regime* (Brussels: Vrije Universiteit Brussel, 1990), pp. 277–306.

Rousseaux, Xavier, 'Doctrines criminelles, pratiques pénales, projets politiques: le cas des possessions Habsbourgeoises (1750–1790)', in Michel Porret (ed.), *Beccaria et la culture juridique des Lumières* (Genève: Droz, 1997), pp. 223–52.

Rousseaux, Xavier and Axel Tixhon, 'Du "sergent à verge" à la "profileuse": pistes pour l'histoire des polices dans l'espace belge, du Moyen Age au 21e siècle', in Jonas Campion (ed.), *Les archives des polices en Belgique: des méconnues de la recherche?* (Brussels: Algemeen Rijksarchief, 2009), pp. 11–34.

Ruberg, Willemijn, 'Travelling knowledge and forensic medicine: infanticide, body and mind in the Netherlands, 1811–1911', *Medical History*, 57:3 (2013), 359–76.

Rublack, Ulinka, 'Fluxes: the early modern body and the emotions', *History Workshop Journal*, 53 (2002), 1–16.

Ruller, Sibo van, *Genade voor recht: gratieverlening aan ter dood veroordeelden in Nederland 1806–1870* (Amsterdam: Bataafsche Leeuw, 1987).

Ruller, Sibo van, 'De territoriumstrijd tussen juristen en psychiaters in de negentiende eeuw', in F. Koenraadt (ed.), *Ziek of schuldig? Twee eeuwen forensische psychiatrie en psychologie* (Arnhem: Gouda Quint, 1991), pp. 23–33.

Sabean, David Warren, *Power in the Blood: Popular Culture and Village Discourse in Early Modern Germany* (Cambridge: Cambridge University Press, 1984).

Sabean, David Warren, 'Production of the self during the age of confessionalism', *Central European History*, 29 (1996), 1–18.

Sabean, David Warren and Malina Stefanovska (eds), *Space and Self in Early Modern European Cultures* (Toronto: University of Toronto Press, 2012).

Scheer, Monique, 'Are emotions a kind of practice (and is that what makes them have a history)? A Bourdieuian approach to understanding emotion', *History and Theory*, 51:2 (2012), 193–220.

Scholliers, Peter, 'The medical discourse and the drunkard's stereotyping in Belgium, 1840 – 1919', in Alexander Fenton (ed.), *Order and Disorder: The Health Implications of Eating and Drinking in the Nineteenth and Twentieth Centuries* (East Linton: Tuckwell Press, 2000), pp. 227–39.

Schwerhoff, Gerd, 'Early modern violence and the honour code: from social integration to social distinction?', *Crime, Histoire & Sociétés / Crime, History & Societies*, 17:2 (2013), 27–46.

Sedgwick, Eve Kosofsky, *Epistemology of the Closet* (Berkeley, CA: University of California Press, 1990).

Seigel, Jerrold, *The Idea of the Self: Thought and Experience in Western Europe since the Seventeenth Century* (Cambridge: Cambridge University Press, 2005).

Sharpe, J. A., *Defamation and Sexual Slander in Early Modern England: The Church Courts at York* (York: Borthwick Insitute of Historical Research, 1980).

Shoemaker, Robert, 'Male honour and the decline of public violence in eighteenth-century London', *Social History*, 26 (2001), 190–208.

Shoemaker, Robert B., 'The taming of the duel: masculinity, honour and ritual violence in London, 1660–1800', *The Historical Journal*, 45:3 (2002), 525–45.

Shoemaker, Robert and Richard Ward, 'Understanding the criminal: record-keeping, statistics and the early history of criminology in England', *British Journal of Criminology*, 57 (2017), 1442–61.

Shrank, Cathy, 'Beastly metamorphoses: losing control in early modern literary culture', in Jonathan Herring *et al.* (eds), *Intoxication and Society: Problematic Pleasures of Drugs and Alcohol* (Basingstoke: Palgrave Macmillan, 2013), pp. 193–209.

Silverman, Lisa, *Tortured Subjects: Pain, Truth and the Body in Early Modern France* (Chicago, IL: University of Chicago Press, 2001).

Sluhovsky, Moshe, *Becoming a New Self: Practices of Belief in Early Modern Catholicism* (Chicago, IL: University of Chicago Press, 2017).

Smeyers, Jozef, 'Mevrouw de mode in de Vlaemschen Indicateur (1779–1787)', in *Literair- en cultuurhistorische bijdragen: van Rousseau en Amerika tot Aalst en Brussel* (Brussels: Studiecentrum 18de-eeuwse Zuidnederlandse Letterkunde, 2004), pp. 72–7.

Sökefeld, Martin, 'Debating self, identity, and culture in anthropology', *Current Anthropology*, 40 (1999), 417–48.

Soly, Hugo, 'Kroeglopen in Brabant en Vlaanderen, 16de–18de eeuw', *Spiegel Historiael*, 18 (1983), 569–77.

Spierenburg, Pieter, 'Knife fighting and popular codes of honor in early modern Amsterdam', in Pieter Spierenburg (ed.), *Men and Violence: Gender, Honor, and Rituals in Modern Europe and America* (Columbus, OH: Ohio State University Press, 1998), pp. 103–27.

Spierenburg, Pieter, *A History of Murder: Personal Violence in Europe from the Middle Ages to the Present* (Cambridge: Polity Press, 2008).

Spierenburg, Pieter, 'The rise of criminology in its historical context', in Paul Knepper and Anja Johansen (eds), *The Oxford Handbook of the History of Crime and Criminal Justice* (Oxford: Oxford University Press, 2016), pp. 373–95.

Spiro, Melford E., 'Is the Western conception of the self "peculiar" within the context of the world cultures?', *Ethos*, 21 (1993), 107–53.

Srebnick, Amy Gilman, 'Does the representation fit the crime? Some thoughts on writing crime history as cultural text', in Amy Gilman Srebnick and René Levy (eds), *Crime and Culture: An Historical Perspective* (Aldershot: Ashgate, 2005), pp. 3–19.

Stearns, Carol Z., '"Lord help me walk humbly": Anger and sadness in England and America, 1570–1750', in Peter N. Stearns and Carol Z. Stearns (eds), *Emotion and Social Change: Toward a New Psychohistory* (New York, NY: Holmes and Meier, 1988), pp. 39–68.

Stearns, Carol Zisowitz and Peter N. Stearns, *Anger: The Struggle for Emotional Control in America's History* (Chicago, IL: University of Chicago Press, 1986).

Stearns, Peter N., *Shame: A Brief History* (Urbana: University of Illinois Press, 2017).

Stearns, Peter N. and Carol Z. Stearns, 'Emotionology: Clarifying the history of emotions and emotional standards', *The American Historical Review*, 90 (1985), 813–36.

Stecher, J., 'Reiffenberg (Baron Frédéric-Auguste-Ferinand-Thomas de)', *Biographie nationale de Belgique* 18 (Brussels: Bruylant, 1905), pp. 887–918.

Steedman, Carolyn, *Strange Dislocations: Childhood and the Idea of Human Interiority, 1780–1930* (Cambridge, MA: Harvard University Press, 1995).

Steedman, Carolyn, *History and the Law: A Love Story* (Cambridge: Cambridge University Press, 2020).

Stein, Edward (ed.), *Forms of Desire: Sexual Orientation and the Social Constructionist Controversy* (New York, NY: Routledge, 1992).

Steinberg, Jessica, 'She was "a comon night walker abusing him & being of ill behaviour": Violence and Prostitution in Eighteenth-Century London', *Canadian Journal of History*, 50:2 (2015), 239–61.

Steinberg, Jessica, 'For lust or gain: perceptions of prostitutes in eighteenth-century London', *Journal of Gender Studies*, 26 (2017), 702–13.

Sturkenboom, Dorothée, *Spectators van hartstocht. Sekse en emotionele cultuur in de achttiende eeuw* (Hilversum: Verloren, 1998).

Sturkenboom, Dorothée, 'Historicizing the gender of emotions: changing perceptions in Dutch Enlightenment thought', *Journal of Social History*, 34 (2000), 55–75.

Tausiet, María, 'From illusion to disenchantment: Feijoo versus the "falsely possessed" in eighteenth-century Spain', in Owen Davies and Willem de Blécourt (eds), *Beyond the Witch Trials: Witchcraft and Magic in Enlightenment Europe* (Manchester: Manchester University Press, 2004), pp. 45–60.

Taylor, Charles, *Sources of the Self: The Making of the Modern Identity* (Cambridge, MA: Harvard University Press, 1989).

Taylor, Chloe, *The Culture of Confession from Augustine to Foucault: A Genealogy of the 'Confessing Animal'* (Abingdon: Routledge, 2009).

Thiel, Udo, 'Self and sensibility: From Locke to Condillac and Rousseau', *Intellectual History Review*, 25:3 (2014), 257–78.

Thomson, Mathew, *Psychological Subjects: Identity, Culture, and Health in Twentieth-Century Britain* (Oxford: Oxford University Press, 2006).

Tinková, Daniela, 'Protéger ou punir? Les voies de la décriminalisation de l'infanticide en France et dans le domaine des Habsbourg (XVIIIe–XIXe siècles)', *Crime, Histoire & Sociétés / Crime, History & Societies*, 9:2 (2005), 43–72.

Tlusty, B. Ann, 'Crossing gender boudaries: women as drunkards in early modern Augsburg', in Sibylle Backman *et al.* (eds), *Ehrkonzepte in der frühen Neuzeit. Identitäten und Abgrenzungen* (Berlin: Akademie Verlag, 1998), pp. 185–98.

Tlusty, B. Ann, *Bacchus and Civic Order. The Culture of Drink in Early Modern Germany* (Charlottesville, VA: University Press of Virginia, 2001).

Tobin, Robert Deam, *Peripheral Desires: The German Discovery of Sex* (Philadelphia, PA: University of Pennsylvania Press, 2015).

Tricaud, François, 'Le procès de la procédure criminelle à l'âge des Lumières', *Archives de Philosophie du Droit*, 39 (1994), 145–67.

Trousson, Raymond, 'Le Prince de Ligne et l'autobiographie', *Nouvelles annales Prince de Ligne*, 12 (1998), 93–115.

Trumbach, Randolph, *Sex and the Gender Revolution. Volume One: Heterosexuality and the Third Gender in Enlightenment London* (London: University of Chicago Press, 1998).

Valverde, Mariana, *Diseases of the Will: Alcohol and the Dilemmas of Freedom* (New York, NY: Cambridge University Press, 1998).

Van Bruaene, Anne-Laure and Sarah Van Bouchaute, 'Rederijkers, Kannenkijkers: Drinking and Drunkenness in the Sixteenth and Seventeenth-Century Low Countries', *Early Modern Low Countries*, 1:1 (2017), 1–29. doi:10.18352/emlc.4

Van Damme, Ilja, 'Zotte verwaandheid. Over Franse verleiding en Zuid-Nederlands onbehagen, 1650–1750', in Raf De Bont and Tom Verschaffel (eds), *Het verderf van Parijs* (Leuven: Universitaire Pers Leuven, 2004), pp. 187–203.

Van Der Made, Raoul, 'L'influence de l'ivresse sur la culpabilité (XVIe & XVIIe siècles)', *Tijdschrift voor Rechtsgeschiedenis / Revue d'Histoire du Droit / The Legal History Review*, 20:1 (1939), 64–88.

Van De Steene, Christine, *Satan en zijn trawanten volgens de achttiende-eeuwse predikatie* (Aartrijke: Decock, 1991).

Van Dijck, Maarten F., 'Towards an economic interpretation of justice? Conflict settlement, social control and civil society in urban Brabant and Mechelen during the late middle ages and the early modern period', in Manon van der Heijden *et al.* (eds), *Serving the Urban Community: The Rise of Public Facilities in the Low Countries* (Amsterdam: Aksant, 2009), pp. 62–88.

Vanhemelryck, Fernand, *De criminaliteit in de ammanie van Brussel van de late middeleeuwen tot het einde van het Ancien Régime (1404–1789)* (Brussels: Koninklijke academie voor wetenschappen, letteren en schone kunsten van België, 1981).

Vanhulle, Bert, '"Uitmunten door vlijt": Gratie in het gevangeniswezen tijdens het Verenigd Koninkrijk der Nederlanden (1815–1830)', in Dirk Heirbaut, Xavier Rousseaux and Alain Wijffels (eds), *Histoire du droit et de la justice: Une nouvelle génération de recherches / Justitie- en rechtsgeschiedenis: Een nieuwe onderzoeksgeneratie* (Louvain-la-Neuve: Presses universitaires de Louvain, 2009), pp. 411–22.

Van Oostveldt, Bram, *The Théâtre de la Monnaie and the Theatre Life in the 18th Century Austrian Netherlands: From a Courtly-Aristocratic to a Civil-Enlightened Discourse?* (Ghent: Academia Press, 2000).

Van Oostveldt, Bram, *Tranen om het alledaagse: Diderot en het verlangen naar natuurlijkheid in het Brusselse theaterleven in de achttiende eeuw* (Hilversum: Verloren, 2013).

Van Osselaer, Tine, *The Pious Sex: Catholic Constructions of Masculinity and Femininity in Belgium, c. 1800–1940* (Leuven: Leuven University Press, 2013).

Van Uytven, Raymond, 'De drankcultuur in de Zuidelijke Nederlanden tot de XVIIIde eeuw', in *Drinken in het verleden* (Leuven: Stadsbestuur Leuven, 1973), pp. 17–49.

Vanysacker, Dries, 'Enlightenment and witchcraft. The dangers of denying the existence of the devil', *Hexenforschung*, 114 (2016), 25–33.

Vanysacker, Dries and Erik Aerts, 'Hekserijbestraffing met twee snelheden. Peilen naar geografische verschillen in de Zuidelijke Nederlanden', in Michiel Decaluwe, Véronique Lambert and Dirk Heirbaut (eds), *Inter amicos: liber amicorum Monique van Melkebeek* (Brussels: Koninklijke Vlaamse academie van België voor wetenschappen en kunsten, 2011), pp. 317–43.

Velle, Karel, 'Gerechtelijke archieven en lokale geschiedenis (19de–20ste eeuw)', in Jan Art (ed.), *Hoe schrijf ik de geschiedenis van mijn gemeente?* (Ghent: Stichting Mens en Kultuur, 1996), pp. 219–55.

Vercruysse, Jeroom, 'Les pamphlets de la Révolution belge (1787–1791) et les Lumières philosophiques', *Revue belge de philologie et d'histoire*, 91:2 (2013), 317–26.

Verhoeven, Gerrit, '"Le pays où on ne sait pas lire": Literacy, numeracy and human capital in the commercial hub of the Austrian Netherlands (1715–75)', *European History Quarterly*, 44:2 (2014), 223–43.

Verreycken, Quentin, 'The power to pardon in late medieval and early modern Europe: New perspectives in the history of crime and criminal justice', *History Compass*, 17:6 (2019). doi:10.1111/hic3.12575

Verschaffel, Tom, *De hoed en de hond: geschiedschrijving in de Zuidelijke Nederlanden, 1715–1794* (Hilversum: Verloren, 1998).

Verschaffel, Tom, *De weg naar het binnenland: geschiedenis van de Nederlandse literatuur 1700–1800, de Zuidelijke Nederlanden* (Amsterdam: Bert Bakker, 2017).

Vigarello, Georges, 'L'émergence du mot "émotion"', in Georges Vigarello (ed.), *Histoire des émotions. T. 1: De l'Antiquité aux Lumières* (Paris: Seuil, 2016), pp. 219–24.

Vincent-Buffault, Anne, *Histoire des larmes: XVIIIe–XIXe siècles* (Paris: Rivages, 1986).

Voyé, Liliane and Karel Dobbelaere, 'Portrait du catholicisme en Belgique', in Alfonso Pérez-Agote (ed.), *Portraits du catholicisme. Une comparaison européenne* (Rennes: Presses Universitaires de Rennes, 2012), pp. 11–61.

Vrolijk, Marjan, *Recht door gratie: gratie bij doodslagen en andere delicten in Vlaanderen, Holland en Zeeland (1531–1567)* (Hilversum: Verloren, 2004).

Vyverberg, Henry, *Human Nature, Cultural Diversity and the French Enlightenment* (New York, NY: Oxford University Press, 1989).

Wahrman, Dror, *The Making of the Modern Self: Identity and Culture in Eighteenth-Century England* (New Haven, CT: Yale University Press, 2004).

Warner, Jessica, *Craze: Gin and Debauchery in an Age of Reason* (London: Profile, 2003).

Watt, Jeffrey R., *Choosing Death: Suicide and Calvinism in Early Modern Geneva* (Kirksville, MO: Truman State University Press, 2001).

Watt, Jeffrey R. (ed.), *From Sin to Insanity: Suicide in Early Modern Europe* (Ithaca, NY: Cornell University Press, 2004).

Weiner, Dora B., 'The madman in the light of reason: Enlightenment psychiatry. Part I: Custody, therapy, theory and the need for reform', in Edwin R. Wallace and John Gach (eds), *History of Psychiatry and Medical Psychology* (New York, NY: Springer, 2008), pp. 255–77.

Wiener, Martin J., *Reconstructing the Criminal: Culture, Law, and Policy in England, 1830–1914* (Cambridge: Cambridge University Press, 1990).

Williams, Owen, 'Exorcising madness in late Elizabethan England: "The seduction of Arthington" and the criminal culpability of demoniacs', *Journal of British Studies*, 47:1 (2008), 30–52.

Wils, Kaat, *De omweg van de wetenschap: het positivisme en de Belgische en Nederlandse intellectuele cultuur, 1845–1914* (Amsterdam: Amsterdam University Press, 2005).

Ylivuori, Soile, 'Rethinking female chastity and gentlewomen's honour in eighteenth-century England', *The Historical Journal*, 59:1 (2016), 71–97.

Index

EU authorised representative for GPSR:
Easy Access System Europe, Mustamäe tee 50,
10621 Tallinn, Estonia
gpsr.requests@easproject.com

www.ingramcontent.com/pod-product-compliance
Lightning Source LLC
Chambersburg PA
CBHW070411100426
42812CB00005B/1707